THE
PROPHETS
FOR
YOUNG PEOPLE

THE PROPHETS FOR YOUNG PEOPLE

*To Brynn, Joslyn +
Benjamin —
with my best wishes
for a happy future —
Esta Cassway
1995*

written and illustrated by
Esta Cassway

JASON ARONSON INC.
Northvale, New Jersey
London

The author wishes to thank her son Nicholas Cassway for creating "The Call of Ezekiel" and for his tremendous assistance in designing this book. Also, many thanks to Jessica Hansen for her cheerfulness and efficient organizing, and to Joanna V. Hill for her good counsel.

This book was set in 14 pt. Garamond 3 by Alpha Graphics of Pittsfield, New Hampshire, and printed by Haddon Craftsmen in Scranton, Pennsylvania.

Library of Congress Cataloging-in-Publication Data

Cassway, Esta.
    The prophets for young people / written and illustrated by Esta
Cassway.
      p. cm.
    ISBN 1-56821-148-1
    1. Bible stories, English—O.T. Prophets (Nevi'im) 2. Bible.
O.T. Prophets (Nevi'im)—History of Biblical events—Juvenile
poetry. [1. Bible stories—O.T.] I. Title.
BS551.2.C385   1995
224'.09505—dc20   94-2498
                                             AC

Manufactured in the United States of America. Jason Aronson Inc. offers books and cassettes. For information and catalog write to Jason Aronson Inc., 230 Livingston Street, Northvale, New Jersey 07647.

This book is dedicated to my husband, Robert.

Blessed are You, Lord our God,
Ruler of the universe,
Who has blessed us with health, sustained us,
and enabled us to reach this happy day.

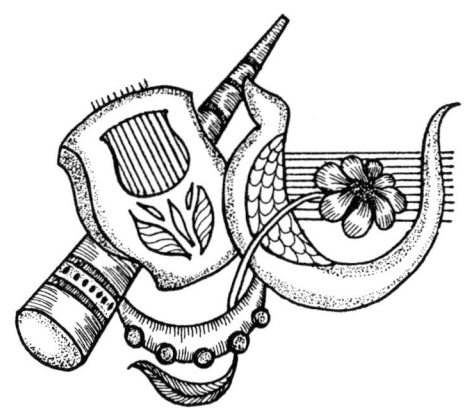

Contents

JOSHUA

JUDGES

I SAMUEL

II SAMUEL

I KINGS

II KINGS

ISAIAH

JEREMIAH

EZEKIEL

THE TWELVE PROPHETS

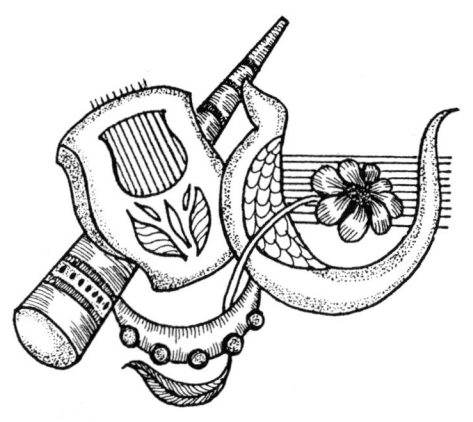

Joshua

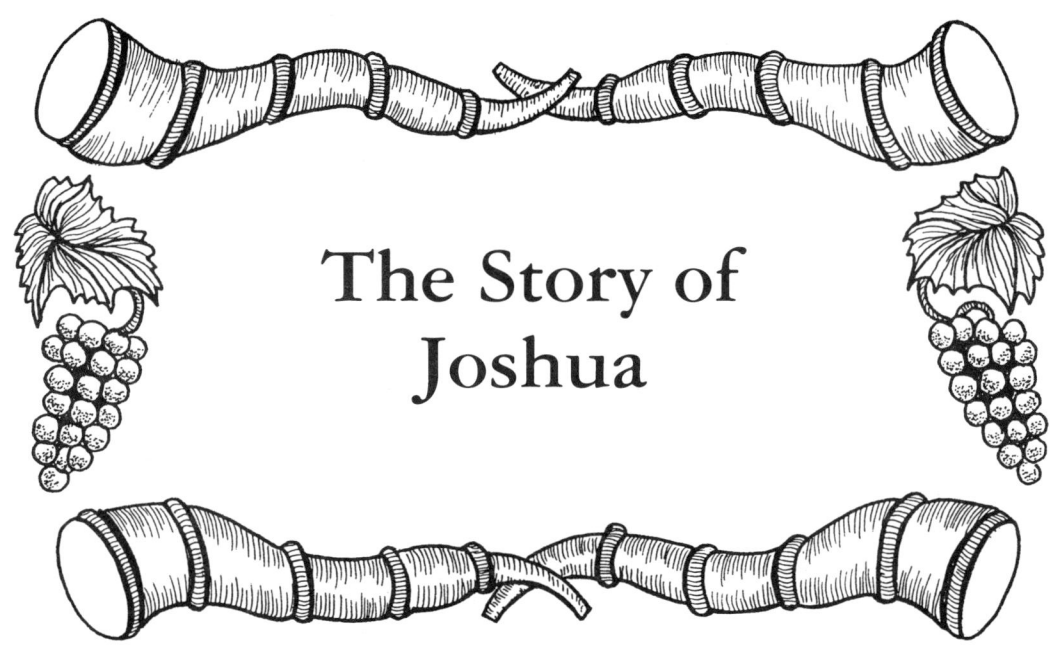

The Story of Joshua

At sunset, the moon waits patiently for the colors of day to bid farewell to God's beautiful world. As the last purple streak fades into night, the moon, having gained strength and light from the sun, rises slowly and takes command over stars and seas alike. So it was with Joshua, chosen by God to succeed Moses and lead the Children of Israel into the Promised Land.

When Moses was very old, God told him to stand before Eliazar, the high priest, and all the Israelites and to place his hand upon his trusted friend Joshua. In this way, a portion of the Spirit of God—the wisdom, courage, and faith that had made Moses so very special—would be passed on to Joshua. As the light that was the life of Moses disappeared into God's own cloud, Joshua, like the moon, waited patiently for his turn to shine.

Remembering Moses

For thirty days, the Children of Israel mourned the death of their great leader Moses. The sound of weeping rose above the wind, and tears, like rain, formed salty pools on the dry ground. During this sad time, people did not stay home feeling sorry for themselves. Instead, they visited their neighbors, shared the sadness, and remembered, with smiles, wonderful stories about Moses.

THE LIFE OF MOSES

Moses was found by Pharaoh's daughter,
In a basket that floated through reeds in the water.
He was raised like a prince, but always remembered
What his true mother taught him, his mother who nursed him
For Pharaoh's own daughter.
She told him, "My son, though you live in a palace
With servants and gold and a fine horse to ride,
You must always remember that you are a Hebrew,
And that all through your life God will be at your side."

When Moses grew up, he killed an Egyptian
Who was beating a Hebrew, a poor Hebrew slave.
Moses left Egypt fast; he feared for his life.
After crossing the desert he met seven daughters
Of Jethro the shepherd, and picked for his wife
The lovely Zipporah, and they soon had two boys.

One day, while Moses was tending the sheep,
He heard his name called, and when he looked up
Saw a bush filled with fire that did not consume it.
And out of the flames came the Voice of the Lord:
"You will help Me deliver My people from Egypt.
I will put out My Hand and with signs and with wonders
Pharaoh's might will be broken!
Tell the Children of Israel the Lord God has spoken.
I will speak to you just like I've spoken today.
I will give you directions, and, since I know
That your own speech is slow, have Aaron, your brother
Speak the words that I tell you to tell him to say."

Moses went back to Egypt, as the Lord said to do,
And showed Pharaoh the signs and the wonders of God.
His rod he turned into a huge snake that ate
All the slippery snakes made by Pharaoh's magicians.
Moses told the cruel Pharaoh, "Your fate is with God.
Pain and sorrow will follow,
If you don't let the Children of Israel go."

The rivers turned blood red, frogs hopped all around.

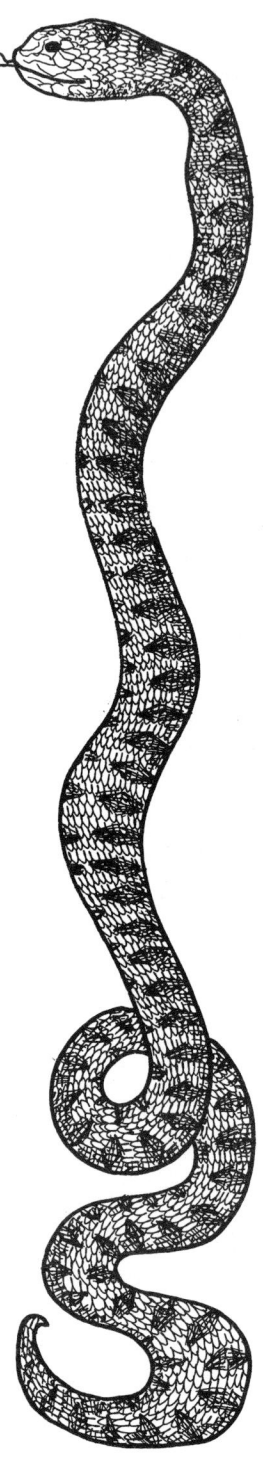

The Egyptians were itching from flies and from fleas,
Cattle died of disease, people's bodies had pimples,
There was hail, there was darkness,
Locusts came with the wind.
Then God showed His Hand
And death came to the firstborn
Of all Egypt land.

The Children of Israel left in a hurry;
There was not even time for their good bread to rise.
And God, Who is wise, led them not by a straight line,
But roundabout lands where people were wicked.
He did not want His children to think about war.
To the shore of the sea, Pharaoh's army pursued them,
Six hundred chariots and thousands of men!
But Moses said,
"Fear not,
The Lord will protect you!"
Then he stretched out his arm
And the sea broke in two!
The water, like fountains,
Flowed left and flowed right!
The Children of Israel walked on dry ground!
When every last foot had crossed over the sea,
And as Pharaoh's great army
Stepped on the dry land,
Moses stretched out his hand
And the sea flowed back on them!
Chariots and riders fell into the sea!

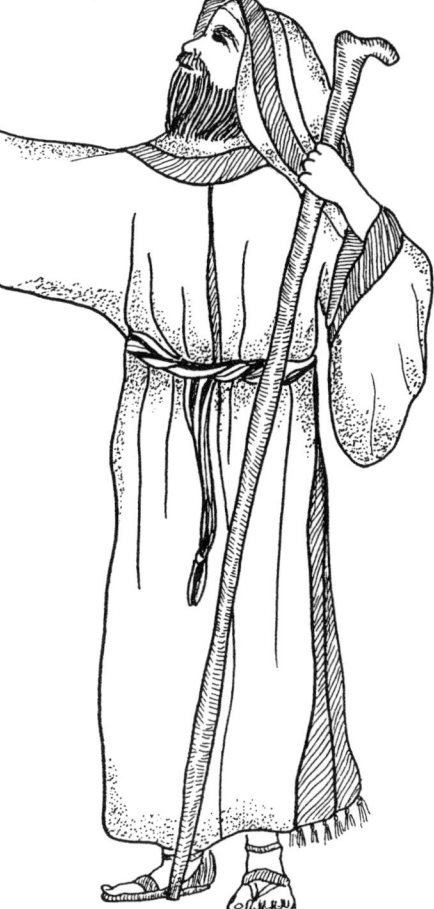

The Israelites let out a sigh of relief;
They were saved by the Hand of the Lord!
As they stood on dry land,
They sang praises to God:
"Who is like You, God on high?
Who is like You, God so holy?
With awesome deeds and wonders
Who is like You, God on high?"

The people went forward, into the dry desert.
God made bad water sweet, and sent "Manna" to eat.

But the Children of Israel did not stop complaining.
Moses cried to the Lord, "They are ready to stone me!
Again they want water; what shall I do?
I'm fed up with explaining!"
God said, "I'll help you.

Take your rod and strike it against this big rock.
Water will flow from it, water will pour
Like a cloud that has burst."
Moses did as God said.
Water flowed, water poured!
Israel's thirst was quenched by the Lord!

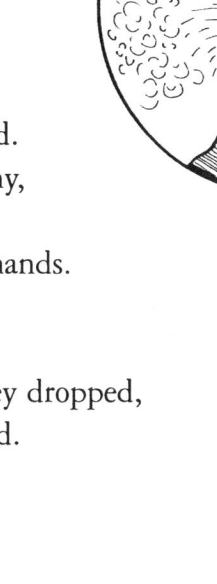

Then came Amalek, a fierce tribe of the land.
Moses told Joshua, who was head of the army,
"Choose men who can fight.
I'll stand on the hill with God's rod in my hands.
And as long as I hold it high
Israel's might will prevail!"
But his arms soon grew heavy and when they dropped,
Amalek and his warriors couldn't be stopped.
Then Moses sat down, defeat was in sight;
Aaron sat on his left, Hur sat on his right.
And they lifted his arms until the sun set!
That's how Joshua's sword overcame Amalek!

The Children of Israel came to a mountain,
A mountain whose top was covered with smoke.
As they stood there they heard the long cry of a trumpet.
It grew louder and louder until Moses spoke
To the Lord, and God answered, His Voice strong and clear,
And told Moses that he must let no one come near.
Only Moses and Aaron the priest were allowed
To come near the Lord.
There was thunder and lightning; the whole earth was quaking!
The people were trembling, the people were shaking!
As the trumpet grew louder, its voice like a wail,
The Lord gave His law to the Children of Israel.

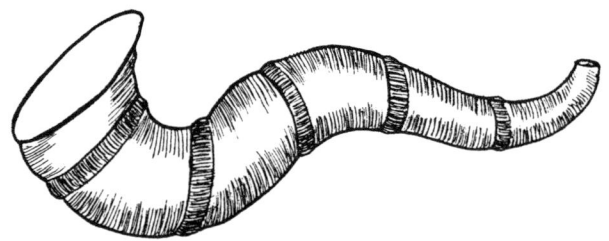

For forty long days and forty long nights
Moses stayed on the mountain with God, alone.
God taught him His rules and gave him directions
For building an Ark, covered with gold,
That would hold the commandments, written on stone,
By the Finger of God, and God alone.

While Moses was learning the laws of the Lord
The Children of Israel soon became bored.
They had no self-control, they got out of hand.
Down in the camp there was shouting and screaming,
Music and dancing, laughing and singing.

God told Moses, "Leave. Go back to your people.
I am angry with them; they have all turned aside
From My commandments!
I will stretch out My Hand and deal harshly with them!"
"Forgive them," cried Moses,

"Do not wipe them out from the face of the earth.
Remember the promise You made to Your people,
And to Abraham, Isaac, and Jacob before,
That one day they'd number like stars in the sky,
That one day they'd enter the Lord's Promised Land!"
The Lord listened to Moses,
And put down His Hand.

As Moses came down from the mountain of God,
He heard the commotion, his ears soon were ringing
With shouting, and screaming, with laughing and singing!
And when Moses saw what his people had done,
His heart ached with pain; anger showed on his face!
They had built a golden calf to worship in God's place!

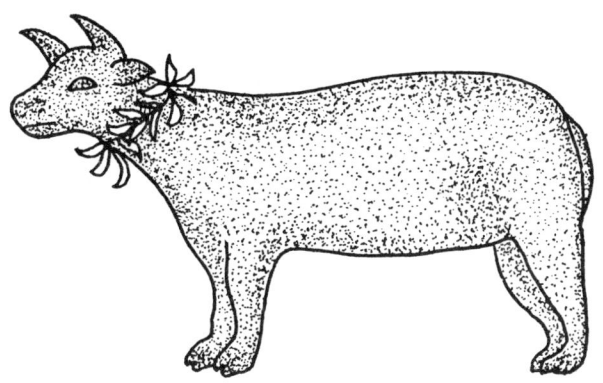

Moses smashed the Ten Commandments,
The two tablets made by God!
He told the foolish people he would go back to the Lord
And ask Him to forgive them, he would plead on their accord.
"I will punish only those who sinned," said God,
"They were the fools!
The rest shall live, and you shall teach them
My commandments, laws, and rules."

11

For forty long days and forty long nights
Moses stayed on the mountain with God, alone.
He wrote on two tablets the words of the Lord.
When he carried them down to the people below,
His face was like sunshine, so radiant, it shone!
He gave them the laws, he gave them the rules
And said,
"If you keep God's commandments,
And don't act like fools,
And never again worship idols of stone,
Then God will forgive you
And He'll lead you home."

Moses led them onward, Israel's twelve tribes,
Reuben, Simeon, Judah, Issachar,
Zebulun, Ephraim, and Manasseh,
Asher, Gad, and Benjamin,
Naphtali and Dan.
And in the middle,
Levite priests carried the Ark
That held God's laws and rules.
For forty years they marched,
With laughter and with tears,
Their worries and their fears were soothed by Moses,
Their great leader,
Who taught the children's children
In preparation
For the end of their long journey.
A whole new generation
Learned God's laws and rules.

God's own servant, Moses, made a big mistake one day.
Everyone can make mistakes, but when it comes to God
His directions must be followed,
His rules must be obeyed.
In his haste to help his people, who were thirsty once again,
Moses asked the Lord for help.
God said, "Speak to this rock and it will flow
With water cool to ease their thirst."
Moses didn't listen carefully to the Lord's command.
Instead of speaking to the rock,
Moses raised his hand!
He struck it once, he struck it twice!
Water poured out, water spilled!
Man and beast both drank their fill.
But God said, "Moses, you have disobeyed.
Now you shall not lead your people
Into the Promised Land."

When Moses brought his people close to the Jordan River,
He climbed a mountain there to see
The land the Lord had promised.
Though he was old his eyes were sharp;
Nothing did they miss.
And when he finished looking,
Moses, servant of the Lord,
Disappeared into God's cloud,
Taken gently with a kiss.

Where he lies, nobody knows,
But he lives on inside the hearts
Of the Children of Israel.
They recall his signs and wonders.
They remember him with awe.
And there's never been a prophet quite like Moses,
Whom the Lord knew face to face,
And who brought Israel God's law!

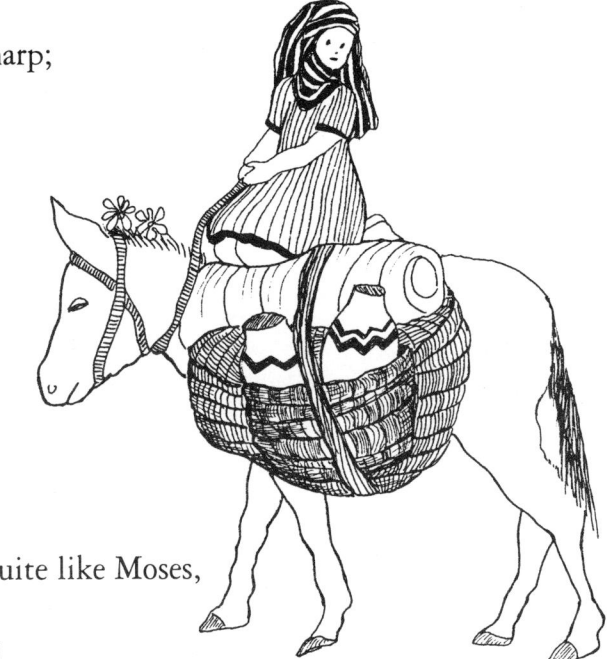

13

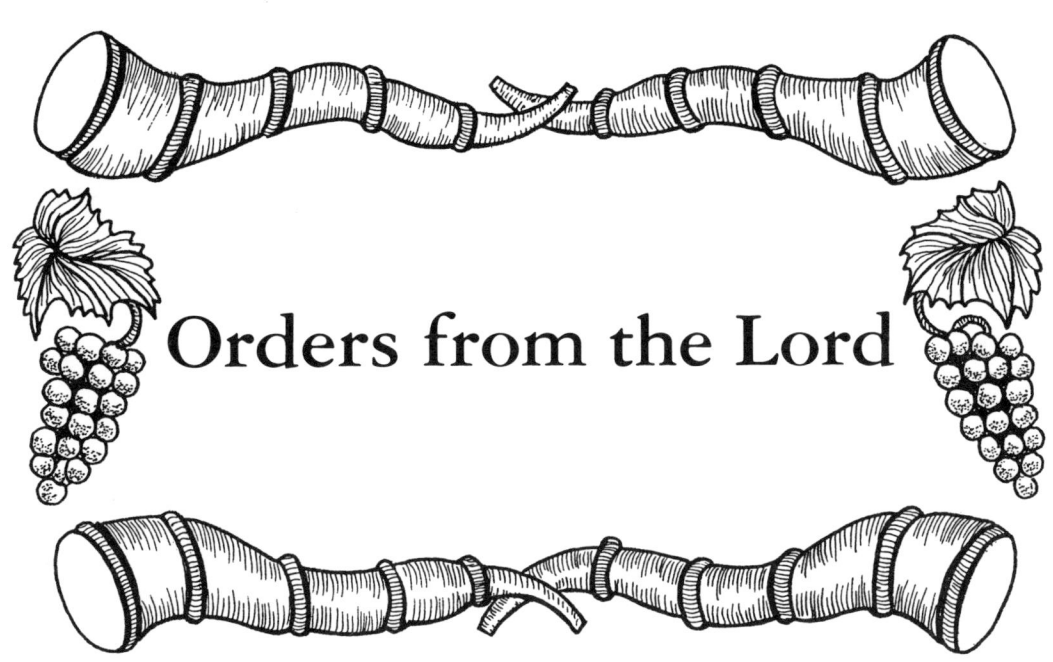

Orders from the Lord

Everyone will always miss somebody sometime. The end of an official mourning period does not mean that people no longer miss the one who has died. As life continues, remembering the names and good deeds of those who are no longer here helps us create the world that is to come.

When the thirty days of mourning for Moses were over, the grownups went back to their everyday work, weaving cloth, sewing patches on the goatskin tents, and sharpening arrows for hunting bows. Since they were so close to the river, the children looked for tadpoles in the little streams and began to have frog-jumping contests. And the animals, who had been on their best behavior, began stomping their feet and their neighbors' feet.

There was mooing and grunting,
Clucking and braying,
Baaing and barking,
What were they all saying?

15

Joshua, the son of Nun, had been Moses' trusted helper and the head of his army. The Lord spoke to Joshua and said:

"Moses, My servant, is dead. Take everyone and cross over this Jordan River into the land which I have given to the Children of Israel. Every place where the soles of your feet tread shall be yours:

From the wilderness of Zin,
To the snow-capped peaks of Lebanon,
From the land ruled by the Hittites,
To the sea where the sun goes down.
No man shall lead but you.
I helped Moses
And I'll help you, too.
I won't fail you or forsake you.
Be strong and be courageous!
You'll lead these people to the land
I promised those who lived before
To give you,
By My Hand.
Be strong and be courageous!
Remain faithful to My rules
That Moses gave to you.
Don't ignore these teachings.
Don't forget My book of law.
It should be with you night and day.
Observe all My commandments,
And success will come your way.
Be strong and be courageous!
Never be dismayed.
The Lord your God is with you.
You must not be afraid."

Joshua then made this announcement to the officers of the twelve tribes:

"Tell the people to begin to prepare food. In three days you will pass over this mighty Jordan River into the land that the Lord your God has given to you."

16

Different portions of the Promised Land were to be given to each tribe. The Levite priests, who were in charge of the Ark and the traveling Tabernacle, would be given small parts of everyone's land. This way, the Ark would always have a home when it was carried from tribe to tribe. Two and a half tribes had asked to remain on the eastern side of the river, where the land was green and fertile. They were the Reubenites, the Gadites, and half the tribe of Manasseh. These people had large herds of sheep, goats, and cattle, and this ground was especially good for grazing. Joshua reminded these tribes that Moses had given them permission to remain on one condition: all the strong men must first cross the river and be ready to help the other tribes in case of trouble. They could return to their wives and children on the sunrise side of the river after the Promised Land had been possessed. The men of the two and a half tribes said to Joshua:

"All you have commanded us, we will do. And wherever you send us we will go. We listened to Moses and now we shall listen to you."

Joshua Sends Spies into Jericho

Every spring, the Jordan River descends swiftly from its mountain home, overflows its banks, and creates green valleys filled with beautiful trees. The Israelites' camp was in a valley full of acacia trees. These were the same kinds of trees that God had instructed Moses to use for building the Ark and the Tabernacle. Across a narrow part of the Jordan, tucked into a valley of palm trees, was the walled city of Jericho. Most of the Canaanite cities were small, and their walls helped protect them from enemies. Some of these walls were slanted and covered with slippery, white plaster. During battles, this helped prevent big, wooden machines called "battering rams" from breaking apart the bricks. Gates, big enough for chariots and horses, were built into the wall. At night, these gates were locked with metal bolts.

Joshua picked two brave men to cross the river and spy out the city of Jericho. Disguising themselves as traveling salesmen, the two men snooped around the town. With curiosity, they looked at the mud-brick houses jumbled together, their flat roofs serving as outdoor living rooms. They were fascinated by the clay trenches lining the narrow, dirt streets. These were designed to carry off sewage and rainwater. In the center of town they saw the king's palace, a sturdy, two-story building, and next to it a small temple honoring Baal, the storm god. Jericho seemed both strange and marvelous

18

to the Israelites. Because they had been wandering through deserts and wild places for so many years, they had no real knowledge of what a city was like.

The two men found an inn built right into the thick wall. Staying there would be a new experience for them; they had never slept away from their tents before! The house was owned by a lady named Rahab. Here, they thought they could safely blend in with the other men coming and going from the place. But news travels fast in a small town, and soon the king of Jericho suspected that these two strangers were Israelites. He sent this message to Rahab:

"Bring out the two foreign men who are in your house!"

Rahab had also heard the news buzzing around the town. And because she was a good woman, she had already hidden the two men.

Rahab said to the king's messengers: "You are correct. Two men did come to my house. But I don't know where they came from. They were trying to sell me some pots and pans. They left when it became dark, right before the city gate was locked. If you go quickly, you might overtake them."

Rahab was a quick thinker! The king's men raced their horses toward the Jordan River. Then, the gates to the city were locked, just in case the two strangers were hiding inside. After the king's men left, Rahab ran up to her roof and uncovered the men, who were hiding beneath stalks of drying flax, the plant that is used to make linen cloth.

HOW TO TURN FLAX INTO CLOTH

1. Pick bundles of flax, a tall flower with pretty blue petals.
2. Soak flax in water to loosen its inside fibers.
3. Spread the flax outside on a flat surface and dry it in the sun.
4. When completely dry, beat and comb out the fibers until they separate.
5. Roll these separated fibers on your thigh until they make long strands of yarn.
6. While standing, spin the yarn like this: Work your two arms in an up-and-down rhythm as they dangle two heavy twisting spindles. These are connected to a bowl fitted with a guide that separates the yarn.
7. Using a tall loom, weave the fine threads of spun yarn into linen, a beautiful cloth.

Rahab said to the two men: "I know that the Lord has given you this land. All the people here are frightened; they will melt away like snow when they see you. We have heard how the Lord dried up the Sea of Reeds and brought you out from Egypt. We have heard of the cities that your army has destroyed. Because of you, there is no more fighting spirit here. I know that the Lord your God is the God of heaven above and the earth below. Because I have been kind to you, promise me that you will deal kindly with me and all my relatives."

The men replied, "When the Lord gives us this land, we will deal kindly with you."

Rahab got a strong, red rope and put it through a window. As the men began using the rope to climb down the wall Rahab said: "Go to the hill country and hide for three days in one of the caves. After that, you will be safe."

The men said: "When we come back with our army, gather your family together. If you keep quiet about us, we promise to save all who are in your house. Just make sure that this red rope is hanging in the window where we can see it."

"I will do as you say," promised Rahab.

And so she sent them away, remembering to put the red rope back in her window.

After three days, the pursuers gave up. The two spies made their way back across the river and told Joshua all that had happened. They said:

"The Lord has delivered into our hand,
All of the land we can see today.
The people have heard of us,
And they are frightened.
Like snow, they will melt away!"

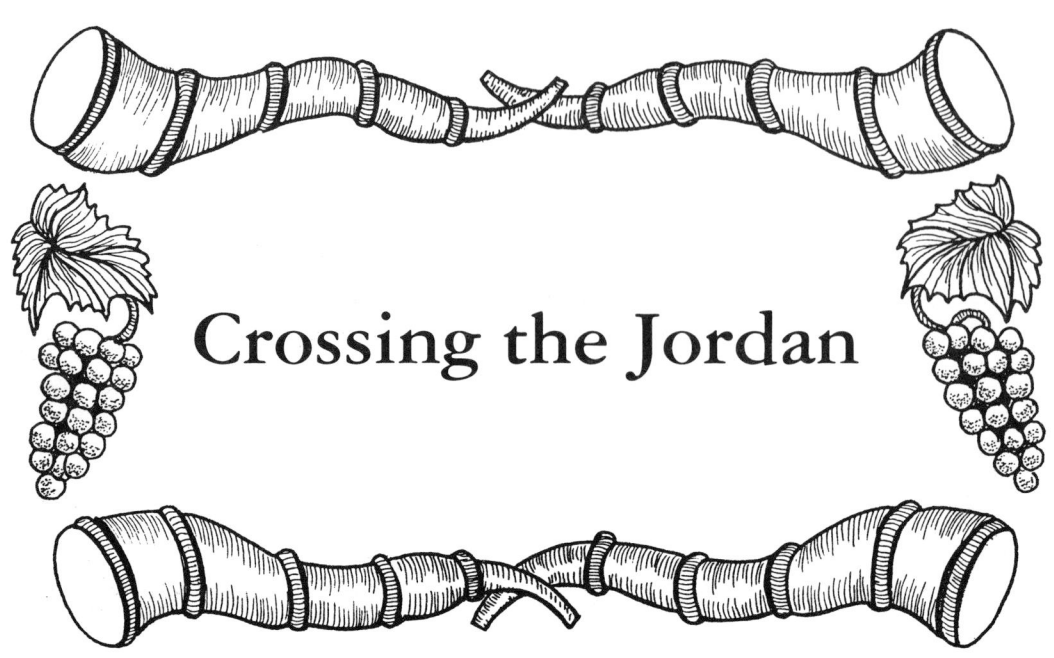

Crossing the Jordan

At daybreak, the sun peeks over the hills and, with a gentle kiss, awakens the world. Early in the morning, as butterflies tickled sleepy eyelids, Joshua and the Children of Israel moved their tents to the banks of the Jordan River. The flags of each tribe waved in the breeze, and nobody was ever lost for long.

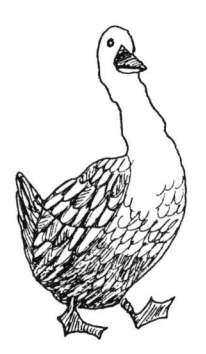

There were thousands of men,
And thousands of women,
Thousands of children,
And thousands of sheep.
There were thousands of camels,
Goats, ducks, and donkeys,
Chickens and dogs,
Fourteen doves and one crow.
There were lots of pet fish,
And a few silly geese,
Who wandered from camp to camp,
Honking hello.

22

While they waited for the signal to begin crossing the river, the Israelites washed their dusty clothes and greasy pots. All the children had their hair washed. Shrieks and howls filled the air as mothers and fathers tried to untangle curls and braids. Even the pet dogs received a bath. Afterward, looking like skinny, wet rats, they shook themselves dry, giving anyone in their path an extra shower!

Although very excited, the Israelites kept their self-control. They had been waiting a long time to enter the Promised Land and were not about to do anything to anger the Lord.

SELF-CONTROL

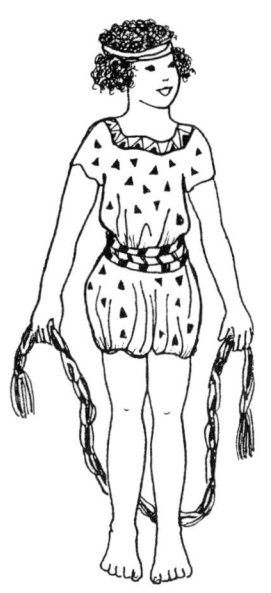

Sometimes it's hard
To keep your self-control.
Sometimes you can't wait
To do something great,
Or go somewhere cool.
Sometimes you wish
Time would please hurry up,
Especially when others
Are fed up with hearing
"Are we there yet?
Can I jump in the pool?
Can I eat my dessert?

When can I talk?
Do I have to be quiet?
Will it cause a riot
If I scratch my nose,
Or muss my new clothes,
Or wriggle,
Or giggle,
Or ask one more question?"
It's hard keeping still.
Self-control is a skill
That needs to be practiced.
Perhaps when you're older,
Calmer and slower,
And you want time to last
Just a little bit longer,
You'll be patient and stronger.
Then your self-control
Will be under control!

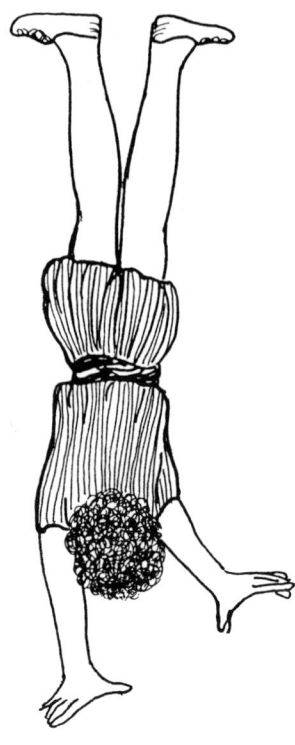

Finally, it was time to leave. Officers went from tribe to tribe giving these orders: "As soon as you see the Levite priests carrying the Ark of the Covenant of the Lord, you must pack up your tents and belongings, round up all the animals, and follow behind." The Ark, which was always in the center of the camp, would now be in front. God was ready to lead His people home.

The Lord said to Joshua: "Today I will make you a great man in the eyes of the Children of Israel. They will know that I will be with you as I was with Moses. You must now command the priests to walk past the water's edge and stand still in the Jordan River."

Joshua followed these instructions and then said to the Children of Israel:

"Hear the words of the Lord your God:
The living God is with you.

He is not made of stone.
Before you He will drive out
The wicked from your home:
The Canaanite, the Hittite,
The Hivite and the Perizzite,
All worshipers of idols,
Gergashite, Amorite, and Jebusite."

Next Joshua directed the Israelites to pick a man from each tribe. He would later have a very important job to do. Then, he continued giving directions:

"When the feet of the priests who carry the Ark
Stand in the Jordan's swift waters,
This fast-moving river shall stop its flow,
No water above, no water below.
From shallow to deep
It shall stand in one heap!"

The Children of Israel, following Joshua's orders, lined up a good distance behind the priests. They were not allowed to come too close to God's holy Ark.

As the feet of the priests
Stood in the river,
The fast-moving water
Rose up in a heap.
Like Moses before them,
The Children of Israel
Passed over on dry ground,
God's promise to keep.

When all the Israelites had crossed over the river, God said to Joshua: "Tell each of the twelve men selected from each tribe to return to the middle of the river, where the priests are holding the Ark. Each one is to find a very big stone, lift it onto his shoulder, and carry it back to his tribe. When your children ask, 'What do these stones mean?' you shall say, 'This is to remind us that the waters of the Jordan stopped flowing before the Ark of the Lord.'"

Joshua then set twelve big stones in the river bed to mark the places where the priest's feet were standing. They are still there today!

All the Children of Israel, including forty thousand soldiers from the two and one-half tribes who had chosen to stay on the river's eastern side, had passed before God's holy Ark and reached the Promised Land!

The Lord said to Joshua, "Command the priests to come out of the Jordan." And just as the soles of their feet reached dry ground, the heap of still water dissolved into a churning, rushing torrent that overflowed its banks as it raced to its final home in the Dead Sea.

The people camped in Gilgal,
Not far from Jericho.
There Joshua set up the stones,
The twelve stones from the Jordan.
He said, "Someday when you are asked
The meaning of these stones,
You'll answer 'God dried up the Jordan,
As He did the Sea of Reeds,
Until you had passed over.
The Lord God's Hand is mighty!
You must respect the Lord forever!'"

Joshua, the Angel, and Jericho

Angels are the messengers of the Lord. Sometimes they have important information to deliver, and sometimes they announce God's Presence. Angels told Abraham that he would have a son named Isaac, and angels warned Lot that Sodom was to be destroyed. Jacob saw angels climbing up and down a beautiful ladder; Moses saw an angel in the flame of a burning bush, right before God spoke to him for the first time; and an angel with a sword blocked the path of Balaam and his talking donkey.

As Joshua waited outside the city of Jericho, a man appeared, sword in hand. "Are you for us or for our enemies?" asked Joshua.

The man answered, "I am the captain of the Lord's angels."

Joshua lay face down with his hands outstretched. This was a sign of reverence. The angel, speaking for the Lord, said, "Take off your shoes because the place where you are standing is holy."

Joshua did as he was told, and the Lord said: "I have given to you the city of Jericho, its king, and all its brave men. Here is what you must do to capture it:

Take your men of war
And seven priests with seven ram's horns,

27

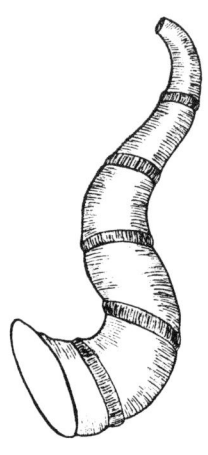 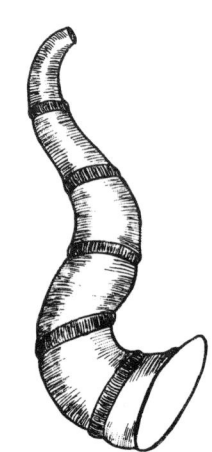

And for each of seven days
Tell them to walk once round the town,
Blowing loudly on their horns.
They'll make a terrifying sound!
On the seventh day,
Walk seven times around the town.
Tell your priests to blow their horns,
And when they make their last, loud sound,
Have all your people shout!
The sturdy walls of Jericho
Will all fall down!"

Joshua called the priests and said: "Tomorrow, you will take the Ark of the Covenant and have seven priests carrying seven ram's horns walk before it. Armed soldiers are to be in front and behind the Ark."

Joshua then told his people that they were to follow behind this procession as it circled the town. He warned them: "Let no sound escape from your mouth until I tell you to shout. Then you can yell as loud as you want."

Early the next morning, Joshua supervised the lineup. Once around the town they went, the ragged wail of the ram's horns piercing the soft air of morning.

The horns made such a racket
Donkeys folded back their ears!
Birdsong, bee-buzz,
Moo and cackle,
All but disappeared
Into the noise of seven ram's horns,
And their wailing, shrieking sound!
Even camels put their heads
Between their feet,
Close to the ground!

On the seventh day, as the sun peeked warily over the horizon, the Israelites marched seven times around the town. As they began the final circling Joshua ordered: "Shout! For the Lord has given you this city! Jericho and all that is in it shall be dedicated to the Lord! Only the family of the good woman Rahab, who took care of our men, shall be spared!"

As the last shrill wail of the ram's horns sounded, the Children of Israel began shouting, louder and louder! The walls of Jericho shook with the noise and came tumbling down! The two spies found the red rope hanging in Rahab's window and rescued her and her family. All the rest of the people of Jericho perished.

War is terrible. People are hurt, some die, and some are captured. Towns and countries are destroyed. However, long ago, when God was trying to make His young world perfect, He gave Joshua permission to wage war against the sinful people of Canaan, who were breaking His commandments. These people worshiped idols made of stone and clay. Sometimes, they were cruel to children and did dreadful deeds. God had already told Moses: "It is not because of your goodness that you are going to possess the Promised Land, but because of the wickedness of the Canaanites. This is why the Lord your God will be driving them out before you!" And so Joshua, the mighty warrior and leader chosen by God, did exactly as the Lord commanded.

The Day the Sun Stood Still

Joshua, the mighty warrior, never forgot that he was the successor to Moses, the great teacher. One day, after a large battle for the city of Ai, Joshua assembled the Children of Israel. He wanted to remind them, once again, of the important lessons taught by Moses. Half the Israelites stood in front of Mount Ebal, and the rest, in front of Mount Gerizim. The direct center of the Promised Land was between these two hills. There, Joshua followed the directions found in Deuteronomy, the fifth book of Moses. He took the twelve big stones from the Jordan River, covered them with white plaster, and set them up in front of Mount Ebal. Then, he built an altar to God of stones untouched by iron tools.

A sword is made of iron,
Which symbolizes strife.
In battles during warfare,
Iron shortens life.
An altar made to God
Of stone untouched by iron,
Symbolizes peace
Between the Lord and all His children.

31

A burnt offering, to ask God's forgiveness for any wrongdoings, was given on this altar, followed by a peace offering of thanks. Next, Joshua wrote all the laws of Moses on the newly plastered stones. He wrote very carefully, so that all the people, young and old, would be able to read the words. After reciting these laws to the Israelites, Joshua, like Moses before him, recited the Blessings and the Curses. These were God's promises and warnings, all the "dos" and "don'ts" of life in this Promised Land. And Joshua reminded his people to love God and to always walk in His ways.

As the Children of Israel moved through the land of Canaan, they had many new things to learn. Since they had been shepherds, wandering in the desert, they knew little about farming. In Canaan, they learned how to clear forests and fields and how to plow, plant, and fertilize the earth. They were clever people and soon made terraced gardens that descended, like wide steps, from the many hills that rambled through the center of Canaan. Where once they moved from oasis to oasis searching for water, they now learned to make cisterns, big containers to hold the precious water that nourished the Promised Land.

Joshua's reputation as a great warrior was known far and wide. When the townspeople of Gibeon, one of the four Hivite cities God had promised to the Israelites, heard what the mighty Joshua had done to Jericho and Ai, their leaders devised a trick to save themselves from the same fate. They put old, ragged sacks on their donkeys, filled patched-up wine containers with water, and dressed themselves in worn-out shoes and ripped clothing. For their food, they prepared some dry, crumbly bread covered with green mold. Gibeon was only nineteen miles, or a three-day walk uphill, from Gilgal, the Israelites' home base. In Joshua's day, people were used to walking for years and years; a few days' walk must have seemed like a leisurely stroll. The Gibeonites walked the short distance downhill to Gilgal and found Joshua, who asked these decrepit-looking men, "Who are you and where do you come from?"

"We have come from a country far away and wish to make peace with you," answered the disguised Hivites. "We have heard about the Lord your God, what He did for you in Egypt, and how you have conquered kings. Our leaders sent us to you. We took clothes and food with us but, because of our long journey, our clothes are torn and our food is spoiled."

These men told a very convincing story. They certainly fooled Joshua, who made a sacred covenant with them and spared their lives.

Three days later, Joshua found out the truth: these imposters were really his neighbors, the Hivites! The Children of Israel were very angry about being deceived!

"Why did you lie to us, saying you lived far away, when you really live close by?" asked Joshua, controlling his temper.

The men replied: "We heard that your Lord commanded Moses to give you all this land and to destroy its inhabitants. Now that you have reached Canaan, we are afraid for our lives. That is why we did not tell the truth. We place ourselves and our people in your hands. Do with us what you think is fair."

Promises are not made to be broken unless, of course, there is a very good reason. Sacred promises, like the Lord's covenants, are never to be broken. Since Joshua had already made a sacred covenant of peace with these imposters, it was his duty to save them from destruction. As punishment, the Gibeonites were given the difficult jobs of being woodcutters and water carriers. They would work hard for their lives!

TELLING LIES

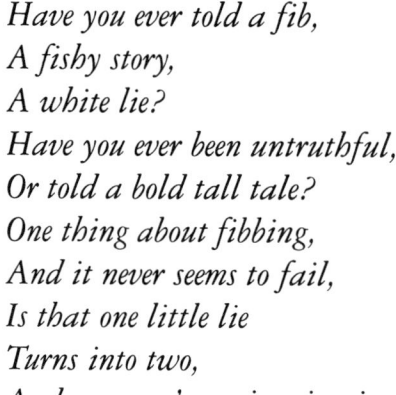

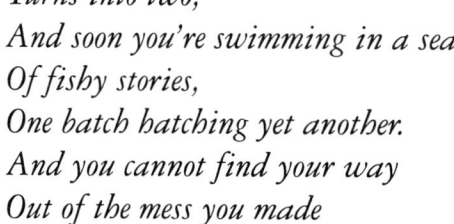

Have you ever told a fib,
A fishy story,
A white lie?
Have you ever been untruthful,
Or told a bold tall tale?
One thing about fibbing,
And it never seems to fail,
Is that one little lie
Turns into two,
And soon you're swimming in a sea
Of fishy stories,
One batch hatching yet another.
And you cannot find your way
Out of the mess you made
When first you told
That fib, or fishy story,
White lie, untruth, or tale.
And then finally, of course,
Like hungry fish,
You will get caught!
And you'll surely be embarrassed!
You forgot what you'd been taught
About NEVER EVER telling
Fibs, or fishy stories,
Or tall tales that seem odd.
You must always tell the truth.
You must be honest every day.
Remember God is listening
To every word you say!

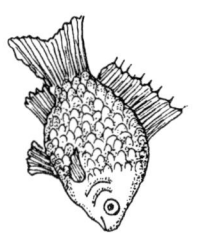

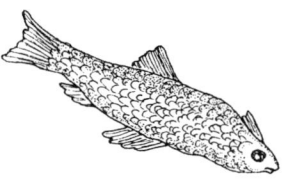

When the Amorite king of Jerusalem, Adoni-Zedek, heard the amazing stories about Joshua and how the inhabitants of Gibeon had made peace with the Israelites, he became frightened. Gibeon was known as a great city with a strong army. This was a disgrace! How could they have betrayed the rest of the Canaanite tribes and let this happen? The king sent messages to four other Amorite kings to come and help him destroy Gibeon!

As the five armies gathered outside the high walls of Gibeon, the townspeople sent Joshua this message: "Do not abandon your servants! Come quickly and help us against these enemies!"

Joshua did not abandon his new servants. After he assembled his warriors, the Lord said to Joshua: "Do not fear this great army. I have delivered them into your hands. Not one man will fight you!"

The rich city of Gibeon sat on top of a great hill. Joshua and his men marched uphill very quickly, all through the night, and surprised the Amorites. The Lord had helped by making the enemy weak, and they were easily conquered. Some did try to run away downhill, but the Lord sent hailstones, as big as duck eggs, which knocked down the fleeing warriors!

Just then, the sun began to slip into the blanket of night. Since darkness would help any remaining Amorites to flee, Joshua spoke these words to the Lord, in front of the Children of Israel.

"Sun, stand still over Gibeon;
And moon, in the valley of Aijalon."

The sun stood still,
And the moon stayed put
Until Joshua conquered the Amorites.
Never before had there been such a day!
Never again would there be such a day!
The Lord God listened to the voice of a man,
And granted His people a miracle!
By the helpful light of the sun at night,
God stood by their side
In His Promised Land!

Thirty-one Kings

These are the kings whom Joshua conquered,
  As he marched with his army through God's Promised Land.
  Though his warriors only had swords, slings, and daggers,
They had lots of courage and heads that were clever.
They never gave up!
They never gave in to fear of their enemies
Riding in chariots,
Pulled by swift horses across the flat plains.
The Israelites lured them to come to the hills.
The pride of Canaan, swift horses and chariots,
Could not climb the hills!
There was no place to hide!
And they soon were defeated by Israel's army!
The great leader Joshua had God by his side!

These are the kings whom Joshua conquered,
As he marched with his army through God's Promised Land:

The great king of Jericho,
The strong king of Ai,
The kings of Jerusalem,
Hebron,
And Jarmuth.
The kings of Lachish,
Of Eglon,
And Gezer,
Of Debir,
And Geder.
The king of Hormah.
The kings of Arad,
Of Libnah,
And Adullam.
The king of Makkedah.
The king of Beth-El.
The kings of Tappuah,
Of Hepher,
And Aphek.
The king of the Sharon.
The king of Madon.
The kings of Hazor,
And Shimron-Meron.
The king of Achshaph,
And the king of Taanach.
The king of Megiddo.
The kings of Kedesh,
Of Jokneam in Carmel,
And Dor.
The fierce king of Goiim
   in the Gilgal,
And the king of Tirza.
Thirty-one kings in all!

37

These are the kings whom Joshua conquered,
As he marched with his army through God's Promised Land.
From the north to the south, his army went forth.
From the hills to the valleys, from the east to the west.
Thirty-one kings and all of their lands
Were given, by God, into Joshua's hands.
And after these wars
There was peace,
There was rest.

Joshua Distributes the Promised Land

When most of Canaan was conquered, Joshua, leader of the Children of Israel, began dividing the land between the twelve tribes. Although this job was difficult, Joshua acted wisely and with patience. Joshua's people respected him and were grateful for what they received. They knew he would not allow quarreling and jealous behavior to disrupt this important duty.

LEADERS

Leaders stay calm
When there's work to be done.
Leaders stay cool,
They're not nervous.
They don't get the jitters,
The quivers or dithers,
They're not shook-up or jumpy,
Upset or uptight.
They don't lose self-control,

Or get overexcited.
They don't throw a fit
Or walk off in a snit!
When leaders stay calm,
They make wise decisions.
Their thinking is clear;
Their heads are on tight.
They use common sense,
And they don't show their fear.
When leaders stay calm,
Their people will listen
To all their directions,
And do what is right!

Joshua began the distribution of land by describing the portions that Moses had already given to the tribes of Gad, Reuben, and half of Manasseh. These people were in the cattle-raising business, and this green valley bordered with hills, on the Jordan's eastern side, was perfect. As promised, the men of these tribes had helped their friends settle in Canaan. Now they could cross back over the river and return to their families. After reminding them to observe the laws of Moses, to love God, and to keep His commandments, Joshua blessed these people and sent them away.

Next, Joshua gave the tribes of Ephraim and the other half of Manasseh land that included the towns of Shechem and Shiloh. This area was full of trees. The tribes would have to learn to clear the forests, dig wells, and save water in cisterns. Soon, grapes and cucumbers would tumble over terraced gardens, butterflies would help the flowers help the bees make honey, and lemons and pomegranates would shine like yellow and red polka dots against the clear blue sky.

The large tribe of Judah was given the southern hill country. These shepherds were strong people accustomed to hard work. Although this land was rugged and rocky, they were determined to make some of it fertile. To their delight, there would also be plenty of grazing ground for their spotted sheep, long-haired goats, and chubby cows.

After assigning these portions of land, Joshua decided to erect the Tent of Meeting in a central location. Shiloh, twelve miles north of Shechem, was selected. Abraham had built the first altar to God at Shechem, and ever since that time, the people living around Shechem had been friendly toward the Israelites. Also, because it was in the middle of high hills, Shiloh seemed to be safe from attack.

The tribes of Ephraim and half of Manasseh were very proud to hear that the Ark of the Covenant would rest on their land. This turned out to be a good choice; the Ark remained there for the next three hundred eighty-nine years!

Shiloh would be the gathering place for worship during the three big festivals honoring the Passover, the giving of the law at Mount Sinai, and the final harvest. This last, joyous festival, was to remind the Israelites of how they had lived outdoors, in flimsy huts, for forty years. Shiloh would also serve as a convention center, a place for tribal meetings and business discussions. There was plenty of room for tents and the mountain scenery was spectacular!

Seven tribes had not yet received their inheritances. Joshua told these people, who were getting bored and lazy as they waited: "Wake up! Get a move on! This is no time to relax! I want three men from each tribe to walk through and survey the remaining land. They are to return with seven written descriptions of seven different portions of land."

He reminded them that the Levites were not included in this assignment because the priesthood was their inheritance. All twelve tribes were to set aside for the priests a portion of land surrounded by open fields. This way the Levites would have somewhere private to stay, wherever they might travel.

When the men returned from their sight-seeing trip, Joshua held a lottery. He took two large, round containers, called urns, and placed the names of the tribes in one and the seven land descriptions in the other. He shook each urn to mix up the contents, and then reached in and selected one name from urn number one and one from urn number two. This was called "drawing lots." The first name he picked was the small tribe of Benjamin. It was paired with a narrow piece of the Jordan valley that included the city of Jericho and the unconquered city of Jerusalem.

Next, the tribe of Simeon received land practically on top of that of Judah. They were so close together that eventually Simeon would decide to give up its inheritance and become part of Judah.

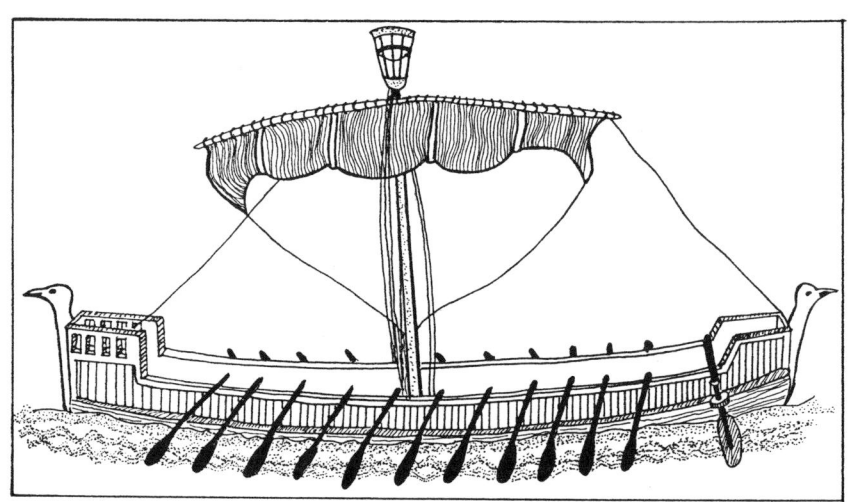

The third lot drawn was for the tribe of Zebulun. They received mountainous land near the sea. This would fulfill Jacob's words from long ago: "Zebulun shall live at the shore of the sea." These people soon learned the art of shipbuilding. In time, their descendants would become merchant-sailors who traveled to distant lands trading or selling goods such as

Lemons and apricots,
Sweet grapes and wine,
Wheat, barley, and lentils,
Pistachio nuts,
Olive oil, honey,
And the bright purple cloth
That had made Canaan famous.
It was traded like money!

These early sailing trips took a long time. After two or three years, the sailors might return with a cargo of

Marvelous perfumes,
Soft cotton, new spices,
Fine gold, and strong iron,
Strange animals, too.
There were monkeys and peacocks,
And camels with two humps,
Aardvarks and cats.
Were they building a zoo?

In the future, sea travel would make God's world, as the Israelites knew it, more and more wondrous.

The tribes of Issachar, Asher, and Naphtali also received land not far from the sea. Unfortunately, Issachar's fertile land contained many unconquered Canaanite cities. The tribe had a hard time keeping order and soon became weak.

The tribe of Asher won the best land of all! It had rich soil, green pastures, and a sparkling seacoast. They became a wealthy people and, as Moses had predicted, "they would dip their feet into the oil of their olive groves." Asher's land was truly filled with milk and honey. However, when people get too many good things at one time, they often become careless. The tribe of Asher spent more time having fun than working hard. These people did not know how to save money and soon lost their importance.

The tribe of Naphtali was allotted a large portion of the eastern mountains leading down to the sea. They did well, raised big families, and had a large army that could be relied on to help out in emergencies.

The tribe of Dan was given a nice piece of land in the southeastern part of the hill country. Soft breezes blew in from the sea, and the sunny countryside was ideal for growing olive trees and wheat. They were happy with their inheritance and did not know that a fierce tribe of people, called Philistines, would someday force them to move from this lovely place.

When all the land had been distributed, Joshua accepted the city of Temnath-Serah, in the mountains of Ephraim, for himself. There he built a nice stone house in the shade of an old cypress tree. Joshua could finally take a rest, go fishing in the nearby streams, and have the time to do a little bird watching.

Some years later, Joshua called a meeting of the Children of Israel. He said:

"I am old now, my years are many.
You have seen what God has done
To the nations who once lived upon your land.
He fought for you before,
And he will do so until all
The lands of your inheritance are conquered.
He will thrust them out before you!
He will drive them from your sight!
Therefore, be courageous, follow Moses and his law.
Do not turn aside; go neither left nor right.
When you meet up with these nations,
Make no mention of their gods.
Neither swear by them nor serve them.
Hold on to the Lord your God, as you have done up to this day.
Remember, it was easy to chase thousands,
Because God first drove them away!
If you turn back and hold onto these strange nations in your land
Or if you marry with them,
Know that, for sure, God nevermore
Will drive them from your door.
They will become a snare, a trap, a pain in both your sides.
Your eyes will hurt as though they're pricked with thorns.
And you will surely die.
Though I depart from this good earth remember, in your heart,
That everything told you by God
Has come to pass.
Not one has failed!
But if you break the sacred promises,
And disobey what He commands,
The Lord's anger will be great,
And you will perish from this land!"

Joshua's Farewell

Reunions are special meetings filled with hugs and kisses and shared memories, both happy and sad. When Joshua, the mighty warrior, was one hundred and ten years old, he asked all the Israelites to come to Shechem for a reunion. Everyone was excited; many people hadn't seen each other for a long time. There were proud mothers and fathers showing off beautiful babies, and many young people taking their first steps away from childhood. There were new stories to memorize, new dances to practice, and new music to learn, although naturally, some grown-ups complained about the noise. Everyone brought food and, as they waited for Joshua to speak, the Children of Israel had a delicious picnic!

There was cucumber salad and red-lentil stew,
Whole wheat and barley bread, raisin bread too.
Ripe watermelons, and sweet lemonade,
Date cakes and yogurt, and hard-boiled duck eggs.
They had leeks and tomatoes and plenty of wine
Made from fat purple grapes grown on leafy green vines.
And then all became quiet, not a cough or a giggle.
Children sat still, trying hard not to wiggle.

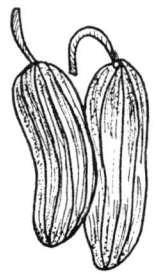

As fluffy white clouds played tag with the sun,
They listened to Joshua, son of Nun.

Although old in years, Joshua stood tall and straight as he spoke to the Children of Israel. He said:

"Here are the words of the Lord your God:
'I took your father, Abraham, and led him through Canaan.
I gave descendants to him, and Isaac was his son.
To Isaac I gave twins, Esau first and Jacob last.
I gave Mount Seir to Esau.
Jacob and his children went away to Egypt,
Where they lived for many years.
I sent Moses, I sent Aaron, to bring you up from Egypt.
Chariots and horsemen pursued you to the sea.
And the sea was turned back by the Lord
Right before your eyes.
You were in the desert forty years
And others fought against you.
Then Balak, king of Moab, called Balaam in to curse you.
I wouldn't listen to his pleas,
And he blessed you instead.
You crossed the Jordan river and came to Jericho.
You fought against strong people; I drove them out before you.
And I gave you land and cities, leafy vineyards, olive trees.'
Now, therefore, fear the Lord!
Serve Him sincerely and be true!
But if you do not wish to serve the Lord,
Then you must choose whom you will serve.
But as for me
And my own family,
We will serve the Lord!"
The people answered,
"We will not forsake the Lord for it is He
Who brought our fathers up from Egypt land.
He showed us signs and kept us safe.

He drove away our enemies.
He is our God and we will serve Him."
Joshua said to his people,
"He is a holy God and jealous;
He won't forgive your sins.
If you forsake the Lord and serve strange gods
He'll turn and do you evil."
The people said out loud,
"No, we will serve the Lord."
And Joshua, son of Nun, said,
"You are witnesses today.
You have chosen to serve God, the Lord.
Now therefore put away
Any strange gods still among you.
Give your heart only to the Lord."
The people answered Joshua,
"We will serve the Lord our God, listen to Him and obey."

On that special day, Joshua made a covenant with the Children of Israel. He wrote down the story of the renewal of God's sacred promises. Joshua then took a great stone and set it up beneath the oak tree that stood by the Tent of Meeting. He proclaimed:

"This stone shall be our witness, for today it has heard the words of the Lord."

The Children of Israel went back to their homes, carrying with them the great gift of God's words. Soon after, with the hope that his people would remember their covenant, Joshua, the mighty warrior, died and was buried in the hills of Ephraim. And the bones of Joseph, which had been brought up out of Egypt, were also buried in those hills, in the same parcel of ground purchased by his father, Jacob, so many years ago in this, God's Promised Land.

Judges

The Story of Gideon

It was not easy to farm the stony hills of Canaan. First, the Israelites had to cut flat spaces, like steps, into the hillsides. This is called "terrace gardening." Then, after digging and loosening the soil, big stones, large rocks, and old tree roots had to be carried away. For twelve months a year, six days a week, from dawn to sunset, farmers planted and harvested, weeded and watered. If they were lucky, the cucumber, zucchini, and melon vines would spill over the hills, like colored polka dots on the brown earth. Good luck is like a surprise gift: you never know when it might come your way. Bad luck is also a surprise, but it certainly isn't a gift!

*Sometimes there was no rain,
And sometimes it flooded.
Some years there were locusts
Who ate every leaf.
Sometimes a hot wind blew,
Sometimes there was mildew.
Sometimes enemies attacked
Leaving nothing but grief!*

53

When the farmers found nice, flat spaces, they planted fields of barley and wheat. If the weather cooperated, these long, graceful stalks swayed with the breezes, their plump tops golden in the sun. Good luck is something for which the farmers hoped; good weather is something on which they depended!

Ripe olives are picked in September
And pressed into green olive oil.
Then in late October, when winter rains come,
Barley and wheat seeds are placed in the soil.
All through the winter the farmer has patience,
Waiting and watching and pulling out weeds
While the little seeds grow into
Fat ears of barley and long sheaves of wheat,
Which are ready to cut in April and May.
On a nice, sunny day,
The farmer is ready to beat
The cut barley and the cut wheat.
This loosens and separates all of the grains.
He tosses these grains when a light breeze is blowing.
The chaff blows away,
And only the heaviest grains remain.
This is called "threshing" and "winnowing."
In summer, the sweet scent of roses and lilies
Perfumes the air.
While eggplants and squash turn their dark, shiny faces
Up to the sun,
Onions and radishes, carrots and leeks hide
Under the ground, until they are picked
By the hardworking farmer
Filling the baskets he keeps at his side.
Lemons and apricots, pears and red cherries
Hang from the trees,
While below them the berries
Can't wait to be picked and made into pies!
If August is filled with fair days and blue skies,
The ripe figs and dates will have doubled in size.

After planting, and picking,
Raking, and baking,
The farmer now comes to his most joyous time:
In late August when grapes almost burst on the vine,
He prunes and he cleans.
Then it's time to make wine!
Ripe olives are picked in September,
When the earth starts its journey
Away from the sun.
The days become cool,
There is work to be done.
Once again, the farmer's long year has begun.

With bad luck hanging over them like heavy clouds, plus the constant threat of bad weather, the Children of Israel did what was evil in the eyes of the Lord. They forgot the second commandment, *"You shall have no other gods before Me,"* and began building altars to Canaanite gods. The crops belonging to their idol-worshiping neighbors seemed to be bigger, greener, and riper than their own. The Israelites thought that by imitating the Canaanites, their own luck would change.

The Lord became very angry with His people. As punishment, He allowed the Midianites to attack the Israelites for seven terrible years. The Midianites were a dangerous tribe who made great use of swift, galloping camels. Sitting high up on these snorting animals, they raided Israelite towns and fields. Stealing everything that had taken the Israelites a full year to grow, the Midianites, along with some of their ferocious friends, would ride off into the sunset. The Israelites, trying to hide themselves and whatever food they could carry in mountain caves, were in great distress. Finally, they asked the Lord for help.

In the town of Ophah, an angel of the Lord came and sat under a terebinth tree. Gideon, the son of Joash, was beating grains of wheat in an old winepress, an oblong-shaped bowl cut into the rocky hill. He was a smart young man, and this was a clever solution to the wheat-stealing problem. Nobody would think to look in a winepress for kernels of wheat! Gideon was a good, kind son, who took over much of his father's hard work. He was also courageous and a fast thinker. The angel, watching Gideon, liked what he saw and said, "The Lord is with you, brave warrior."

Gideon replied: "If the Lord is with us, then why have we had all this bad luck? Where are God's wonderful deeds, such as bringing His people up from Egypt, that our ancestors told us about? Now He has thrown us away into Midianite hands."

Because He saw that Gideon had remembered the lessons about God, the Lord Himself, answered, "Go, and with your great courage, you shall save the Children of Israel from the Midianites."

Gideon was not afraid to tell God how he felt. He said: "O Lord, how can I save my people? My family is the poorest in the tribe of Manasseh, and I am the youngest son."

The Lord answered, "I will be with you and you shall completely destroy the Midianites!"

Gideon was amazed that God had spoken to him. He asked the angel, who had reappeared, to do something special as proof of this wondrous event. "Please don't leave," said Gideon, "until I come back with a gift for you."

"I shall wait until you return," replied the angel.

Gideon went into his tent and prepared a young goat and a bushel of cakes made of unleavened, ground meal. Putting the goat meat and the cakes in a big basket and the cooking broth in a pot, Gideon carried his gift out to the waiting angel.

"Pour out the broth," ordered the angel of God, "and place the meat and the unleavened cakes on this rock."

Then, the angel took the staff that was in his hand and touched the meat and the cakes. Suddenly, a great fire came out of the rock, burned up the food, and the angel disappeared!

"O Lord," cried Gideon, "now that I have seen proof that he truly was the angel of the Lord, I know I shall die!" Gideon remembered that God had said to Moses, "You shall not see Me and live." Thinking that this also meant God's angels, Gideon was terrified.

But God, in His kindness, eased Gideon's fears. "Do not be afraid," said the Lord. "There is peace. You shall not die."

That same night, God ordered Gideon to destroy the altar the Israelites had made to the god Baal. He was to build an altar to God, and take his father's ox as a burnt offering. Gideon took ten good men and obeyed the Lord's command.

When the townspeople saw that their altar to Baal had been destroyed, along with the idol that stood by its side, they asked each other, "Who could have done this?" When they found out that Gideon was the culprit, they said to his father, Joash: "Bring out your son. He must die because he tore down the altar to Baal and destroyed the idol."

Joash was a good father. He defended his son by saying to the angry crowd: "Are you going to fight for Baal? Any person who is so reckless as to try and save such a powerful idol will surely be dead by morning. If he is such a great god, let him take care of his own business!"

On that day, Gideon was given the name "Jerubaal," which means, "Let Baal fight against him because he has torn down his altar."

COURAGE

It's good to believe in what's right and what's wrong.
It's good to be brave and not take off and hide.
It's good to have someone stand by and support you.
And it's good to have good friends taking your side.

Gideon's Surprise

Every morning, tiny fingers of light reach out from the rising sun. Song-birds, awakened by this warm caress, sing their hellos to the dawn. These joyful birdsongs awaken the sleeping world. All who live on God's beautiful earth give thanks for the gift of a new day.

Gideon, the brave warrior, always got up with the birds, climbed the highest hill, and searched the surrounding valleys for enemies. One clear day he overslept; the sun had already begun its climb toward heaven and the only sound he heard was the breeze rippling through the tall grass. The birds were silent. Was this a warning? Sensing that something was very wrong, Gideon quickly ran up the hill. Turning slowly, he saw the Midian-ites, Amalekites, and several other unfriendly tribes preparing, once again, to raid Israelite villages. They had crossed a shallow part of the Jordan River and were pitching tents and building campfires. Thinking fast, Gideon blew a loud blast from a ram's horn. Immediately, the men who lived in the area came running to his side. He sent messengers throughout all of Manasseh and to the tribes of Asher, Zebulun, and Naphtali; they soon joined Gideon and his men. The Spirit of the Lord wrapped Itself around Gideon and helped give him the strength and courage to fight back!

59

Gideon said to God: "I am putting a fleece of lamb's wool on the hilltop threshing ground. If there is dew only on the fleece and not on the ground, I will know that You will save Israel through me, as You promised."

When Gideon awakened
Very early in the morning,
He pressed the fleece together
And squeezed out a bowl of water.
As the sun rose in the sky,
The ground beneath the fleece was dry!

Gideon again spoke to God: "O Lord, please do not be angry with me, but I need another sign that You are with me. This time, when I awake, let the fleece be dry."

When Gideon awakened
Very early in the morning,
As the sun rose in the sky
A pool of dew was on the ground.
And though it lay upon the dew,
The fleece was fluffy, white, and dry!

Filled with the assurance of God's help, Gideon and all the men who were with him set up camp in a green valley by a fast-flowing stream. The Midianites and the other enemy troops were camped next to a hill about four miles away.

The Lord said to Gideon: "There are too many people with you. If I deliver the Midianites into their hands, they might give themselves all the glory." The Lord wanted to remind the Children of Israel that it was not by numbers or strength but by the Lord's Hand that they would be saved.

The Lord continued, "Tell your people that whoever is trembling with fear may leave this place."

Twenty thousand men took advantage of God's offer and went home. Ten thousand men remained.

The Lord said: "There are still too many people. Bring them down to the water and I will decide who shall or shall not go with you."

Gideon did as the Lord commanded. He listened carefully as the Lord gave further directions: "Set aside every man who cups his hand and laps the water with his tongue, like a dog. Make another group of the men who go down on their knees to drink." The Lord knew that really good soldiers would not kneel down or turn their backs on their enemies. In this way, three hundred men were chosen and the rest were sent home.

That same night, the Lord instructed Gideon to sneak into the enemy camp and listen to what they were saying. He knew that this would help Gideon have the courage to attack. By campfire light, Gideon saw so many soldiers that they looked like swarms of locusts. And the swift camels were too numerous to count. As Gideon walked around on tiptoes, he heard a man telling this dream to a friend:

"I dreamed this dream about
A cake of barley bread.
Round and flat
It tumbled over,
It flip-flopped
Into our camp.
And when it came
Up to a tent
It didn't stop
Until the tent fell down
And lay upon the ground.
Now friend,
What do you think of that!"

61

The other soldier answered fearfully:
"This cake of barley bread
Can only mean bad news for Midian.
Their God will place us, by His Hand,
Before the sword of Gideon."

This was all Gideon had to hear! Filled with encouragement, he first gave a prayer of thanks to God and then said to his men: "Arise. The Lord will deliver our enemies into your hands!"

Gideon divided the three hundred men into three companies. He gave each man a ram's horn and an empty pitcher with a flaming torch hidden inside. He said: "Watch me carefully and do exactly as I do. After we surround their camp, I will blow my horn. All of you are then to blow your horns and shout: *'For the Lord and for Gideon!'*"

Three hundred men and Gideon
Moved softly round the camp.
Three hundred ram's horns wailed their warning
Through the still night air.
Three hundred pitchers fell
And hidden torches lit the sky.
Three hundred men and Gideon let out a fearsome cry:
"The sword for the Lord and Gideon!"
The great army fled in fright!
Three hundred men and Gideon
Watched them flee into the night!

As the enemy scattered, Gideon sent this message to the men living in the hill country of Ephraim: "Come down to the banks of the Jordan River and seize the Midianites!" The men of Naphtali, Asher, and Manasseh chased the Midianites and their fellow invaders toward the river. Waiting there, on the banks, were the men of Ephraim. The enemy was trapped! Two Midian leaders, Oreb (which means "raven") and Zeeb (which means "wolf") were captured. Their heads were cut off and brought to Gideon, who was rounding up stray enemy soldiers. In Gideon's day, there was no quick way to tell someone in another place the results of a good or bad deed. That's why they sometimes used rather disgusting methods of proof, like cut-off heads!

"Why didn't you call for us when you went to fight against this enemy?" complained the men of Ephraim after they delivered the gruesome proof.

Gideon, who was a tactful leader, answered: "What I have done is nothing compared to your achievements. God delivered into your hands these two leaders!"

It is good to answer a complaint quietly. This helps the complainer to calm down and think clearly. By making the Ephraimites feel good about their own success, Gideon was able to stop the anger and bring the tribes closer together.

Soon after the kings of Midian had also been captured and slain, peace finally came to the Promised Land. The Children of Israel said to Gideon, "Rule over us, you, then your son and also your grandson, because you saved us from the hand of Midian."

Gideon answered them, saying: "I will not rule over you. Neither shall my son rule over you. The Lord shall rule over you!"

And Gideon, son of Joash,
Went home and lived a good life,
With his many wives and children.
They all lived happily;
No more fighting, no more fears.
And the country was at peace
While Gideon lived there
Forty years.

The Story of Deborah

Keeping large groups of people together is a difficult job. Making sure that they obey rules and laws is even harder. A good leader knows when to ask for help and how to appoint others to share responsibilities. When Moses told God that he was having trouble dealing with the burden of so many people, God instructed him to choose good men from all the tribes to help judge the Israelites. These important people acted as assistant leaders; they settled arguments and squabbles and, when enemies threatened the tribes, they helped create a well-disciplined army.

Joshua, the successor to Moses, was also a great leader. He managed to keep the twelve tribes organized because they all had the same goal: to settle in the Promised Land. And, since Joshua was also a great warrior, he was able to help his people conquer most of Canaan. The Children of Israel kept the memory of God's wonderful signs and miracles close to their hearts. They remembered the words of Moses, and Joshua made a solemn promise to serve God and always listen to His Voice.

After Joshua died, the Israelites continued to serve the Lord, as they had promised. However, in time, the assistant leaders, who had outlived Joshua, also died and were buried with their ancestors in the large family tombs.

A new generation of Israelites was growing up all over Canaan. Their towns had simple stone huts, with sleeping mats for beds and goatskin water bags. These towns were often surrounded by unconquered Canaanite cities full of all sorts of beautiful things.

The Canaanite people dressed in fine linen;
Their clothes were embroidered with colorful thread.
They were famous for making a dyed purple cloth
Which was traded like money for other nice things
Such as spices and jewelry, tables and beds.
In their sturdy stone houses were jars of all shapes
And sizes for water, for wine, and for grain.
Some jars had long straws for sipping and straining
The beer made from barley; this too gave them fame.
There were special small jars for babies just learning
To drink by themselves, with spouts on the side
That they sucked when they wanted
Some goat's milk or grape juice. When these babies cried,
Their mothers would put them in fancy carved cradles
Which they rocked as they sang their sweet lullabies.
The Canaanite ladies wore all sorts of makeup,
They made their lips red and they outlined their eyes.
Their long, shiny hair was curled up at the ends.
The men also had long hair, now that's no surprise!

Wherever the Israelites looked, there were statues of strange gods called Baal and Asherah. Worshiping Baal, the god of nature and weather, was supposed to ensure good crops. Worshiping Asherah would help people produce beautiful children. Since these young Israelites had not personally seen God's miracles, they were tempted to try their luck with these gods of the Canaanites, Hittites, Amorites, Perizzites, Hivites, and Jebusites. Perhaps these idols might really help them have many healthy children, bigger crops, and full rivers. Maybe these gods would cause the sun to shine and the moon to dance with the stars.

The Children of Israel forgot that the Lord was watching their every move! When He had had enough, God made the very people whom they were imitating become their enemies!

BEING YOU

Trying to be who you're not
Will cause trouble,
Mostly for you.
The people you copy
Have had many years
Of being themselves,
And you with your years
Of just being you
Can never catch up and be
Someone you're not.

Who needs a person
So like someone else
In the way that they think,
Do a job,
Wear their hair,
Or their hat,
Tie their shoes,
Or choose colors?
It's better
Just to be you.
This way you won't lose
Your own personality
Being
Someone you're not.

Learn what you can
From the others around you.
Then take what you learn
And add it to
Everything else that you know.
Take it slow.
Think and stop,
Before you try too hard to be
Someone you're not!

66

When the Lord saw that the Children of Israel were behaving in evil ways, He placed them in the hands of Jabin, the mighty king of Canaan. The captain of his army was Sisera, a ferocious man. For twenty years he tormented the Israelites. Animals and birds stopped in their tracks when Sisera made his way across Canaan. They were afraid to move an ear, chirp a note, or swish a tail. Men feared him and bowed before Sisera. If they displeased him, they were slain!

Sisera had nine hundred iron chariots, each one carrying a skillful archer armed with a bow and arrow that could shoot long distances. His foot soldiers had iron spears, shields, and helmets and wore protective metal body coverings.

The Israelites had never seen such frightening sights. They still fought on foot using bronze or copper daggers and swords, along with stones and slings. Their small bows and arrows only went a short distance. They had leather-covered wooden shields but no protective body clothing. Finally, when they could no longer defend themselves, the Children of Israel cried to the Lord for help.

This was not an easy time for the Israelites. They were scattered all over the Promised Land and had no unity. They relied on judges, temporary leaders appointed by the Lord, to rescue them from terrible times. In the land of Ephraim, the judge was a woman named Deborah. Every day she sat under a tree called the Palm Tree of Deborah, high in the hills, and people would come to her for advice and to settle arguments. When Deborah learned that Sisera's army was about to attack, she sent for Barak, a famous warrior from the tribe of Naphtali. He was to command an army of twenty thousand Israelites!

"The Lord has commanded that you go toward Mount Tabor," directed Deborah. "I will lure Sisera's army to the Brook of Kishon and deliver them into your hands."

Barak said: "If you will come with me, I will go. If you will not come with me, then I will not go." Barak thought that Deborah, the judge, would help him have great power.

"I will go with you," said Deborah. "But remember this: You will not take the credit for winning. Sisera will first be given into the hands of a woman!"

Barak assembled the ten thousand men of Zebulun and Naphtali; they followed behind as he and Deborah led the way. From the top of Mount Tabor they saw below them the gleaming chariots of the enemy, each pulled by two fast horses. Deborah ordered: "Arise Barak! Today the Lord will deliver Sisera into your hand! The Lord has gone before you!"

As Barak's army went down from Mount Tabor,
The Lord caused a wild, sudden storm to pour
Buckets of rain and drop heavy, hard hail
Upon Sisera's men, their horses and chariots.
This made them panic, the horses were skidding,
The chariots tumbled one over the other!
Then the Brook of Kishon overflowed,
And the ground
Turned soft and soggy.
There was mud all around!
Fleeing soldiers were up to their knees in the goo;
They couldn't go forward, they couldn't go back.
Barak pursued them, not one man remained.
Except for Sisera, all the soldiers were slain!

The Story of Jael

A good soldier does not desert his troops. Sisera, the famous captain of the Canaanite army, was supposed to be a great soldier. However, in a time of real trouble, he turned himself around and slogged through the mud in the opposite direction!

Looking for shelter, Sisera saw a tent sitting by itself on a gently sloping hill. This belonged to the wife of Heber, the Kenite. Heber liked living in the hills, away from all his tribe's commotion. Sisera did not realize that Jael and Heber were not friends of Jabin, the king of Canaan.

Jael saw Sisera coming and urged him to enter her tent. To ask a strange man to enter your tent was unusual for a woman, but Jael was very brave. She knew all about Sisera's bad reputation and was determined to seek revenge for all the widows and orphaned children he had left in his wake. "This man will never kill again!" she vowed to herself, smiling sweetly as he entered her tent.

"Sisera, my lord, fear not," said Jael softly. Fooled by her kindness, Sisera took off his muddy sandals and lay down wearily on a straw mat. Jael covered him with a goatskin rug; after all the rain and mud, this certainly felt good.

"Give me some water to drink," he said, used to being waited on. "I am thirsty."

Instead of water, Jael gave him a cup of milk. One of the best things to drink when you need a good night's sleep is milk; it actually makes you sleepier! After ordering Jael to stand at the tent door and say "no" if anyone should ask, "Is there a man here?" Sisera quickly fell into a deep sleep.

Without making a sound, Jael walked up to the sleeping man. She picked up a tent peg and a big hammer, took a deep breath, and hammered the tent peg into the side of Sisera's head, all the way through to the ground!

Jael went outside and saw Barak coming up the hill, searching for the mighty Sisera. "Come and I will show you the man you are looking for," said the brave woman.

Barak went into Jael's tent and saw:

Sisera lying dead.
A tent peg in his head!

71

The Song of Deborah

Deborah, the wise judge, was also a great poet. On the day of their victory over Sisera's army, Deborah and Barak recited her wonderful song:

When Israel's men grow their hair long like warriors,
When Israel's people offer to fight,
Thank the Lord!
Listen kings and listen princes,
I will sing praises to God.
Lord, when You went to battle
The earth trembled.
The clouds in the heavens dropped rain.
Mountains quaked at Your Presence,
Even Mount Sinai shook at the Presence of God,
The Lord God of Israel.

In earlier days, enemies filled the highways.
And travelers had to take back roads.

People abandoned their villages,
Their Israelite homes,
Until you arose, Deborah, and took charge
Like Israel's own mother.

When your people chose new gods,
The Lord would not protect them,
And war came to their gates.
Was there a shield or a spear to be seen?
My grateful heart is with Israel's leaders
Who stayed with their people.
Bless the Lord!

All you wealthy people, who ride on white donkeys,
And sit on rich saddle cloths,
And all of you who walk by the wayside,
Retell the story of God's victories,
The victories of His leaders in Israel,
And how God's people went down to the gates
And confronted the enemy.

Awake, awake Deborah;
Awake, awake, sing a battle song!
Rise up Barak and take your captives.
The enemy came,
The kings of Canaan,
And they fought by the waters of Kishon.
The stars fought from God's heaven,
And rain fell from the clouds.
And the old Brook of Kishon,
Swept them away!

May Jael, wife of Heber, the Kenite,
Be the most blessed of women.
The king asked for water;
And she gave him milk.
Her left hand held the tent pin,

Her right hand held the hammer.
With the hammer, she hit him,
Straight through the head.
At Jael's feet he lay curled up.
Sisera was dead!

Sisera's mother
Looks out of her window.
"Why is my son's chariot so late coming home?"
Her handmaid gives this answer,
Which the mother repeats:
"Are they not dividing the treasure they've found,
And taking young women for slaves?
No doubt Sisera will find colorful clothes,
Embroidered garments, two for each warrior."

May Your enemies perish, O Lord.
But they that love God,
May they be strong,
Like the sun at its brightest
Destroying the darkness of night.

The Birth of Samson

Gideon lived a good, long life. He was a wise judge who made important decisions and settled arguments fairly. Due to his calm, thoughtful leadership, the Children of Israel went about their work peacefully. The different tribes cooperated with each other nicely; silly jealousies were forgotten. But when Gideon died, it seemed that all the old problems reappeared.

The Children of Israel again went astray
And worshiped the god named Baal.
They did not remember their God, the Lord,
Who delivered them all from their enemy's sword.
They forgot about Gideon, who was called Jerubaal,
And the goodness with which he had judged Israel.

The Lord saw that the Children of Israel were behaving in evil ways. As punishment, He delivered them into the hands of the Philistines, a war-like group of people who came from islands in the Mediterranean Sea. As the Israelites were entering Canaan from one end, the Philistines, sailing long, goose-billed ships, began settling on its seacoast. They brought with them the secret of making iron and became well known for making very strong iron weapons. Up until this time, the Israelites had relied on weapons made of bronze, a softer metal containing copper and tin. When the Israelites heard about iron, they were forced to come to the Philistines for tools, spears, daggers, and long-lasting parts for their carts and wagons. The Philistines were good businessmen and unfriendly neighbors. One minute they took your money, and the next minute they came after you. Their seaside location made it easy for them to invade the hill country between the coast and the mountains of Judaea. The ruthless Philistines burned Israelite towns, raided their farms, and forced some tribes to give up their land. For forty long years, the Philistines made life miserable for the Children of Israel.

During these troubled times, an angel of the Lord visited the wife of a man called Manoah. "Listen to me," said the angel. "So far, you have not had any children. Now you shall have a son. Please beware. While you carry this child you must not eat any forbidden foods or drink any wine or beer. When he is born, you must never cut his hair. Your son shall be a Nazirite, a man who will spend his life working for God. He shall begin to save Israel from the hands of the Philistines."

When the angel finished speaking, the woman ran to her husband and said in a trembling voice: "A man of God came to me! He looked like God's own angel! I was so awestruck I didn't ask who he was, nor did he tell me his name! He told me that I shall have a son who will be a Nazirite to the Lord from now until the day he dies!"

Manoah did not know what to make of this amazing story. He decided to ask God for help. "Please Lord," he said, "let Your angel come again and teach us what we are to do with this special child."

God listened to Manoah and had His angel appear to the woman, as she sat out in a field drying sunflower seeds. Once again she came running to her husband, the seeds spilling out of her lap. "Come quickly!" she ordered. "The man from God has returned!"

Manoah and his wife ran to the field and the waiting angel. Being very cautious, Manoah asked, "Are you the man who spoke to my wife?"

"I am," replied the angel quietly.

"When this child is born, how shall we behave toward him?" questioned Manoah, who did not like leaving things up to chance. He wanted to be sure that he understood all the details.

QUESTIONS

*It's good to ask questions, it's good to make sure
That you understand which way
To go or to do something new,
Something special, homework or housework,
The rules of a game.
Questions get answers
Which add to your brain's information.
And questions prevent
An event from surprising.
You won't be unsuspecting,
You'll know what to do.
Asking questions
Will help make life easy for you.*

The angel replied to Manoah, "Right now it is only important that your wife follow the orders I gave her about drinking and eating."

Manoah was still not quite sure of the visitor's identity. Since he was a good host, Manoah asked the angel to stay while they prepared a roasted goat dinner in his honor. The angel declined the invitation, saying: "Even if I stay, I will not eat your food. And if you do make a burnt offering, you must be sure to offer it to God."

"What is your name," asked Manoah, still testing the man, "so that we may thank you when your words come true?"

"Why do you ask my name?" answered the angel. "It is hidden and cannot be understood."

With this last reply, Manoah was satisfied that the visitor was truly God's own angel. He built an altar and made a burnt offering and a meal offering to the Lord. And the most wondrous thing happened: as the flame reached toward heaven, the angel of the Lord rose up into the fire and disappeared!

Manoah and his wife lay on the ground, their hands outstretched and their faces hidden. This was an act of honor toward God. Now that he was absolutely certain he had seen the Lord's angel, Manoah began to shake. He remembered hearing that seeing angels sometimes meant death was near! "We shall surely die because we have seen God's messenger!" he cried.

His wife remained calm; she had thought carefully about this marvelous happening. "If the Lord intended to kill us, He would not have accepted

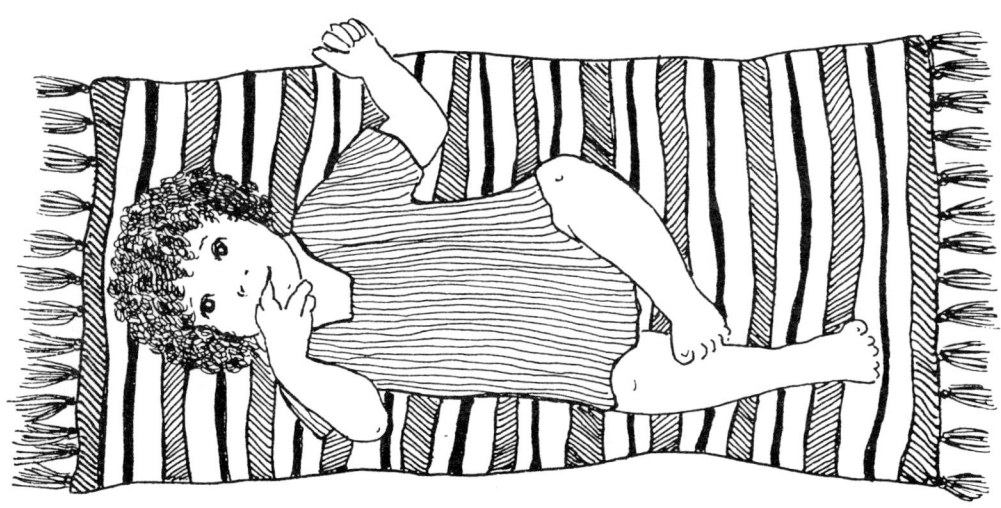

our offerings," she said sensibly. "And if we were going to die, He would not have told us about the child."

In time, just as God's angel had promised, the woman gave birth to a son and named him Samson. The Lord blessed this sunny child, and he grew to be a happy, healthy young man. And Samson began to be filled with the Spirit of the Lord, the superhuman strength that he would use, someday, to help protect the Children of Israel.

ANGELS

God's holy angels
Bring greetings and messages
All in God's name.
They sometimes appear
As women or men,
And disappear in a cloud,
A whirlwind or flame.
God's angels bring blessings.
God's angels bring warnings,
Good news and bad,
Happy and sad.
But most of the time
God's angels bring love
And peace to His children
From God up above.

Samson's Riddle

Sometimes, mothers and fathers find it difficult to deal with strong-willed children. Although children do have a right to their opinions, most of the time, parents get their way because they are the parents and are supposed to know best. However, if they think that parents or stepparents are wrong, and if they speak politely, children can try to get grown-ups to change their minds. Because Samson had been selected by God to be a Nazirite, he was spoiled by his grateful parents, who sometimes did not know how to handle him. Not only was Samson strong in body; he was also exceptionally strong-willed and determined to get his own way.

One clear day, when breezes from the sea made the flowers dance, Samson went for a long run downhill to the town of Timnah. There, he saw a beautiful Philistine woman. He came back and told his parents, "I have seen a Philistine woman and I want you to get her for me as a wife!"

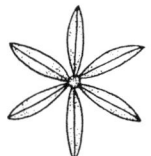 *Now don't you think it's impolite*
To tell another person to
Get you this, or get you that,
Without a please or thank you?

Samson's parents were upset. This was a tricky situation because the Philistines were always making trouble for the Israelites. "Isn't there anyone from our own people that you could take for a wife?" they asked, knowing that when Samson got an idea into his head there was little hope of changing it.

Samson straightened his shoulders, raised his chin and demanded: "Get her for me. She pleases me!"

In Samson's day, it was the father's duty to obtain a wife for his son. Although they objected to Samson's choice and were disappointed by his lack of manners, his parents decided to accompany him back to the woman's town. Perhaps they could talk some sense into him! They did not know that God Himself had planned these events all along. Something important was about to happen that would cause Samson to protect the Israelites by taking revenge against the Philistines.

As Samson and his parents walked down through the hills to Timnah, their rocky path was blocked by a vineyard. Since a Nazirite was not allowed to drink any wine, he was also not allowed to go near a vineyard, the place where the wine grapes grew. While his parents took the shortcut through the grapevines, Samson took the long way around. Suddenly, a young lion came toward him, roaring fiercely. As the animal was about to attack, the Spirit of the Lord came upon Samson and, with superhuman strength, the youth tore the lion to pieces with his bare hands!

When he again joined his parents, Samson kept this story to himself. He knew that most parents become upset just hearing that their child has escaped danger. Samson's parents were upset enough; he did not want to make the situation worse.

As they continued their walk, his parents gave Samson one piece of advice. "Looks aren't everything," they said. "When you meet with this woman, why don't you see if she is as intelligent as she is pretty."

Samson decided to follow this good suggestion. While his mother and father waited in the shade of a cypress tree, Samson went down to the town. There he had a nice, intelligent conversation with the woman, and he was happy to find that she was both beautiful and smart! Samson and his parents returned to their home to feed the animals and water the vegetables. Then they made preparations to go back to Timnah for the wedding.

As Samson and his parents
Traveled once again to Timnah,
He left them for a minute
And turned aside to see
If he could find the fallen body
Of the roaring, fierce young lion.
He found the body of the lion
Lying drying in the sun.
And in the fallen body
Of the roaring, fierce young lion
Lying drying in the sun,
Was a noisy swarm of busy, buzzing bees,
Making honey!
Being careful not to aggravate
The busy, buzzing bees,
Samson scraped the honey out.
Then he shouted to his parents,
"I'll be right there; I've got a treat!
Something wonderful to eat!"
He shared the honey with them,
But didn't tell them that he'd found it in

The busy, buzzing, fallen body
Of the roaring, fierce young lion
Lying drying in the sun.

Samson and his parents licked their sticky fingers clean and continued on to the town of Timnah. There, Samson arranged to have a wedding feast. Thirty Philistine men were invited to this celebration, and soon everyone was telling jokes and laughing. Samson thought that it would be fun to give these men a riddle to unravel.

"Let me now ask you a riddle," he said. "If you can tell me the answer within the seven days of my wedding feast, I will give you thirty soft linen robes and thirty outfits for special occasions. But if you cannot tell me the answer to the riddle, then you must give me thirty soft linen robes and thirty outfits for special occasions."

The thirty Philistine men, thinking that this would be easy, laughed and said, "Let's hear the riddle."

Samson replied:

"Out of the eater came forth food,
And out of the strong came sweetness."

The thirty men began to think.
They thought for three long days.
They turned the riddle upside down.
They turned the riddle sideways.
They turned the riddle right side up.
Three days turned into seven.
Then they said to Samson's wife,
"Entice your husband,
Whine and wheedle till he gives you
The solution to this riddle
Or we'll burn your family home.
Have you asked us to this feast
To make us poor?"

83

Samson's wife could not endure this
So she did as she was told,
And went to Samson, crying,
"You must hate me!
You don't love me!
You've put me in the middle
Of this riddle
You have given to my people.
Won't you please give me the answer?"
He said, "I haven't even told
The answer to my parents,
So why should I tell you?"

Samson's wife began to weep
As she thought of her own father,
Whose house the thirty men said
They would burn
Unless they learned
The answer to the riddle.
And she was in the middle!

All through the week she sobbed
She whimpered, wailed, and cried!
She egged him on, she begged him!
Samson couldn't stand
To hear his new wife weep.
He thought,
"I don't have to keep
The answer to myself."

On the seventh day,
He gave his bride the answer.
She told the thirty men,
Just as the sun was setting.
They came to Samson and they said:
"What is sweeter than honey?

84

What is stronger than a lion?"
Samson knew that he'd been cheated!
Samson knew he'd been defeated!
He knew his wife was in the middle
And he said,
"If you had not plowed with my cow
You'd not have figured out my riddle!"

The Spirit of the Lord came upon Samson. Filled with superhuman strength, he went down to the town of Ashkelon and killed thirty Philistines. He took their clothes and gave them to the men who had solved the riddle. With this debt paid, Samson, who was very angry with his new wife, needed some cooling-off time. He left his wife with her family and went back up through the hills to his father's house.

Samson had no way of knowing that while he was trying to get his temper under control, the wife he had left behind was being given in marriage to another man!

Samson's Revenge

During the month of May, when the tall wheat bows to the gentle wind, Samson began to miss his beautiful new wife. After thinking things through, Samson decided it was time to forgive her for revealing the answer to his riddle. After all, she had been caught in the middle of a difficult situation between her new husband and her old friends. Samson did not know that these same old friends had threatened his wife and her family.

To forgive and forget is a hard thing to do,
Bad deeds and cruel tricks are remembered.
Some people hold grudges a very long time;
They will not budge an inch or give in.
And they walk around mad,
With no smiles on their faces.
They don't know that forgiveness
Most often replaces
The gloom that goes with being angry and mad,
And that when they forgive they'll feel peaceful and glad.

And so, full of forgiveness and carrying a young goat as a gift, Samson went down through the hills to his wife's house. But his father-in-law would not let him in! "Because I thought that you hated my daughter after she told the answer to your riddle, I gave her to one of the thirty men," said her father. "Now, isn't my younger daughter more beautiful than her sister? Why don't you take her instead?"

Samson's great temper boiled up in him once again. His new wife had been given to someone else! He declared, "This time I shall be blameless when I do harm to the Philistines!" Samson knew he had already killed thirty innocent men. This time, he felt that his revenge would not count as a sin.

Samson left his wife's father and took a long run by himself, up and down the hills. This is what he did whenever he needed some thinking time; lots of his problems were solved this way. Running steadily and breathing deeply, Samson devised a frightening plan. After slowing down, he caught three hundred foxes. He tied them tail to tail, put a torch between each two tails, set the torches on fire, and let the foxes loose in the Philistine's wheat fields. The fire destroyed all the bunches of ripe wheat, all the tall, standing stalks, and even the olive trees that surrounded the fields!

The Philistines came running! "Who has done this terrible deed?" they cried.

Other men answered, "Samson, the son-in-law of the Timnite, because his wife was given to another man."

And so the Philistines came and burned both the house of Samson's wife and that of her father!

When Samson heard the terrible news, he thundered, "If this is the way you act, then I shall seek revenge for your revenge!" And with his superhuman strength, Samson slew the Philistines singlehandedly. He then hid himself in a cave.

The Philistines went up into the hills and camped in Judah. "Why have you come up against us?" asked the Israelites who lived there.

"We are here to capture Samson," replied the Philistines. "And to do to him what he has done to us!"

Three thousand angry men of Judah searched the rocky hills and found the cave in which Samson was hiding. "Don't you know that the Philistines rule over us?" they cried. "You have exposed us to attack! What have you done to us?"

Samson answered, "As they did to me, so I have done to them."

The Israelites told Samson, "We have come to tie you up and deliver you to the Philistines!" Judah's people were always being harassed by the Philistines. By giving up Samson, perhaps they would have a little peace.

"Swear to me that you will not kill me," begged Samson. He knew that he would surely defend himself, and he did not want to shed Israelite blood.

His captors said: "We will tie you up and deliver you to them. We will not kill you."

They bound Samson with two new ropes and brought him to the Philistines. The Spirit of the Lord once again came upon Samson. The ropes on his arms became like burnt strands of flax; the bonds melted in his hands! Looking around, Samson found a donkey's jawbone lying among the rocks and weeds. He raised it overhead like an axe and, with his superhuman strength, killed a thousand men!

Samson said:

"With the jawbone of a donkey, heaps upon heaps,
With the jawbone of a donkey I have killed a thousand men."

After he spoke these words, Samson threw away the donkey's jawbone and realized that he was thirsty. He called to the Lord and said: "You have given me the strength to do this job and help my people. Shall I now die of thirst or once again fall into the hands of the Philistines?"

The Lord, Who had planned Samson's revenge on the Philistines all along, listened to his plea and caused a deep hole to appear in the dry ground. As if by magic, it quickly became a flowing spring of cool water. After giving thanks to the Lord, Samson drank his fill, and he soon felt like his old self. And for twenty years thereafter, Samson protected and judged the Children of Israel.

Samson and Delilah

Although the Lord had given Samson his superhuman strength,
It was up to Samson to keep fit and keep himself in shape.
He ate lots of fruits and vegetables,
Whole wheat bread, and yogurt.
He drank eight cups of water every day.
He went running every morning,
Sixteen times around the pastures,
And said hello to cows and sheep along the way.

He worked out by lifting boulders,
His big muscles helped build walls.
He skipped rope and he did push-ups,
Long jumps, pole vaults; he kicked balls.
He carried tree trunks on his shoulders,
He climbed rocks, he plowed the fields.
He shot baskets that were tied to cedar trees.
He did cartwheels, handstands, back flips,
Splits, and somersaults.

He did two hundred sit-ups,
And made sure to bend his knees!

Samson was a handsome man, a Nazirite with uncut hair.
Little girls and grown-up ladies loved his shiny curls
Which flew, like wings, behind him when he ran.
And Samson loved the ladies back,
But his favorite was Delilah, from the valley of Sorek.
He loved her lovely smiles,
And she charmed him with her wiles.

Five leaders of the Philistines came to see Delilah
And they said, "Delilah dear,
Since Samson is in love with you, use your lovely charms
To find out what makes him strong,
So we may capture and destroy him."
If Delilah thought that it was wrong to betray Samson,
She put the thought aside,
For in return for this betrayal
Each leader promised her
Eleven hundred silver shekels,
If she did not fail!

She closed her eyes and thought of what she'd buy
With all these shekels,
Embroidered purple dresses, kidskin sandals,
Beads and bangles.
Delilah figured out the angles and readily agreed
To use her many charms on Samson,
And do this dirty deed!

Delilah used her winning ways and all her wiles
In pleasing Samson.
Then she started teasing him,
With lowered eyes she said,
"Tell me Samson,
What's the secret of your strength?
What could be used to tie you up?
And how could you be captured?"
Although Samson was enraptured with the beautiful Delilah,
He knew this was a trick; she was trying to confuse him.
So he amused himself by saying, "If I'm tied
With seven bowstrings that never have been dried,
Then I shall be as weak as any ordinary man."
The five leaders brought Delilah
Seven bowstrings, never dried.
Delilah tied up Samson;
Soldiers lay in wait to chain him.
She said, "The Philistines are upon you!"
Samson took a good, deep breath,
And the bowstrings broke like yarn touched by a flame!

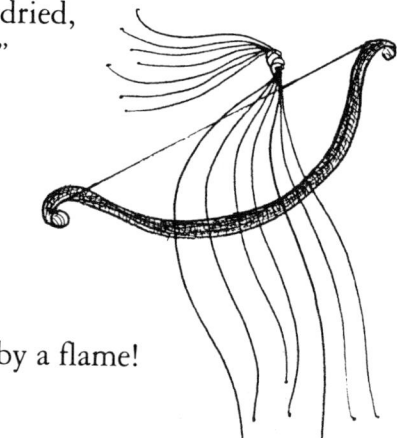

"You've made a fool of me!" Delilah whined,
"You've told me lies!
Now tell me please what can be used to tie you up?"
"They must use new ropes," said Samson,
"Ropes that never have been tied.
Then I shall be as weak as any ordinary man."
Delilah found new ropes and with her hopes up

Bound him tightly,
And said, "The Philistines are upon you!"
While soldiers waited out of sight,
Samson took a good, deep breath
And broke the ropes that tied his arms!
Again he beat Delilah's charms!

Delilah tried once more to trick him.
"Dearest Samson," she said sweetly,
"You've made a fool of me.
You've told me lies.
With what can you be tied?
How can you be restrained?
Tell me, please."
And Samson answered, "Weave
The seven long locks of my hair
Into the web of cloth
That you weave into your loom."
Delilah took the weaving pin
And pinned the weaving in the loom,
To prevent its slipping out,
And wove the hair on Samson's head
As she would do with weaving thread.
Samson slept while soldiers waited in another room.
"The Philistines are upon you!" said Delilah.
Samson sat up!
He was wide awake, and took a good, deep breath.
He yanked the pin out of the loom
And pulled the seven locks of hair upon his head
Out of the web!

Delilah cried, "How can you say
'I love you,' every day,
When your true heart is not with me?
You have made a fool of me three times!
And you have never told me

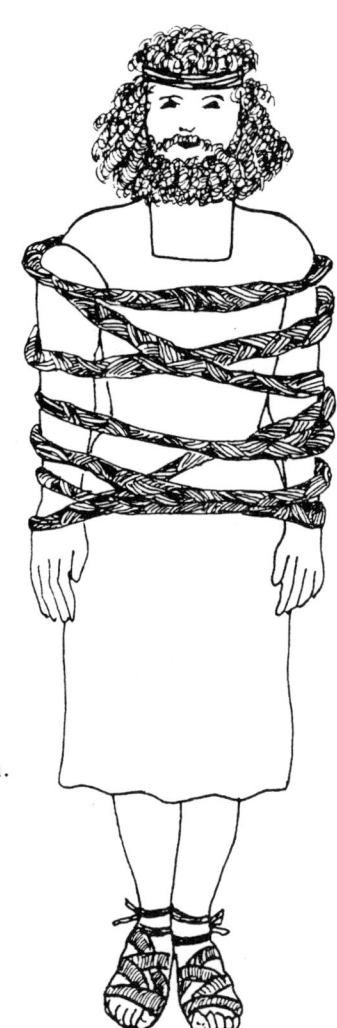

The secret of your strength!"
Delilah then went to great lengths.
She pestered Samson and beseeched him!
Every day she coaxed and nagged him
Until finally she reached him
He was sick of being hounded!
And Samson told the secret that he held inside his heart:

"A razor's never touched my head.
I am a Nazirite for God,
A Nazirite from birth,
And if my hair is cut
My mighty strength will leave me.
Then I shall be as weak as any ordinary man."

Delilah heard him speak and knew he wasn't lying
Because Samson wouldn't take God's Name in vain!
She called the Philistines and said,
"He's told the truth!
Now bring the money!"
Delilah thought of purple dresses, soft new sandals,
Beads and bangles.
And once again she used her charms;
Her voice was soft, and sweet as honey.
"Take a nap, my darling Samson,
Put your head upon my lap."
Samson fell beneath her spell,
Samson fell into her trap.
He didn't smell a rat!
And so he took a nice, long nap!

When he was fast asleep and dreaming,
Delilah called the man appointed
By the scheming leaders.
He took a knife and cut
The seven locks of Samson's hair.

And Samson's strength went from him,
With the cutting of his hair.
As he lay sleeping, he was unaware.
God's Spirit left him there.

Delilah said to Samson,
"The Philistines are upon you!"
Samson woke out of his sleep and thought,
"I'll take a good, deep breath,
In case I've been tied up again."
He was still a little drowsy,
And didn't know what had been done
To his seven locks of hair:
His superhuman strength was gone!
God's Spirit left him there!

The Philistines seized Samson!
They put out both his eyes!
They brought him to the town of Gaza,

And bound him up with chains!
Round and round the prison house Samson pulled the wheel
That ground wheat into flour; he did a donkey's job.
Round and round he went in darkness,
Round and round, never knowing
That the hair that had been cut off from his head
Had started growing!

The Philistines soon gathered all together to rejoice;
They thought their god, Dagon, had brought them Samson.
"Call for Samson!" they said merrily,
"We'll laugh at him and jeer him,
The strong man now is blind and weak,
No one will need to fear him!"
They put Samson near the pillars
In the middle of their temple.
Samson asked the boy who led him by the hand,
"Give me a rest,
And let me lean against these pillars."

All the leaders were together.
Men and women filled the temple.
There was hardly room to stand.
People sat upon the floor.
And on the flat roof of the building,
There were three thousand more!
What a crowd!

And Samson called to God,
His voice was strong and loud,
"O Lord God, remember me, I pray,
And strengthen me, I pray,
Only once, only today,
That I might be avenged for my two eyes!"
And Samson grasped the two great pillars
That were holding up the place,
And with his face turned up to heaven he cried,

"Let me die with the Philistines!"
Samson pushed with all his might!
The temple fell on all the people!
What a sight!

Samson killed more enemies
At his death than in his lifetime.
And his family came and brought his body
Back up to be buried next to Manoah, his father.
For twenty years thereafter, the Philistines were worried;
The memory of Samson kept them frightened, gave them fears.
Now the Children of Israel had peace,
They felt protected.
And so Samson, both in life and death,
Judged Israel forty years.

I Samuel

The Birth of Samuel

A village is a community smaller than a town. A city is a large and important town. A town is a community larger than a village and smaller than a city. After almost two hundred years in Canaan, the Children of Israel were settled in towns and villages perched on grassy hilltops or tucked into shady valleys. Their cozy homes, made of dried or baked mud bricks, had flat roofs for outdoor dining and sleeping. Sometimes grandmoms, grandpops, aunts, uncles, and cousins all lived together in two-story buildings and shared cooking, cleaning, and baby-sitting chores. Fruits and vegetables spilled over the sides of terraced gardens; barley and wheat grew tall with each kiss of the sun. Herds of long-haired goats and spotted sheep nibbled happily on buttercups and dandelions. Restless cows, waiting to be milked, clanked their bells and swished their tails in each other's faces. Donkeys wandered all over the place, perking up their pointy ears and pretending to be dumb. Donkeys are really very smart; they just act dumb when they want to get out of hard work!

A nice man named Elkanah lived in the Ephraimite town of Ramah with his two wives, Hannah and Peninnah. In those faraway days, a man sometimes married a second wife if his first wife did not seem able to have children. Peninnah was always ridiculing Hannah because Hannah was childless. Making fun of another person's misfortune is unkind. After years of this treatment, Hannah could no longer control her feelings; she cried and cried, and would not eat.

"Hannah, why are you weeping and why won't you eat?" asked Elkanah, who loved her dearly. Hannah, too upset to answer him, decided to ask the Lord for a child.

Every year, during the harvest festival, Elkanah and his family journeyed to Shiloh, where Joshua had set up the Tabernacle. There, by God's holy Ark, Elkanah worshiped and made sacrifices. One day, while most of the visitors were taking an afternoon rest, Hannah went to the Tabernacle and began to pray. "O Lord of Creation," she said, "if You will give me a little boy, I will have him serve You all his days. He shall be a Nazirite; no razor shall ever touch his head."

Hannah did not pray out loud. She prayed in her heart, her lips moving silently. Eli, the priest, noticed this and thought that she had drunk too much wine. When Eli accused her, Hannah said, "No, I am only a sad woman, pouring out my deepest thoughts to God."

It's wrong to accuse someone of something unless you know the whole story. Eli was ashamed of his mistake and said kindly: "Go in peace. The Lord will answer your prayers."

With a smile beginning to lift the corners of her mouth, Hannah returned to her husband. And within a year, Hannah gave birth to a beautiful son. She named him "Samuel," which means, "I asked the Lord for him."

Once again, it was time for the yearly visit to Shiloh. This time Hannah stayed home. "I will not go until Samuel is finished nursing," she said. "At that time I'll bring him to stay in the Lord's home forever."

Elkanah, understanding that mothers usually know what's best for their babies, said: "Do what you think is right. May the Lord answer all your prayers."

Hannah rocked her baby,
And sang him lullabies
Until Samuel went to dreamland
Beneath God's starlit skies.

When Samuel was ready to drink from a cup, Hannah prepared all the correct sacrifices and brought her little boy to Eli, the priest, at Shiloh. Hannah announced: "I am the woman who prayed from her heart to the Lord. I asked for this sweet child and God answered my prayers. I am now lending him to God, as I promised, for as long as he lives."

103

HANNAH'S PRAYER

Hannah, Samuel's mother, sang this song of praise:
"My heart is joyful with the Lord;
There is no one holier than He.
There is no one else besides Him;
No protector like our God.

"Do not brag about yourself,
Or speak with too much pride;
For the Lord knows what you do,
And only He decides what deeds
Are worthy of praise.

"In life nothing is sure.
Sometimes strong men break their bows,
And those who stumble
Find that they are filled with strength.
Those who once ate well are poor;
They must work hard for their food.
And those who once were hungry
Are well fed.
The woman with no children
Now has a brood of seven;
And the one with many children
Cries, as every one is taken.

"The Lord brings danger and misfortune.
He makes us poor, He makes us rich.
He brings us to the lowest depths,
And when we feel forsaken,
We are raised up by the Lord.

"He takes the beggars from the street,
And gives them seats of honor
Next to leaders.
For the Lord has made the earth,
And He can place men as He chooses.

"He will guard good men and women,
And the wicked shall be silenced;
They shall no longer live in light.

"Those who fight the Lord
Shall be broken.
He will thunder against them
From His heaven;
The Lord will judge the earth
From one end to another;
He will give strength to His appointed
Kings or leaders,
Those anointed by the Lord
Will carry their heads high."
When Hannah's song of praise was finished,
She kissed her little boy good-bye.

God Speaks to Samuel

Adjusting to new places, new people, and new rules takes patience. It's important to look around carefully and watch how other people go about their everyday life. When Samuel came to live with Eli, the priest, he kept his eyes open and his mouth quiet . . . except for asking questions. Samuel was a regular "question machine"!

"Why, Eli?" he would ask.
"When and how and where?"
"Who's that man?"
"What's this or that?"
"May I eat this pear?"
Questions! Questions!
They could make a person
Lose his mind!
But kind Eli
Answered Samuel's questions
Each and every time!

Samuel's mother, Hannah, was a good seamstress. She made him a miniature ephod, a linen shirt tied at the waist, like the one worn by Eli, the priest. Each year she sewed him a new long coat to wear over his ephod. These special clothes were only worn by special people. Since Samuel was learning God's laws and rules from Eli, he was a very special little boy.

When Hannah and Elkanah came for their yearly visit, Eli blessed them and prayed that Hannah be given more children in return for Samuel, the child she had lent to God. As Samuel grew, watched over by the Lord, his mother gave him three brothers and two sisters. Soon Hannah's hands and heart were full of children.

Eli, the priest, was growing old. His eyes were dim and his spirits were low. He was disappointed in his two sons, whose behavior had angered the Lord. They had grown up dishonest and undisciplined, not knowing right from wrong. Their reputations were terrible! Eli had been a bit too gentle with his boys. He had forgotten to teach them good conduct, and they got away with everything! A priest's sons usually inherited their father's job. Eli was told, by a man who spoke the word of the Lord, that his sons would not live long; God would select a new and faithful priest.

Samuel slept in the Lord's temple; his job was to watch over the holy Ark. One night, right before the dawn said hello to the morning star, Samuel was fast asleep under his favorite blanket. Out of the darkness, a voice called to him.

"Here I am," answered Samuel, running to see what Eli wanted.

"I did not call," said Eli, half asleep. "Go back to bed."

Samuel returned to his bed. Once again he heard his name called. When he went over to Eli, the old priest said patiently: "I did not call you. Go and lie down again."

Samuel heard the voice a third time, and once more went to Eli's bedside. In Samuel's time, it was very rare to hear the voice of God. He had no idea what this strange experience might mean. But Eli had figured it out. "Go lie down," instructed Eli. "And if you are called again, say, 'Speak, Lord, Your servant is listening.'"

Samuel lay down and pulled the covers up to his chin.

"Samuel, Samuel," called the voice.

Samuel answered: "Speak. Your servant is listening." He was afraid to say, "Speak, Lord," because he couldn't quite believe that God was calling him!

The Lord spoke: "I am about to do something that will make the ears of all who hear about it tingle. I must punish Eli's house forever because his sons have sinned, and he was too kind to reprimand them. These sins cannot be wiped away by sacrifices and offerings."

Under his warm, camel's-hair blanket, Samuel was shivering with amazement. He was beginning to understand that he was to be the Lord's prophet, a man who would speak God's words to all the people!

Samuel was afraid to tell Eli what God had said; he loved Eli and did not want to hurt him in any way. However, when Eli begged him to speak, Samuel related God's words. Eli, the kind and gentle priest, said: "It is God's will. Let Him do what He thinks is best."

As Samuel grew into a fine young man, the words of God began to come true. All Israel knew that Samuel was the Lord's prophet.

Once again, the Philistines gathered to invade the Promised Land. This time, they pushed farther and farther into the hill country, determined to destroy the mountain tribes. Although they fought bravely, the Israelites were defeated by these fierce men who wore body armor and used iron weapons. When the surviving soldiers returned to their camp, Israel's leaders asked: "Why has the Lord allowed the Philistines to win over us? Let us go to Shiloh and get the Ark of the Covenant of the Lord. This way, He will be among us and save us."

The Ark was brought from Shiloh,
Carried by the sons of Eli.
When the enemy heard cheers
They said, "Their God is in the camp!
We are frightened! Woe is ours!"
Another group of Philistines said,
"Be strong and stop your worrying,
Or you'll be slaves to the Hebrews.
Act like soldiers!
Go and fight!"
And so the mighty Philistines
Defeated Israel.
Thirty thousand soldiers fell on that sad day.
Eli's sons were dead.
The Ark of God was taken.
Eli, who was ninety-eight years old,
Was badly shaken.
When he heard the Ark was gone
He cried,
Fell backward,
Broke his neck,
And died.

The Philistines brought the
Ark to the house of their god,
Dagon. The next morning, when
the people awakened, the statue of
Dagon was flat on its face before the Ark of the Lord. They raised it up and
set it back in place. Crash! The next day, there it was on the floor! This
time, its head and the palms of its hands were cut off. Only the body was
unbroken.

After toppling the Philistine's god, the Lord brought a terrible plague
of mice and disease to their city, Ashdod. The men of the city were terrified.
"The Ark of the God of Israel cannot stay here!" they cried. "Their God has
done this to us!"

Deciding to let others deal with this problem, they sent the Ark to the city of Gath. Once again, the Lord caused a terrible plague to afflict the people. Good-bye Ark! Its next stop was Ekron. Once again, men died and others were stricken with a plague carried by mice. The people cried, "They have sent the Ark of the God of Israel to slay us!"

After seven months of mice and disease, the Philistines asked their magicians, "What shall we do with this Ark?"

"Send it back to its people," replied the magicians. "And place a box with guilt offerings next to it."

The Philistines filled the box
With symbols of the plagues:
Five swollen, golden pimples,
Five golden, long-tailed mice.
They placed the Ark upon a cart
Pulled by two good cows,
Who didn't look up,
And didn't look down.
They didn't choose to roam,
But headed straight for an Israelite town!
The Ark would soon be home!

Samuel the Prophet

For twenty years, the Ark of the Lord rested safely in the tree-filled town of Kiriath-Jearim. During that time, the Philistines were as nasty as ever, raiding towns and villages, stealing food, and kidnapping animals. The Children of Israel yearned for the Lord; they were ready to open their hearts to God.

Samuel had been traveling from town to village, patiently teaching God's rules and laws, settling disputes, and trying to lift his people's spirits. He now felt that they were almost ready to return to the Lord. "If you get rid of any idols that are still around, and promise to serve only God, then He will save you from the Philistines."

The Children of Israel gave their solemn promise. Samuel gathered everyone together at Mizpah and held a special ceremony. The people said, "We have sinned against the Lord." Apologies flowed from their hearts as Samuel poured water and offered prayers to God. Once again, Samuel went from tribe to tribe, settling arguments and making decisions, all the while reminding everyone of their promise to God.

When the Philistines heard about this big meeting, they planned another attack. "Oh no! Not again!" cried the Israelites to Samuel. "Please beg the Lord to help us!"

Samuel made a burnt offering to God. The Lord answered by causing a great storm to fall on the enemy!

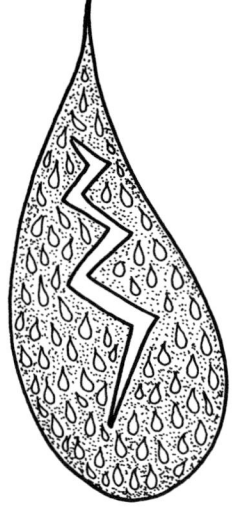
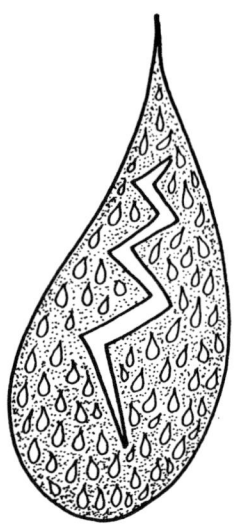

There were flashes of lightning
As bright as the sun,
And crashes of thunder
Like ten thousand drums.
Buckets of rain fell;
Hail dropped by the ton.
In panic, the Philistines
Started to run!
The Israelites chased them
And God, with His Hand,
Kept the enemy out of
His own Promised Land.

Samuel was tired. Bumpy camel rides from place to place were exhausting. Sleeping every night in leaky tents and crowded houses was uncomfortable. Although Samuel loved his job, he felt he needed some help. He decided to appoint, as judges, his sons Joel and Abijah. But as you know, things don't always work out as planned. Despite their good training, Samuel's sons did not follow in all his ways. They acted more like busy businessmen than thoughtful judges. They had little time for listening, and the people became unhappy.

"You are old, Samuel. Give us a king to judge us like all the other nations!" demanded the people.

After so many years of devoted service, Samuel was hurt and upset. After opening his heart to God, the Lord said to him: "Listen to the people. It is not you they have rejected; they have rejected Me from being their King! Give them a good warning about how a regular king would act!"

Samuel told the people all that God had said:

"A king will take your sons to drive his chariots.
They'll run before him and behind him,
And they'll be his bodyguards.

112

They'll plow his fields and pick his harvest.
And your daughters will be taken
To make perfume, cook, and bake.
He'll take your fields, vineyards, and oliveyards,
And give them all away
To his best officers and servants.
He'll take your workers and your donkeys,
And a tenth of all your flocks.
You'll serve him and he won't help you,
Or give you anything.
You'll cry to God
But He won't listen
Because you have another king!"

The people refused to listen. They demanded a king who would bring all the tribes together to fight off enemy attacks. Samuel repeated this request to God and the Lord answered, "Listen to their voice and get them a king."

With a heavy heart, Samuel sent the people home and waited for the Lord to guide him in selecting a king.

WAITING

*It takes patience to wait
For whatever needs waiting for
Playtime or springtime,
Or the next day to come.
Some people wait hours
For food or for shelter,
And some people wait months
To smell the new flowers.
It takes faith to believe
That positive thinking
Will somehow win over
The doubts and the don'ts.
You won't have to wait long;
You'll know just what to do
When the guidance you've hoped for
Comes through for you.
Because calmly and cooly,
You've taken the time
To think clearly and carefully
While waiting patiently.*

Saul the King

Donkeys are wanderers; their four knobby legs carry them everywhere but where they're supposed to be. One day the donkeys belonging to Kish, a Benjaminite, were lost in the hills. Kish asked his son, Saul, to take a helper and search for the missing animals.

There was no Israelite better looking or taller than Saul. Whenever he rode through a town, people stopped what they were doing just to look at him. But all this admiration didn't help him find the donkeys. They were still lost!

Saul said to his helper, "We'd better go home before my father stops worrying about the donkeys and starts worrying about us."

The helper said: "Wait. I heard that Samuel, a man of God, is in this city. All that he says comes to pass. He is a prophet, a man who asks God's help to see the future."

"Let's find him!" said Saul, anxious for any help he could get.

As they climbed the hill toward the city, they met some beautiful maidens drawing water from a well.

"Is the prophet nearby?" asked Saul.

The young women could hardly keep their eyes off such a handsome man. To prevent him from leaving, they gave him the longest, most complicated answer they could invent. Finally, out of ideas, they told Saul where Samuel could be found.

A day before Saul's arrival, the Lord had told Samuel: "Tomorrow, at twilight, I will send a man to you from the tribe of Benjamin. I have heard the sad cries of My people. This man will save them from the Philistines."

As Samuel saw the tall, handsome young man coming toward him, he heard God's voice saying, "This is the man who will rule over My people."

Saul asked Samuel where the prophet could be found. "I am he," Samuel answered. "Go to the top of the hill. Tonight you will be my guest. In the morning, I will have a talk with you. Don't worry about your wandering donkeys. They have been found."

That night, Saul ate in Samuel's house. The meal was wonderful. Saul was given the juiciest portion of meat, the sweetest figs and dates, the biggest olives, and the greenest salad. While night birds sang their bedtime songs, Saul slept on the cool rooftop under a canopy of stars. At daybreak, Samuel awakened Saul from his comfortable sleep. "Wake up, so I may send you on your way," urged Samuel, who then walked Saul to the edge of town. "Ask your helper to go on ahead. I have God's words to tell you."

Samuel took a jar of oil, poured it on Saul's head,
Reached up and kissed the tall young man, and said,
"The Lord's anointed you
To be king over His people."
Then Samuel gave three signs to Saul
To prove to him God's word:
"When you leave today,
You'll find two men by Rachel's tomb.
They'll say to you what only I have known:
'Your donkeys have been found.
Your father's worried about you.
Go home.'

"As you continue on your way
And pass the terebinth tree,
You'll meet three men going to Beth-El,
To sacrifice to God.
One man will carry three young goats,
Another three large breads.
The third a jar of wine.
They'll give you two round cakes of bread
And say,
'May peace be with you.'

"When you come toward your town,
You will meet a band of prophets,
Coming from the place of God,
Singing hymns and playing instruments,
Tambourine, flute, and harp.
The Spirit of the Lord will come upon you,
You'll be joyous,
And you'll start
To join them in their praises
To the Lord your God,
Who raises up the low
And drives the enemy away.

"The day you see these signs,
You shall become a different man.
Prepare yourself as best you can.
Remember, God is with you.
Wait seven days for my return.
Then I'll tell you what to do."

As Saul prepared to do his part,
God gave him another heart
Filled with strength and power.
On his way home, Saul saw the signs
And felt God's Spirit in him.
But when asked what Samuel said,
He was very disappointing,
And only spoke of donkeys.
Saul kept the truth of his anointing
Safely tucked away.

Samuel brought the tribes together,
To have a lottery and pick
A king from all the tribes.
The Benjaminites were chosen
And Saul was bidden to come forward.
But he was modest, and stayed hidden
Until Samuel sent men for him.

Saul stood among the people,
Taller than the rest,
And Samuel said, "He is the best.
There is no one like Saul,
Chosen by the Lord."
The people shouted in accord,
"Long live Saul the king!"

But others were not certain.
They did not bring him any gifts.
This caused a rift among the people
Until Saul proved himself a leader
When the Ammonites declared
That they would take the right eyes out
Of every man in Jabesh-Gilead.

The elders asked for seven days' respite,
That they might send a message
To King Saul.
And when Saul heard the news,
And saw his people weeping,
God's Spirit came upon him!
He was angry at their lack of hope

119

And took a yoke of oxen,
Chopped them into pieces,
Sent the pieces out to every tribe
And cried,
"Whoever does not follow
After Saul and after Samuel,
Will have the same done to his cattle!"

The people feared the Lord,
When they heard Saul's strong command.
They all came as one man,
Three hundred thirty thousand!
By the time the next day's sun was high
The Ammonites were routed!

The people shouted, "Let us put to death
Those men who were uncertain,
And brought no gifts to Saul the king!"
"There will be no more killing!"
Said Saul.
"The Lord delivered us today,
And drove the enemy away!"

Samuel summoned all the people,
In one voice they started singing;
They rejoiced before the Lord,
Thanking Him
For Saul the king.

Jonathan's Victory

A blacksmith works with hot metal. Hammering it on a flat piece of hard metal called an anvil, the blacksmith shapes the hot metal into horseshoes, tools, and weapons. The Philistines had chased all the Israelite blacksmiths from their towns and villages; they did not want God's people to have strong weapons. Whenever a farmer needed new blades for his plow, axe, or digging tools, he had to go to the Philistines and pay outrageous prices for service. Without blacksmiths, Israelite soldiers were left with wooden bows and arrows, old bronze axes, and slingshots and slingstones to use against their enemies. Only King Saul and his brave son, Jonathan, had armor: iron swords, shields, and spears. These had been smuggled to them on moonless nights by captured Israelite blacksmiths, now forced to work for the Philistines.

An armor-bearer carried weapons for a warrior: a large bow with arrows for long-distance shooting, spears for medium-range fights, and swords, daggers, and clubs for close encounters. He had to think quickly, deciding in a split second which weapon to hand to the soldier. Above all, the armor-bearer had to be faithful and trustworthy. This was a very important job.

One day, Jonathan said to his armor-bearer: "Let's go and check out

121

the Philistine guardpost. We will not tell my father what we're about to do. Perhaps the Lord will help us pull off a surprise."

"Do what your heart thinks is best. I will be with you," said the loyal armor-bearer.

At this very moment, King Saul was resting under an olive tree in front of his headquarters in Gibeah. When he wasn't leading his army, he liked exchanging old war stories with the soldiers who dropped by. If he had known what Jonathan was up to, he would have thrown a king's fit!

To get to the Philistines, Jonathan and the armor-bearer had to climb down a steep, rocky cliff, cross a muddy stream, and climb up another steep, rocky cliff. This would be difficult, especially for the one who was carrying all the weapons. Jonathan decided to first announce themselves to the Philistines. He said, "If the Philistines tell us, 'Wait, we're coming for you,' then we won't do any rock climbing. But if they say, 'Come up to us,' that will be a sign from God that we should begin the climb."

When Jonathan announced their presence, the Philistines thought they were coming out of hiding to surrender. "Come up. We've got something to show you," called the Philistines.

Hands over feet, scrambling like spiders on a wall, Jonathan and his armor-bearer climbed down the cliff, slogged through the mud, and climbed up the other cliff, holding on to boulders, weeds, and each other. As they reached the top, Jonathan, using the weapons given to him by his armor-bearer, killed twenty men. The rest of the Philistines were in a panic; they thought a great army had attacked! And then, the Lord terrorized the enemy even more by causing a great earthquake to rumble through the land!

The earth was moving side to side,
Like a boat whose ropes had come untied.
Cracks, like big mouths, split the ground,
Swallowing Philistines with a roaring sound!

King Saul's watchmen saw the Philistines scattering like ants. The king, finding that Jonathan and the armor-bearer were missing, called for the priests who took care of the Ark. He spoke to them, asking them to try, in their secret way, to get some directions from God. As he was talking, he looked across the cliffs and saw that enemy soldiers, who had not disappeared into the ground or run away, were so confused they were beating each other up! "Wait!" shouted the king to the priests. "The Lord has made the situation clear to me!"

King Saul gathered his troops and went after the mixed-up army. Frightened Israelites, who had been hiding in the mountains, came out of their caves, turned into brave soldiers, and joined the chase. They pursued the enemy over tall hills, up and down rocky cliffs, across muddy streams, into shady valleys, and toward the Philistines' own land. Hungry and thirsty, the soldiers pushed on. King Saul, fearing that his men might slow down if they looked for food, prodded them with this threat: "Cursed be the man who eats any food before evening; catching the enemy comes first!"

It's hard for soldiers to do their best when their stomachs are growling with hunger. Good leaders try to think ahead and have their men carry snacks, like raisins and nuts, for energy. Although King Saul was a brave leader, his only thoughts were of winning; he did not think about his loyal, tired troops.

Bees sometimes make honey in tree holes and fallen logs. As the soldiers entered a forest, they saw sweet, sticky honey oozing from honeycombs glistening on the ground. What a temptation! But not one hungry, weak man stuck his fingers in to taste; they all feared King Saul's curse!

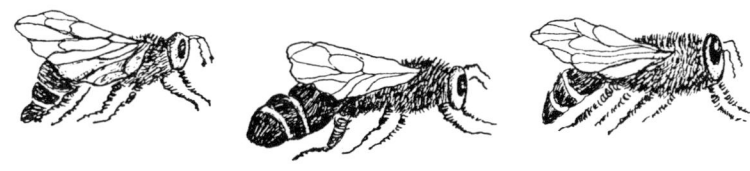

Jonathan had been busy fighting a ferocious Philistine when his father bellowed his warning to the troops. Entering the forest, he took his walking-stick, dipped the end into a honeycomb, put his fingers in the honey, and tasted the gooey sweet. Just that quickly, his tired body was restored with instant energy and his eyes brightened. "Your father threatened us with a terrible curse if we ate any food before evening," said a sweating soldier. "The army is faint with hunger."

Although a son should respect his father, he does not always have to agree with him. Sizing up the situation, Jonathan said: "My father has made things harder for his army. Defeating the Philistines would have been easier if he had allowed his troops to eat what they could find."

King Saul heard that Jonathan had tasted the honey. "Tell me what you have done!" shouted the king.

"I certainly did taste some honey on the end of my walking stick. Here I am. I am ready to die," said Jonathan, not wishing to argue in public with his father.

However, the soldiers knew that Jonathan had not heard the king's curse. They said to King Saul: "Are you going to kill Jonathan, the man who helped deliver us from the enemy? Not one hair of his head shall touch the ground!"

When he calmed down enough to listen to the common sense of his people, King Saul spared his brave son's life. Exhausted from both the battle and the unhappy prospect of losing Jonathan, King Saul went home to his house in Gibeah. He took a straw mat, a jug of cool grape juice, and some date cakes, went over to his olive tree, and took a long nap.

Temptations and Excuses

Once in a while King Saul forgot some of God's rules and laws. He tended to get overexcited, and his strong body often worked faster than his brain. Samuel, who still disliked the idea of a king, had to remind Saul to follow God's orders exactly. He told Saul: "It is I who the Lord sent to anoint you to be king over Israel. Listen now to the words of God: 'I remember what Amalek did to the Children of Israel when they came up from Egypt. I said that I would fight Amalek from generation to generation. You must now get rid of every Amalekite and all their herds of animals, once and for all.'"

King Saul's army of two hundred thousand men waited in the valley below the Amalekites' camp. The Kenites, who lived nearby, were told to leave. Ever since the Exodus from Egypt, the Kenites had been kind to the Israelites. Good army leaders try hard not to hurt innocent people.

After a tough battle, the Amalekites were almost all destroyed. However, King Saul and his soldiers spared the life of their king, Agag, and took the Amalekites' best sheep and cattle. This was against God's orders. In their excitement, Saul and his soldiers could not resist temptation.

TEMPTATIONS

It's hard to resist
When temptations beckon;
In just a few seconds
What was right becomes wrong.
Promises given
And rules and laws learned
Disappear like a dream
And vanish, like steam.

The Lord was angry that his command to completely destroy Amalek had not been followed faithfully. He told Samuel, "I am sorry that I made Saul king!"

Samuel was terribly upset and prayed to God to forgive Saul. Early the next morning, Samuel went looking for Saul. He heard that Saul had erected a large stone to honor his army's success and was on his way to Gilgal, to offer sacrifices to God. When Samuel found him, Saul said, "I have performed the Lord's commandment." Happy with his victory, Saul had no idea that he had offended God.

"Then what is all this sheep bleating and cow mooing I hear?" asked Samuel.

Saul, quickly shifting the blame to his troops, answered, "My men spared the best sheep and cattle to sacrifice to God."

Samuel was furious! He said, "Let me tell you what the Lord told me last night: 'Aren't you head of all the tribes of Israel? A king is supposed to do what's right, not what his people demand.' The Lord anointed you king, and sent you on a journey to utterly destroy Amalek. Why didn't you listen to God's voice? Why did you spare the best animals and do evil in God's eyes?"

A good leader always takes the blame for his people. But once again,

126

King Saul blamed his troops: "I have listened to God's orders, destroyed the Amalekites, and captured their king, Agag. My men took the best animals to sacrifice to the Lord."

With a heavy heart, Samuel said:

"Does the Lord delight in burnt offerings and sacrifices
As much as listening to His voice?
To obey is better than sacrifices.
To listen, better than any fat lamb.
Because you have rejected God's word,
He has rejected you as king."

Upon hearing these terrible words, Saul said: "I have sinned because I feared what the people might say. Please pardon my sin and stay with me as I ask God for forgiveness."

An intelligent person does what he thinks is right and doesn't worry about what others might say. King Saul was still blaming his people for his sin. Samuel answered, "I will not return with you; you have rejected God's word and He has rejected you as king."

As Samuel turned to leave, Saul grabbed his long robe, and it tore. "Today, the Lord has torn the kingdom of Israel away from you," declared Samuel, looking over his shoulder. "God will not take back His orders!"

Finally, in desperation, King Saul blamed himself. "I have sinned," he said. "Come with me that I might ask God for forgiveness."

With this last plea, Samuel came with Saul as he apologized to God. Agag, king of the Amalekites, was then brought to Samuel, who said:

"As your sword has made many women childless
Now your own mother will also be childless."

Samuel did what he thought was right and destroyed the last living Amalekite. Worn-out and sad, the old man went back to his home in Ramah. Samuel mourned for Saul and never saw him again. And the Lord continued to be sorry that He had made Saul king.

EXCUSES

Forgetting to remember
Laws and rules and dos and don'ts,
Won't help you get ahead in life.
Instead you'll get in trouble;
Your problems will be double what they ought to be.
And when you make excuses blaming anyone but you,
You'll see that others won't respect you;
They'll get angry and reject you.
What's the use of laws and rules,
And dos and don'ts if they're forgotten
By the ones for whom they're made?
The world will be a better place if everybody faces up
To whatever they've done wrong
And says, "I'm sorry; please forgive me.
It was I and I alone responsible for this or that."
It only takes a minute to remember to remember.
But it sometimes takes a lifetime
To make up for your mistakes.

The Star of Israel

A long time ago, some kings believed that magic spells and nasty curses could help defeat their enemies. As Moses moved his people closer to the Jordan River, Balak, the king of Moab, began to worry. There were many stories about the Children of Israel, some tall tales, some true. Balak was a nervous king; the more he worried, the more true the stories seemed. When he saw the Israelite camp spread out like thousands of colored pebbles in a stream, he sent for Balaam, a famous magician. Perhaps he could put a curse on the twelve tribes of Israel and keep them away.

King Balak did not know that the Lord, with the help of a talking donkey, had opened the eyes of Balaam's mind. No curses were ever to come from his mouth, only God's words. Looking out over the wide wilderness, Balaam saw the gigantic Israelite camp, flags flying in the desert breeze. He said:

"How lovely are your tents, O Jacob.
Your dwellings, Israel, O how fair!"

King Balak was furious at Balaam, the magician. "I sent you to curse my enemies!" he cried, purple with rage. "And here you have blessed them! Be quick! Leave! Go home!"

As Balaam prepared to climb on his old, faithful donkey, he told the king that he would use his magician's powers just once, to look into the future. As Balaam spoke, King Balak became even more nervous; he could hardly believe what he heard:

"I see these people, the Children of Israel,
And from their heart shall come a star,
A mighty king,
A ruler rising,
Crushing their enemies near and far!"

Many years after Balaam, the magician, made this prediction, the Children of Israel did have a king. But King Saul had not turned out as God had hoped. Although his body was big and strong, his heart had little room for kindness. Victories meant more to him than God's laws; winning was more important than good behavior. King Saul was hardheaded; his brain had trouble recognizing his own mistakes.

The Children of Israel needed a leader who would, first of all, honor God. His strength would come from his heart, not his height or powerful body. The Lord told Samuel: "Enough of this mourning for Saul. Rise up, fill a ram's horn with oil, and go to see Jesse, the Bethlehemite. Among his sons, I have found a new king who will serve and obey Me."

"How can I go?" Samuel asked the Lord. "If Saul hears about this he will kill me and Your orders will not be fulfilled."

The Lord told Samuel how to hide his true reasons for coming to Bethlehem: "Take a nice cow with you and say, 'I am here to make a sacrifice to God.' Call Jesse to the sacrifice. I will tell you what to do and you shall anoint as king the one I choose."

Once more, old Samuel rode his donkey up and down bumpy roads, over green hills, and through shady valleys till he came to Bethlehem. The townspeople were excited to see him. "I have come to sacrifice to the Lord," he told them. "Go to your homes, prepare yourselves properly, and come with me."

Samuel found Jesse and accepted his offer of a cool glass of goat's milk and a much-needed rest on soft pillows. Going home with him would give Samuel the chance to take a close look at Jesse's seven big sons as they washed and dressed for the sacrifice ceremony. Eliab, tall and handsome, seemed perfect. "Surely he must be the Lord's anointed," thought Samuel, remembering how Saul, so tall and handsome, had been chosen. As his memory flipped through unforgettable pictures, Samuel heard the voice of God say, "What someone looks like is not important; rather, it is what is in his heart that matters."

The seven sons of Jesse passed before Samuel. "The Lord has not chosen any of these young men," said the old judge to a bewildered Jesse. "Are these all of your children?"

Jesse replied: "One son remains. He is my youngest and he's out taking care of the sheep."

"Send for him," ordered Samuel. "We will not have our sacrifice meal until he arrives."

131

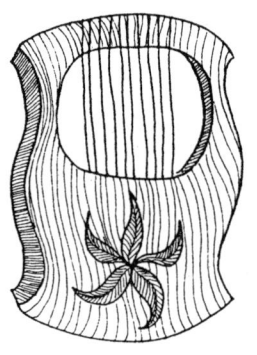

David the shepherd was out in the meadow
Bringing baby sheep back to their mothers
Who bleated so mournfully, thinking them lost.
Happily singing, he walked among sheep,
Tossed them balls made of sweet grass,
And talked to them often about this or that.
Sometimes he sat on a flat rock and played
Songs he called "psalms,"
On his beautiful harp with ten strings,
Called a "lyre."
David the shepherd never got tired;
His beautiful music strengthened his heart.
As David was singing his favorite psalm
Praising God, his own shepherd,
And was up to the part
Where he is anointed with oil by the Lord,
His brothers came for him
And brought him to Samuel, who looked at him closely,
This beautiful boy with large, almond-shaped eyes,
Bright with spirit and strength.
Sunlight and clean air made his cheeks rosy.
His reddish-brown hair curled the length of his neck.
The Lord said to Samuel, "Arise, this is he.
Anoint him."
Was this boy the star Balaam spoke of?
A ruler?
A king?
Samuel, anointing, did not say
To David the shepherd, on that special day
What the Lord God had planned his future to be.

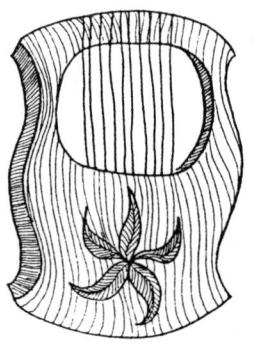

The Spirit of God came upon David mightily,
And it waited within him until the right time,
When Israel's star
Would be ready to shine.

132

Sweet Psalms
for
King Saul

Once in a while a person's brain might show signs of illness. There are many different symptoms. For example, a happy person might begin to cry at odd times, and a friendly person might suddenly become afraid of people. How the brain works and why it does what it does can be mysterious. When someone's brain develops an illness, it takes patience and understanding to deal with the one who is sick and to help the person recover.

As he grew older, King Saul began to behave strangely; his moods changed quickly, without any reason. Some days he was terrified that people were trying to kill him; he kept his spear next to him at all times, even when he slept. Some days he was so unhappy he wouldn't eat or sleep, and he stayed by himself in a dark room. When the king had one of these dreadful spells he felt miserable, and because of this, his servants and soldiers were miserable too.

MOODS

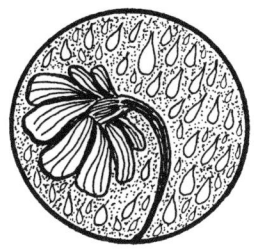

Moods come and go
Like the wind, or the rain.
Some people don't know
How to explain
Why they feel how they feel,
Glum, gloomy, or blue.
Some moods hit like a big wave,
And take over you.

If you feel like your feelings
Are on the outside,
And your insides are hurting
And you don't know why,
Talk to a friend,
Somebody you trust.
You must try; it's important.
And, if you cry you might
Feel better after.
The sad mood,
Glum and gloom
Will move on and make room
For smiles,
And for laughter.

Beautiful music has a way of calming people. Little babies fall asleep to lullabies, children sing nursery rhymes over and over, and teenagers are happy to "disappear" into their own special kind of musical sounds. King Saul's servants had an idea. They begged the unhappy king to let them find a person who could play a stringed instrument called the harp. Since music works its wonders with children, perhaps it would help the king crawl out of his dark moods and once again allow the sun to shine on his handsome face.

The king agreed to this and said, "Find a man who can play well and bring him to me."

One of the men already had someone in mind. "David, a son of Jesse the Bethlehemite, sings and plays the harp while he watches his father's sheep. He's a fine young man and writes wonderful psalms, and I think that the Lord is with him."

"Sounds good," said King Saul, and sent a message to Jesse:

"Send me your son David, the shepherd."

Jesse still did not know why David was suddenly so popular. However, an order from the king was an order one did not question. He loaded a donkey with gifts: loaves of barley, whole wheat and raisin bread, a goatskin filled with wine from the latest harvest, and a young goat seasoned with garlic and rosemary, ready for roasting. He sent these with David, who led the donkey with one hand and carried his wooden harp with the other.

King Saul took one look at this fine young man and gave him the honor of being his armor-bearer. Because he was not in the habit of taking people's sons whenever he wished, King Saul sent a polite message to Jesse requesting that David be allowed to work for him.

And so, when the bad moods, sad feelings, and strange, sometimes dangerous, behavior came over the king, David played his harp and sang his soothing psalms. This beautiful music helped push away the black clouds that had forced King Saul to hide inside himself. As the sweet sounds touched him like gentle fingers, the king would slowly open his eyes and once again return to God's sun-filled world.

David and Goliath

The Philistine army was gathered for war
On a row of hills lining one side
Of a passage, called a ravine,
Cut into the earth by mountain streams joining,
Becoming a brook running swiftly down into a valley.
The army of Israel took up positions
Across this ravine on a row of hills lining
The opposite side of this passage
Cut into the earth by mountain streams joining,
Becoming a brook running swiftly
Down into a valley.

Like alley cats on their toes
With their bushy tails up,
Each army waited the other one out.
Who would make the first move?
Who would give the first shout?
One morning at sunrise a terrible sight

137

Filled Israel's army with horror and fright:
Goliath, the giant,
Nine feet eight inches tall,
Came forward and bellowed a loud warning call!
A helmet of bronze was on top of his head;
His body was covered with pieces of armor
Like scales on a fish,
Weighing one hundred fifty or more pounds in all.
His legs were protected with armor that gleamed
As the morning sun beamed its wide smile on the day.
The hard iron head of his extra long spear
Weighed nineteen pounds,
And he carried an extra large shield for protection.
Between two broad shoulders a javelin hung;
It was deadly when thrown by this man with no fear!
Goliath, the giant, yelled in the direction
Of Israel's army,
"Why are you waiting here dressed for a battle?
Choose a man to come fight me,
We'll see if he rattles me.
And if he kills me, then we'll be your servants!"
Goliath was teasing;
Goliath was taunting.
King Saul was dismayed,
His army,
Afraid.

David the shepherd went to and fro
From his job making music
To feeding his father's large flocks of sheep.
He was trying to keep them from running away
In search of new green grass.
(Sheep don't like dry hay.)
His three eldest brothers had gone with King Saul
Into the hills to wait out Goliath.
The gigantic giant appeared twice a day
At sunrise and sunset.
For forty long days he would not go away!
For forty long days he continued to shout!

Jesse, David's father, asked his young son
To carry some good home-cooked food to his brothers:
Roasted grain, loaves of bread,
And ten soft ripe cheeses to give to their captain.
David arose while the sun was asleep,
Left his sheep with a keeper, and carried the food
To the Israelite's camp,
Left the grain, bread, and cheese
With the keeper of baggage,
And then ran to greet his three eldest brothers.
As he talked with them, out came the Philistine giant.
"Can you imagine what riches will come
To the one who will kill him?"
The men asked each other.
David the shepherd asked, "Who is this man

139

Who dares to make fun of the army of God?
Let no man be upset," David said to the king.
"I will go fight the giant!
I'm good with a sling!"
Saul said, "You're too young.
He's a great man of war."
David answered, "Before, when I cared for the sheep,
And a lion or bear took a lamb in its jaw,
I went out and killed both the lion and bear!
And this Philistine giant shall be like them to me.
He has taunted God's army!
The Lord, Who delivered me out of the paws
Of the lion and bear with sheep in their jaws,
Will help me subdue this mean Philistine!"

Saul took off his armor and put it on David.
But David was not used to wearing such things.
The weight of the armor was much too great for him.
So David removed King Saul's armor and said,
"I can't move wearing these.
King Saul, if you please,
Allow me to do it my own way instead."
With only his staff and his slingshot in hand,
David went to the brook and chose five smooth stones,
Put them in his bag,
Held on tight to his sling,
And drew near to Goliath, the mean Philistine
Who, looking at David, saw only a boy,
Red-cheeked and handsome.
He looked like a toy to be played with!
"Come to me," he growled, "I'll feed you
To the birds in the air!
And the beasts of the field!"
David answered,
"You come to me with shield and with sword.
But I come to you in the name of the Lord!

140

On this day, the Lord will place you in my hand.
You will be dead,
And I'll cut off your head
And feed you to the birds of the air
And the beasts!
Everybody will know that the Lord God is near,
And that He doesn't save with a sword or a spear!"

Goliath, the giant, came close to the boy
Whom he thought he could toss around
Just like a toy.
David ran toward him,
Put his hand in his kit,
Took a smooth stone and slung it!
Goliath was hit
In the forehead!
The giant fell flat on his face.
David took the man's sword
And cut off his head!
When the Philistine soldiers saw David the shepherd
Lift up Goliath the giant's dead head,
They couldn't believe what their eyes said was true!
For a moment they stood across the ravine
On the row of hills lining this passage
Cut into the earth by mountain streams joining,
Becoming a brook running swiftly down into a valley.
They took one more look.
Yes!
Goliath was dead!
Then they threw off their armor,
Turned quickly
And fled!

David and Jonathan

A shepherd lives a lonely life. For weeks on end, no other voice but his own echo returns his call. With only cloud puffs and winking stars for company, a shepherd becomes one with the silence of the heavens.

David the shepherd was often lonely. He was the youngest of eight boys, and his older brothers were always going places, joining the army, selling wool at busy markets, or hanging out at the water well, helping pretty girls lift heavy buckets of water. Since nobody wanted a little child tagging along, David learned ways to amuse himself. He taught himself to play a lyre, a harp with ten strings, and he began writing his own songs, called psalms. When his father, Jesse, felt he was responsible enough to tend his large flock of sheep, these talents came in handy; music made him feel less lonely. Living under the canopy of God's great sky, David was thankful that he was part of such a wonderful world. In his clear voice David would sing:

My heart is loyal and faithful.
I will sing praises.
Wake up stringed instruments!
I will awaken the dawn.

After amazing everyone with his stone-slinging, giant-killing feat, David the shepherd became David the hero. Wherever he went, people wanted to meet him, to shake his hand or pat him on the back. Only Jonathan, King Saul's son, wanted to be his true friend. He was impressed with David's courage and his way of not bragging about himself. Having grown up in an army camp full of men filled with tales of victories, true or imagined, Jonathan needed an honest friend. To Jonathan, David seemed perfect; to David, Jonathan seemed perfect. The two young men became soul mates, the very best of friends. They made a covenant, an unbreakable promise of loyalty and love that would last forever. As his special gift of friendship, Jonathan gave David his army uniform, his sword with two sharp sides, one of his big, beautiful bow-and-arrow sets, and his purple sash, made only for princes. David was no longer lonely, and he thanked his best friend with a psalm that began like this:

How good and how pleasant it is
For men to live together in brotherhood.

King Saul made David an army leader and sent him on many important missions. When David returned victorious, women from all over Israel came out to greet the king and his new captain. Shaking silver tambourines and plucking little, three-stringed harps, the women sang:

"Saul has slain his thousands,
And David his ten thousands."

King Saul did not like this at all! "They have given David credit for destroying more enemies than me! All he needs now is his own kingdom!"

From that day on, King Saul was jealous and suspicious of David. And when the strange sickness once again took over his mind, he became dangerous and uncontrollable. Twice, as David tried to calm him with music, the king hurled his spear at David. Both times, David ducked and the spear clattered to the floor. Luckily, David always kept one eye on this

143

unpredictable king; he never knew what might happen next!

The king began to think that God was truly with David. How else could he so easily escape death? He sent the young man on even more dangerous missions. Again and again David won the battles and returned, more popular than ever. The king had another scheme under his crown. He offered his eldest daughter, Merab, to David as a wife. "Who am I to be so worthy of a king's daughter?" asked David, confused by this invitation.

"Just win more battles for me," ordered Saul, hoping that the Philistines would do to David what his own spear had failed to do.

But King Saul, who could not be counted on to think clearly, abruptly changed his plans and gave Merab away to another man! For once, King Saul's mixed-up mind helped do David a favor: Saul's youngest daughter, Michal, fell in love with the handsome hero. And David fell in love with Michal!

"I have no dowry, no gifts or money to give to you for your daughter Michal," said David to the king.

"All the king wants is proof that one hundred Philistines have been eliminated," the king's servants told David.

To King Saul, this seemed like an impossible order. Surely, David would not survive! To his great dismay, however, David brought him proof of two hundred dead Philistines! Reluctantly, the king allowed Michal to marry David.

Nobody but King Saul knew what Samuel, the judge, had related: God was replacing him with someone else. Saul carried this prediction around like a heavy sack on his shoulders. Every day it weighed him down a little more. If only he could get rid of it! As Saul's mind became more and more jumbled, he devised all sorts of plans to do away with his new son-in-law. When he told his own son to kill David, Jonathan spoke sharply to his father: "Don't hurt David; he has not hurt you! He has slain the Philistines and saved Israel. Why kill him for no reason?"

These strong words from his son helped Saul's mind regain its clearness. He swore that he would not hurt David. Once again David came to play his harp and sing a sweet song:

Unto You, O Lord, I lift up my soul.
O my God, I have put my trust in You;
Let me not be ashamed.
Do not let my enemies defeat me.
No one who serves You shall be ashamed;
Only those who deal treacherously without a reason.
Show me Your ways, O Lord;
Teach me to walk in Your path.

Unfortunately, Saul's clear head soon became cloudy. One day, as David was playing his soothing music, the king sent his big spear flying! Out of the corner of his eye, David saw a flash of metal and hit the ground! Thwack! Into the wall it went as David scrambled to his feet and ran home. He hoped to return as soon as King Saul recovered his senses. But the king sent soldiers to surround David's house. "If you don't leave," cautioned David's wife, Michal, "they will kill you in the morning."

Michal helped David climb out the window and escape over the flat rooftops. She then made a dummy David out of bedclothes and a goat-hair pillow and told the waiting men that he was sick.

"Bring him to me in his bed!" demanded the king when he heard this piece of news.

In the bedroom, the soldiers discovered the trick! "Why have you deceived me and allowed my enemy to escape?" screamed the king at his daughter.

Michal answered in a shaky voice, "David said, 'Let me go. Why should I kill you?' I was afraid for my life and I let him go." This was, of course, a made-up story. In times of great danger, certain kinds of fibs are sometimes necessary.

David ran the few miles to Ramah, where Samuel had opened a school for prophets. He wanted the old man to know what had happened. "Don't worry," said Samuel. "The Lord is with you."

When Saul's men finally caught up with David, the Spirit of God came over them. They joined the students in singing, dancing, and praising God and forgot their reason for coming. Two more groups of soldiers arrived and they too began singing, dancing, and praising God.

"If you want something done right, you have to do it yourself," grumbled King Saul, when none of his men returned. He climbed on a donkey, went to Ramah, and was instantly overtaken by the Spirit of God. Saul took off his clothes, danced in wild circles, sang song after song of praise, and then lay down, naked and exhausted, in front of Samuel. This gave David a chance to escape. Surely the Lord was with him!

David arranged to meet Jonathan secretly. "What have I done wrong?" he asked his dearest friend. "Why does your father want to kill me?"

"You shall not die!" vowed Jonathan. "My father does nothing without consulting me." Jonathan had trouble believing that his father really wanted to kill David. He thought this behavior was only another attack of King Saul's strange illness.

David devised a plan. "I'm supposed to eat with your father tomorrow night. I will hide out in the fields. If your father misses me, say that I am in Bethlehem with my parents. If he stays calm, all will be well. But if he gets angry, know that he has evil up his sleeve."

"Good plan," agreed Jonathan. "Try to hide behind some big rocks. I will come to the field with my bow and arrows. If I shoot the arrows to the side, I will say to my arrow chaser, 'Go find the arrows. They are on this side of you.' If I say, 'The arrows are beyond you,' then you must leave here fast. Remember, David, the Lord is witness to our promise of friendship."

When King Saul heard that David was away, he became very angry—so angry that he threw his spear at Jonathan! Jonathan was furious and left the table. He was much more upset about now having to say good-bye to David than about his father's spear throwing. A true best friend always thinks of the other friend first.

On the third day, as planned, Jonathan went out to the field with his bow and arrows. He shot his arrows far beyond the arrow-chasing boy and shouted: "The arrows are beyond you. Quickly go! Do not stay!"

After these added words of warning, Jonathan sent the boy away. The two best friends put their arms around each other, hugged and kissed and cried, and said farewell. "The Lord shall be with us forever," said David. "You are my very best, my dearest friend."

SOMEWHERE THERE'S A FRIEND

Sometimes, when the world is in a spin
You begin to think the road will never end,
Somewhere, there's a someone who will care
To take the time to be a friend.

If you look beyond the gray skies
And move the clouds away for just a while,
You'll find someone waiting for you
With a hand to hold, and a smile.

Sometimes, when the going gets too rough
And it's tough to get the tallest tree to bend,
Somewhere, there's a someone who will care
To take the time to be a friend.

David Escapes

It is always hard to say good-bye to someone you love. David felt sad after saying farewell to his best friend, Jonathan. However, he could not waste time feeling blue; he had to get away fast, before King Saul found him.

David pointed his trusty donkey toward the town of Nob, where the Tabernacle of the Lord rested. He hoped that the priests who took care of God's holy Ark would give him food, weapons, and some instructions from the Lord. Because it was the end of the week and new holy bread was being baked, the priests shared the old bread with David. For a weapon, they gave him the great sword of Goliath, which had been wrapped in cloth and hidden behind the priests' special robes. David did not know that on that very day, a spy was also visiting the priests of Nob: King Saul's chief herdsman, Doeg.

David left Nob quickly. Not feeling safe anywhere in his own land, he offered his services to Achish, the Philistine king of Gath. Unfortunately, the king's servants were very suspicious of David. They had heard people singing:

"Saul has slain his thousands,
And David his ten thousands."

They could not imagine why David was about to change sides! David realized he had made a big mistake in coming to Gath. Thinking quickly, he pretended to be insane, running around in circles, scribbling nonsense on the walls of the gates, and drooling on himself like a hungry dog. The king of Gath, watching this wild behavior, said to his men: "That man is mad! I've got enough problems! He shall not be allowed to stay!" The king walked away, shaking his head and mumbling: "Just what I need. Another madman!"

David climbed on his donkey, which, doing his best horse imitation, wobbled jerkily away. David remembered that there was a big cave in Adullam, about twelve miles from Bethlehem, his hometown. As he rode the narrow road through the hills, David sang this psalm:

I shall praise the Lord at all times;
His praise shall always be on my lips.
My soul shall glory in the Lord.
Those who have also been afraid shall rejoice.
Proclaim with me the Lord's greatness!
Let us praise His name together.
I sought the Lord and He answered me.
He delivered me from all my fears.

Some news travels all by itself on the wings of the wind. No sooner did David reach the big, dark cave than his brothers arrived! Then, four hundred men who were angry, in debt, or unhappy also made their way to the cave. David was now the head of a tough little army! After making sure that his parents had a safe place to stay with the king of Moab, David and his men left the dark, damp cave and entered a dark, dry forest.

News about David continued to fly back and forth like a bird building its nest. It wasn't long before King Saul heard that David had been seen in the hills. With his dangerous spear in hand, the king threw a temper tantrum in front of his men.

"You are all against me!" he bellowed. "Nobody told me that Jonathan was helping David and nobody feels sorry for me!"

Then Doeg, his chief herdsman, spoke up: "I saw the son of Jesse when he came to see the priests of Nob. They gave him bread and Goliath's sword."

"Bring the priests to me!" ordered the king.

When the priests arrived, King Saul asked, "Why did you plot against me and give David bread and a sword?" Purple with rage, he screamed, "You have asked God questions for him and you are now my enemy!"

Ahimelech, the priest, answered calmly: "Who is more trusted than David, your son-in-law? I don't know anything about him being your enemy."

150

"You and all your families shall surely die!" roared the king.

He then ordered his servants to kill the priests. But not one guard raised his hand. They knew that poor King Saul was at this moment barely sane, and that the punishment he had ordered was wrong. In a fury, King Saul turned to Doeg, the herdsman. "You kill them!" he demanded.

And this man with no mind of his own did as the king wished. All the eighty-five priests of Nob and their innocent families were slain. This was a terrible tragedy.

One of Ahimelech's sons managed to survive. He found David and told him the dreadful story.

"I had a feeling this would happen," said David. "This is all my fault. Stay with me now," he said to the man. "Do not fear. Whoever is looking for me is also looking for you. You'll be safer here."

As a great, dark wave of sadness washed over David, he recited this psalm:

Do not let evildoers worry you;
Do not envy their success.
For they shall soon wither like grass
And dry up like green herbs.
Trust in the Lord and do good;
Live in His land and be faithful.

With God's help, David and his men fought many more successful battles against the Philistines. When King Saul heard that David had saved the people of Keilah, he again began plotting against him. David asked the Lord's help.

"Will Saul come down to get me here?" he asked.

"He will come down," said the Lord.

"Will the men of Keilah hand me and my men over to Saul?"

"They will hand you over to him," answered the Lord.

With thanks for this additional help from God, David and his army were able to leave Keilah and disappear into the hills. Jonathan found his dearest friend in the wilderness of Ziph. He reminded David that God was with him and said: "My father will not find you. Someday you will be king of Israel and my father knows this already!"

151

The two friends pledged their love and loyalty and once again said farewell.

Saul and his men continued to chase David through the forests and into the wilderness of Maon, till they were on either side of some big, rocky hiding places. David and his loyal army ran swiftly as Saul's men began to encircle them, spears and daggers glinting in the sun. Suddenly, a young runner appeared with a message for the king. "Hurry and come!" he cried breathlessly. "The Philistines have raided our land!"

Saul and his army stopped pursuing David, turned around, and went back to fighting the Philistines. Once again, David was able to escape!

That night, in a forest of oak trees, David made his bed on a soft pillow of leaves. Looking up through the swaying branches, David watched the happy stars dance across the sky. As in his shepherd days, David felt at peace under the blanket of God's quiet heavens. Before he fell asleep, David felt the need to sing silently, within himself, parts of one of his earliest psalms:

The Lord is my guide and my help,
Of whom shall I be afraid?
The Lord is my tower of strength,
Whom shall I fear?
When evil men closed in on me,
Seeking, like wild animals, to devour me,
It was my enemies who stumbled,
It was my foes who fell.
If an army came against me,
My heart would not be afraid;
If war raged against me,
Even then I would still be confident.
What if I had not had faith!
But I did have faith
That I would know God's goodness here on earth.
Put your trust in the Lord;
Be strong and let your heart be patient;
Put your trust only in the Lord.

David and Abigail

There once was a rich man who lived in Maon.
He owned three thousand sheep and one thousand goats.
He came to Carmel for the sheep-shearing days,
And they called him "Nabal";
He was rough in his ways.
His wife, Abigail, was good, kind, and smart.
A beautiful woman with peace in her heart.

David heard that Nabal was shearing his sheep.
He sent men to greet him and say,
"Peace be with you, and all of your house.
I have heard that you're shearing the sheep
From your shepherds,
Who've been in the hills with us
Far from their farm.
We've done them no harm, and took nothing from them
Ask them, they will tell you.
Today is a good day to give away gifts.

154

Would you please give some food
To us and to David."
"Who is David?" asked Nabal, nasty and rude.
"Nowadays many servants
Are leaving their masters.
Shall I give my bread, my water, my meat
That I've fixed for my shearers
To those I don't know?"
The young men went back and told David these words.
"Gird on your swords!" he said.
"Nabal's our foe!"

One of the shepherds happened to meet
Nabal's wife, Abigail,
And he told her the tale of how Nabal, her husband,
Flew at David's men like a bird swooping down.
He was rough, he was mean!
He said, "These men were good to us out in the fields
Away from our farm, they did us no harm.
They took nothing from us by night and by day.
Like a wall they protected us.
What can you do?
Evil's coming this way
For us and our master and all of his house.
There will be a disaster!"

Abigail listened; they all might be dead!
Using her head, she took two hundred breads,
Two containers of wine,
Five sheep for roasting,
Five baskets of grain,
One hundred clusters of juicy black raisins,
And two hundred fig cakes,
Some napkins and plates.
She loaded the goodies on twelve sturdy donkeys.
"You go on before me," she said to her men.
Abigail, saying nothing to Nabal, her husband,
Climbed on her donkey and rode down the mountain.
To her surprise, in front of her eyes,
There were David and all his men
Climbing the mountain!

Abigail gracefully got off her donkey,
Bowed to David, and said, "My lord, may I speak?
Don't listen to Nabal.
He's just like his name,
Nabal means churl, which means 'rough and mean,
Stingy and vulgar.'
He's a real pain!
Here are some presents for you and your men.
I didn't meet the men you sent to greet us.
I see that the Lord has held back your hand.
It would be on your conscience if you used your sword.
God will be sure to make you a prince.
You will fight the Lord's battles.
And you will not fail.
You'll be bound in the bundle of life, evermore.
You won't have to atone for
Needless blood shed.
And I hope you'll remember my name,
Abigail."

David said to the woman, "Blessed be the Lord,
Who sent you to meet me.
Blessed be your good judgment,
And may you be blessed too for helping to keep me
Away from my hand and away from my sword.
If you hadn't cared
No one would have been spared."
David accepted the presents she brought him,
Including her wisdom; her words would prevail.
With thanks, David said,
"Go in peace, Abigail."

When she returned home,
Nabal, the churl, was holding a feast,
Like the feast of a king.
Singing and shouting, he'd drunk too much wine.
This was not the right time to do any talking.
Abigail waited till he had a clear head.
When she told him the story
His heart felt like lead!
Ten days later old, mean, nasty Nabal was dead!
When David heard this he said,
"Bless the Lord.
He took revenge for me and held back my sword."
David asked his young helper to ask Abigail,
Who now was a widow,
To be David's wife for the rest of her life.
(Men could have many wives in those faraway days.)
And so Abigail, good, kind, and smart,
Found, besides peace, there was love in her heart!
After giving some thought to this sudden proposal,
She bought a new dress,
Packed her bags,
And said, "Yes."

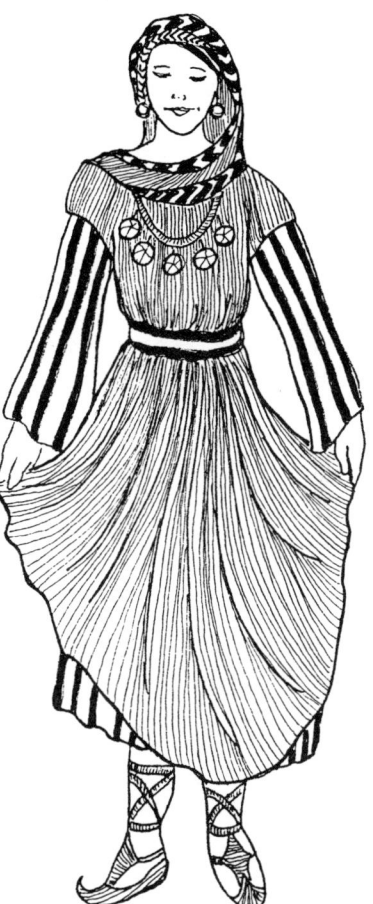

David Spares
King Saul's Life
at En-Gedi

The Dead Sea is the lowest body of water on earth. Bordering most of its edges is a desolate wasteland of rocks and caves. On its western shore, like a precious blue jewel, is the oasis of En-Gedi, whose name means "the spring of the wild goats." Surrounded by palm trees and flowers, this pool of cool water is filled by waterfalls cascading from high, rocky cliffs. Long-haired goats and their adventuresome kids walk carefully down narrow rocky paths to nibble the green grass touched by the waterfall's spray. Fleeing again from King Saul, David came to En-Gedi. He knew that the huge caves sheltered shepherds and animals during bad weather. These would make good hideouts for his army.

After Saul returned from his latest Philistine battle, he took three thousand men and followed David to the rocks of the wild goats. The king, needing some private time, went into one of the dark caves. When you come from bright sun into darkness, it takes a while before your eyes get adjusted. This is why King Saul could not see David and his men, who just happened to be deep inside this same cave!

The soldiers whispered to David: "Here's your chance. The Lord has given King Saul into your hands."

David tiptoed up to Saul, whose mind was busy plotting and planning, and cut off a piece of his robe! David tiptoed back and, to his men's surprise, whispered: "I could not hurt the Lord's anointed king. Leave him alone."

King Saul, who had not noticed David, looked up when he thought he heard things flapping and whizzing overhead. "Uh-oh," he thought. "Bats! I'm getting out of here!"

David followed King Saul as he ran out of the cave. "My lord, the king!" he called, bowing in honor.

"Why do you think that I'm out to hurt you?
God placed you near me.
Some said 'kill him';
I spared you.
I would not raise my hand at you.
Look at this piece of your robe in my hand.
I did not kill you;
I've not sinned against you.
Although you are waiting to take my life,
Wicked deeds come from wicked men.
I will not hurt you.
Why does the great king
Continue to seek me?
I'm not important,
A dead dog, a flea.
Let God judge and give sentence
Between King Saul and me."
When David finished, King Saul said,

"My son? Is this your voice?
Oh dear, what have I done?"
Saul wept as he said,
"You are better than me.
You've done good, I've done evil.
God placed me in your hand
And you did not kill me.
May God reward you.
I know you'll be king.
Now swear to me that you will not hurt
My family
Or my good name."
David gave Saul his word
And let him depart,
Though he knew in his heart
Saul would soon change his mind again.
David said, "Men,
We will stay at En-Gedi
To wait out Saul's good mood.
Keep alert and be ready!"

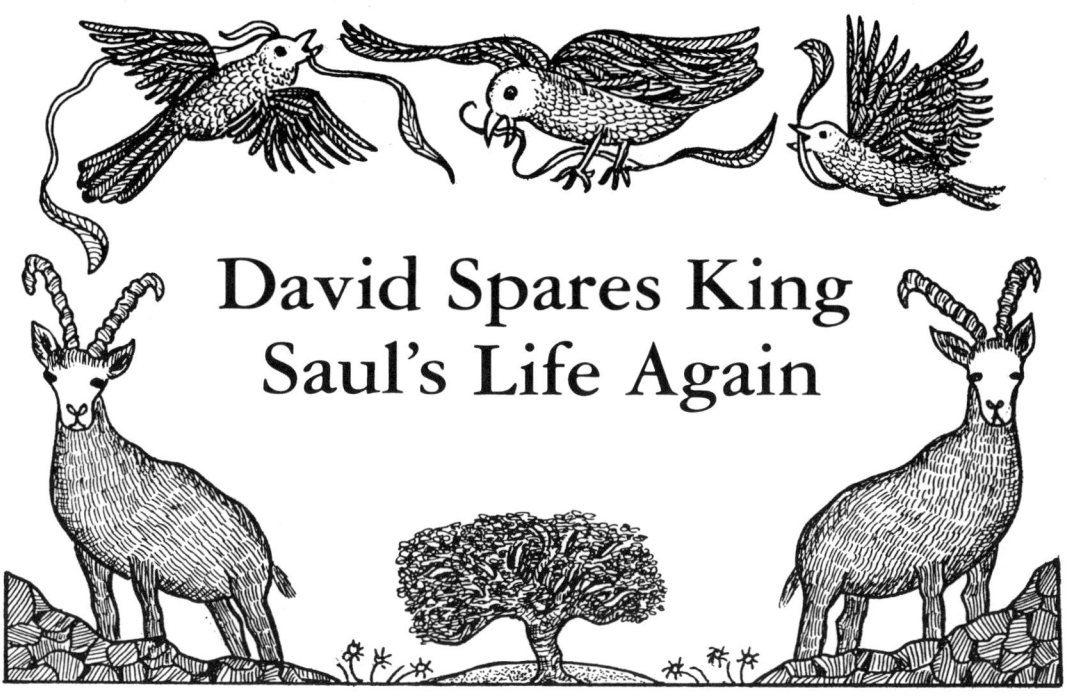

David Spares King Saul's Life Again

When it came to dealing with David, King Saul usually promised one thing and did the opposite. Fortunately, David realized this and kept his eyes and ears open.

One of Saul's spies reported that David was hiding in the wilderness of Ziph. Saul took three thousand men and camped on a big hill about six miles from this area. David had men hiding in trees as lookouts. When they saw the big army, they sent for David. Climbing a tall oak tree, David saw for himself where Saul was sleeping encircled by his general, Abner, and all the soldiers.

"Who will go down with me to King Saul's camp?" asked David.

Abishai, a brave soldier, volunteered.

Later that night, David and Abishai quietly made their way to the camp. They were used to walking softly; living outdoors, they often watched animals and birds silently stalk smaller animals, insects, and worms.

Inside the camp, King Saul was asleep with his sword stuck in the ground by his head. Abishai said to David: "God has delivered your enemy. Let me pin him to the ground with his sword."

David answered: "Do not take his life. Who can hurt the Lord's anointed and not have guilt? His day will come, perhaps in a battle. We'll only take his spear and his water jug."

David tiptoed up to the king, got the spear and the jug, and left. Nobody saw them; the Lord had put Saul and his men into a very deep sleep.

STALKING

Stalking means a careful walking,
Following another person, animal or bug.
Cats are good at stalking,
Walking quietly on paws so soft that no one knows
When they're around.
When they're done stalking,
They pounce!
They've caught a bug or grabbed a dog's tail!
Or ouch!
A mouse!
Poor thing.
Just hear him squawking!

David crossed the valley and called out loud to Abner,
"Answer me!"
And Abner answered, "Who are you who wakes the king?"
David said, "You are supposed to be
A brave man.
There's none like you.
Why haven't you kept watch over the king?
Someone tried to hurt the king!
This is bad!
And you should die!
King Saul, the Lord's anointed,
Will be very disappointed
When he hears that someone took his jug and spear!"
Saul knew David's voice and said,
"Is that you, my son?"

162

David answered, "It is I,
Tell me why you chase me.
Tell me what I've done.
What awful evil thing is in my hand?
Listen to me, now I pray,
If God wants you to punish me for sins,
Let Him accept my offering.
But if men are responsible,
Let them all be cursed
For driving me and all my men out of this land!
Don't let me die a violent death
In a foreign country.
King Saul seeks a single flea;
He hunts me like a partridge."
"I have sinned," Saul said.
"Return to me.
I promise not to hurt you.
You've spared my life today;
I've been a fool.
I've made a big mistake."
And David answered,
"Tell a man to come and take your spear."
Saul said, "May you be blessed,
And succeed in all you do."
King Saul left and David went his way.
He knew not to depend
On King Saul's word and said,
"Someday, this all will end.
King Saul will capture me.
So I'll go to the Philistines,
The king of Gath might have me."
When King Saul heard
Where David went,
He stopped his search
And kept his word!

David Stays with the Philistines

David was desperate. He had to find a safe place for himself, his family, his men, and their households. His last resort was asking Achish, the Philistine king of Gath, to take them in. To David's surprise, the king allowed them to stay; David's well-trained army would be a great help to him.

David was a good actor. He pretended that living in the king's own city was too great an honor and asked Achish if he and his people could live in the country. Achish agreed and gave David the town of Ziklag. With their own town, David's people would stay better organized and be able to practice their religion away from the curious Philistines.

One day, David's army made a raid on some of their old enemies, including the swarms of Amalekites, who kept reappearing like termites after tree trunks. When Achish asked him, "Where did you make a raid today?" David answered, "On the south of Judah, the south of the Jerahmeelites, and on the Kenites. I left no one alive."

This was a good story; Achish was convinced that David had raided his own people. The king said with a smile on his face, "He has made his own people despise him; he shall be my servant forever."

Once more the Philistines gathered their troops to fight against Israel. Cheerfully, King Achish told David, "You and your army are coming with me to this battle."

David was in a dilemma: how could he avoid fighting against his own people and at the same time not show disloyalty to Achish? He gave the king this wishy-washy answer: "We'll see what I'll do."

Achish, taking this answer for loyalty, said, "You shall be my bodyguard forever."

Thousands of Philistines prepared to fight the Children of Israel:

There were chariots, horses,
Riders and foot soldiers,
Archers, and spear throwers,
Dagger and sword fighters.
Wood fetchers, fire builders
Water bearers, food cookers.
The mean Philistines
Were orderly warriors.

David and his men followed behind Achish. The other Philistine leaders were surprised to see a Hebrew army marching with them. "What are these people doing here?" they questioned Achish.

"This is Saul's servant, David. He's been with me for a while and I've found no fault with him," explained Achish.

But the leaders were angry with Achish. They had heard many stories about David and did not trust him.

"Make this man return home!" they insisted. "Do not allow him to fight because he might turn against us. Isn't this the famous David of whom people sing:

'Saul has slain his thousands
And David his ten thousands'?"

Achish felt terrible about this. The fact that a soldier fights for a different side does not always mean he's a bad guy. Achish was genuinely fond of David. He said sincerely, "You have behaved well and have been good to me. I have found no evil in you. Go in peace before these other leaders get too angry."

David, still being a good actor, pretended to be hurt by this change of plans. "What have I done wrong? Why can't I fight against your enemies?" he asked plaintively, inwardly rejoicing that his dilemma had been solved for him.

"You have been like an angel of God to me," said the king, putting his arm over David's shoulders. "But you must go at first light with the morning star."

David and his men returned to Ziklag and found, to their dismay, that the hordes of Amalekites had captured their wives and children and taken everything they owned: cattle, flocks, chickens, bags of wheat and barley, jugs of wine and grape juice, honey, vegetables, dried fruit, and baskets of almonds.

David's two wives, Abigail and Ahinoam, were gone. In David's absence, King Saul had given away Michal, David's first wife. Now, there was no one left! David and his men wept until they had used up all their tears.

David was now in danger; his own soldiers wanted to stone him! Sometimes, in their grief, people don't think straight and will speak or act in angry ways.

David's great faith in the Lord helped him know what to do next. He asked God, "Shall I pursue this army?"

And the Lord replied, "Pursue, for you shall overtake them and recover all you have lost."

David took six hundred men and started out to follow the Philistines. But the long journey back to Ziklag had been rough; two hundred men were not feeling well. David left them by a brook to look after supplies and baggage.

As they continued on, they found a tired, hungry Egyptian lying in the road. After reviving him with water, a fig cake, and some raisins, David asked, "For whom do you work?"

"I am a Egyptian servant to an Amalekite. My master left me here because I was sick. If you promise not to kill me or return me to my master, I will show you where they are."

What luck! This was the army they had been looking for! David gave his word and soon found the Amalekites. They were sprawled out all over the ground like bugs, eating, drinking, feasting, and snoring. David and his men fought them from dawn to dusk. Not one man escaped, except for

two hundred swift camel riders, who were harder to catch than slippery gold-fish! David found his two wives and hugged them both. He recovered everything that had been stolen, plus all kinds of loot taken from other raids. His men rounded up the cattle, and the younger boys whistled to the sheep and goats and shepherded them home. The army's mascot, an old yellow goose that had almost lost its head squawking nasty goose words at its captors, followed along quietly, happy to be going home.

David went back to the brook and greeted the two hundred men who had been left behind. Some men who had fought said selfishly, "Since they didn't come with us, they cannot share our good fortune. We'll give them nothing except their families."

David thought this was unfair and made this rule:

"The Lord has given us this victory and good fortune. The share of the one who goes to battle will be the same for those who stay behind to protect supplies and baggage."

As a sign of goodwill, David sent gifts to all the people in the land of Judah. He wanted them to know that he was loyal to Israel and no longer living with the Philistines. Then, as the sun disappeared, leaving trails of purple and red remembrances across the sky, David recited this psalm to all who would listen:

I will give thanks to the Lord with all my heart;
I will tell of all Your marvelous works.
I will be glad and rejoice in You;
I will sing praises to Your name, O Most High.

King Saul
and
the Witch of Endor

After Samuel the judge died, all Israel mourned.
He was buried in Ramah, his beloved old city.
King Saul then got rid of all witches and sorcerers.
People who talked with ghosts and with spirits
Were sent from the land without one ounce of pity.

When the Philistines once again planned an attack,
King Saul's heart lost its strength.
How could he fight back?
"What will I do now? This army is violent."
Saul asked God for help, but He remained silent.
Saul then asked his servants if they, by chance,
Knew of a witch who was left in the land.
The men said, "There's one left in Endor, you know,
A woman who talks to ghosts."
Saul cried, "Let's go!"

168

On this darkest of nights
While the stars hid from sight,
Frogs gave up their croaking
And crickets their song.
The leaves in the trees
Stayed still as the breeze
Disappeared.
Before long,
Nothing moved.
Not a whisker or tail switch.
King Saul in disguise
Went in search of the witch,
Past enemy eyes.
Round a Philistine guard post
King Saul walked with care.
On this darkest of nights
While the stars hid from sight
King Saul found the woman
Who spoke with ghosts!

Alone in her tent,
She was small and bent over.
Her long, knobby fingers
Were weaving a shawl.
Her wispy, white hair
Was pulled back in a braid.
Seeing Saul and his men,
She was very afraid.

"Do magic for me," Saul said.
"Bring me the ghost of whomever I name."
The woman replied, "By King Saul's own wishes
The witches who did this have all left this country.
Why are you trying to bring death upon me?"

Saul swore by the Lord, "You will not be punished
For this ghostly thing."
"Whom shall I bring up?" the witch asked the king.
"Bring me up Samuel," he said, "if you please."

When the woman saw Samuel, she cried,
"You've deceived me, you're Saul!"
The king answered softly, "Do not be scared.
Tell me, what do you see?"
"I see, in a fog, a being so holy
Floating up from the dead;
Long hair flows from his head.
And he's wearing the long robe of one who, when living,
Went from village to town, judging and giving
Advice and God's words to the people around him."
Saul knew it was Samuel and bowed to the ground.

Samuel spoke in a strange hollow voice from beyond,
"Why have you disturbed me;
Why have you brought me up
From my place in forever?"
Saul, flat on his face, said,
"I am so worried; I am so upset.
The Philistines threaten another war yet.
God has left me; He no longer answers my call
By prophets or dreams.
It seems I'm all alone, so I have called you
To tell me what to do."

Samuel answered from far away,
Though he was close,
(This is the way of a spirit or ghost.)
"Since God has left you,
Why do you ask me?
The Lord told me, Himself,
What your future would be.
Your kingdom was torn from your hand,
Like your robe.
And David will one day rule over this land.
You did not listen.
You did not obey and destroy Amalek.
And that's why today
God has brought you distress.
The Lord will deliver Israel's army
Into the hands of the mean Philistines.
And you and your sons
Will soon be here with me."

On this darkest of nights
While the stars hid from sight,
Saul lay on the ground
And no sound came from him.
There was no more strength in him.
Saul felt weak,
He felt broken
When Samuel had spoken.
Saul's future was told him;
No one could console him.

The woman took pity and got Saul to eat.
Then his servants helped him up onto his feet.
In this darkest of nights
While the stars hid from sight
King Saul walked home in sorrow
To wait for tomorrow.

The Philistines fought.
Arrows went flying;
Saul's three sons were dead.
Many soldiers lay dying.
The archers with large bows
Aimed them at Saul.
The king said in anguish,
"Do not let me languish!"
He ordered his servant,
"Draw your sword now,
Before they come near me
To mock me and jeer me!"

Saul's armor-bearer refused his king's orders.
King Saul, who was used to getting things done,
Took out his own sword
And fell down upon it.
When the brave armor-bearer saw King Saul fall dead,
He fell on his own sword
As Saul's army fled.

II Samuel

David the King

Bad news is difficult to deliver and even harder to receive. The arrival of bad news can reduce a brave man to tears and a strong man to weak knees. After David returned from rescuing his people from the Amalekites, he received the terrible news about Saul and Jonathan's deaths. He tore a piece of his clothing to symbolize his broken heart and said, "Blessed are You, Lord our God, Ruler of the universe, Who is the True Judge."

David and his men wailed and wept for Saul and his son, Jonathan; this was a great loss to the army and all the Children of Israel. Though tormented by Saul, David never lost his respect for God's anointed king. And though separated by circumstances, David never lost his love for his best friend, Jonathan.

On the darkest of days it often helps to put your feelings into words. By sharing these words with others, the heavy burden of grief will lighten, and the day, once gray and cloudy, will slowly open its heart to the sun. A "lament" is a poem written to express great sorrow. David, the wonderful writer of psalms, wrote this lament for King Saul and his brave son Jonathan:

HOW ARE THE MIGHTY FALLEN

Israel's finest are slain on the mountaintop.
How are the mighty fallen!
Do not tell of it in Gath.
Do not proclaim it in the streets of Ashkelon;
The Philistine women are liable to celebrate it
In song and dance.
O mountains of Gilboa,
Let neither dew nor rain fall upon you,
Nor fields of choice fruits grow upon you.
For there the shield of Saul was lost and left to rust
Like that of a common soldier.
Jonathan's bow was always accurate,
And Saul's sword always found its mark.
Saul and Jonathan, the beloved and the pleasant,
In both life and death they were together;
They were swifter than eagles,
They were stronger than lions.
Daughters of Israel, weep for Saul
Who clothed you in rich cloth,
Who dressed you with golden jewels.
How are the mighty fallen in the midst of the battle!
Jonathan slain upon the mountaintop!
I am upset about you, my brother, my true friend, Jonathan.
You have pleased me;
Your special love was deeper
Than the love of women.
How are the mighty fallen;
Two great weapons of war have perished!

Though grieving, David knew that he had to act quickly in order to take Saul's place as king. "Shall I go into any of the cities of Judah?" David asked the Lord, as he always did before taking important steps.

"Go to Hebron," answered the Lord.

The city of Hebron, with its long ridge of tree-filled hills, was twenty miles south of Jerusalem. It was here that Abraham purchased the cave of Machpelah for Sarah's burial, and where he, Rebecca, Leah, Isaac, and Jacob were eventually buried. Jacob's wife Rachel, who died giving birth to Benjamin, was buried on the right side of the road leading from Jerusalem to Bethlehem. The twelve spies sent into Canaan by Moses brought back a gigantic cluster of grapes from Hebron. And Joshua gave Hebron and its surrounding villages to Caleb, his trusted helper. Now it was David, his family, and all his men and their families who were going to Hebron. A long line of people, loaded donkeys, wooden-wheeled carts, woolly sheep, long-haired goats, chickens, ducks, and a pet ostrich wound its way up to Hebron. Two loud-mouthed, long-necked, know-it-all geese led the way through tangled grapevines, piles of pine needles, and crunchy oak leaves.

With its line of hills a natural dividing point, Hebron was home to the large tribe of Judah and whoever was left of the tribe of Simeon. When David and his group arrived, the men of Judah came and anointed him king. Although Samuel had performed this ceremony years ago in secret, it was now the right time to make it public. After the drops of olive oil had been poured on David's head, the women formed a circle and, with their hands held high, danced around the new king. To David's surprise, they serenaded him with one of his own psalms:

May God arise, may His enemies be scattered;
May those who hate Him flee before Him.
May they be blown away like smoke,
Like wax melted by fire.
May the wicked perish in God's presence.
May the faithful be glad, may they rejoice before God.
May they all rejoice with happiness.

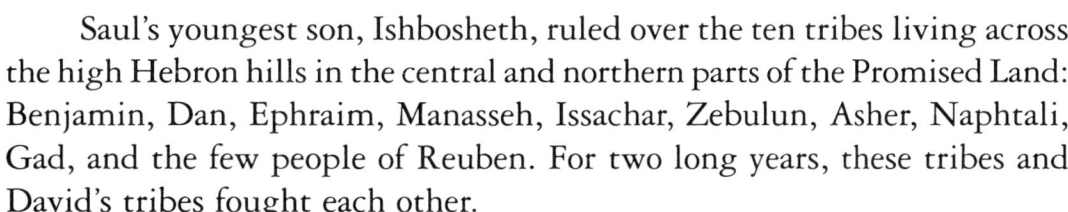

Saul's youngest son, Ishbosheth, ruled over the ten tribes living across the high Hebron hills in the central and northern parts of the Promised Land: Benjamin, Dan, Ephraim, Manasseh, Issachar, Zebulun, Asher, Naphtali, Gad, and the few people of Reuben. For two long years, these tribes and David's tribes fought each other.

Jealousy, envy, stubbornness, greed.
These are some of the reasons why people fight.
Sometimes brothers and sisters, mothers and dads,
Cats and dogs, blue jays and squirrels
Become mad, get annoyed, fed up, or sad.
It would be great if nobody used the word
"Hate"
In a sentence,
And opened the gates to forgiving, forgetting,
To hugs and handshakes.
After mending the fences
They'd come to their senses!

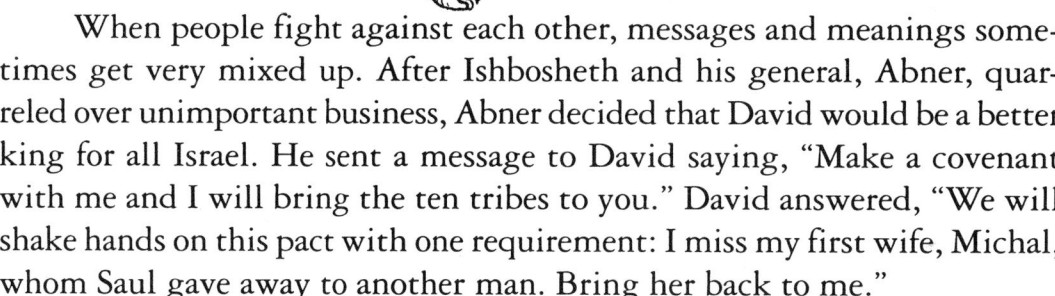

When people fight against each other, messages and meanings sometimes get very mixed up. After Ishbosheth and his general, Abner, quarreled over unimportant business, Abner decided that David would be a better king for all Israel. He sent a message to David saying, "Make a covenant with me and I will bring the ten tribes to you." David answered, "We will shake hands on this pact with one requirement: I miss my first wife, Michal, whom Saul gave away to another man. Bring her back to me."

Michal was sent for and, as her new husband wept, packed her two sets of dishes, her candlesticks, soup pot, ladle, and the bronze spearing fork she used to take boiled meat out of the pot. Any good cook has favorite knives; Michal wrapped her collection of bronze kitchen knives in a piece of strong cloth. These household items were then stuffed into two big baskets hanging on either side of a patient donkey. Michal left her black-and-white goat's-hair quilt, her pretty striped pillows, and the curtains that matched the color of the floor mats for her husband; after all, he might marry again and Michal didn't want his next wife to think she had no taste!

180

Abner told the remaining tribes, "The Lord said that by the hand of David He would save His people from the Philistines and all their other enemies." He then brought Michal to Hebron, and he and David shook hands and became friends.

But signals got crossed; not everyone had heard about the truce between the tribes. When David's general, Joab, returned with his men from a battle, he heard that Abner had visited David and left peacefully. Joab thought this was a trick. He did not know all the facts; he let his temper rule his head, sent for the unsuspecting Abner, and killed him!

This news upset David. He arranged for all the people to mourn their old enemy and new friend, Abner. And when Saul's son Ishbosheth heard that Abner was dead, he became depressed and lost his will to fight. When the northern tribes realized they would soon be united under David, two of their generals killed Ishbosheth as he took his afternoon nap. They thought this dreadful deed would impress David. Perhaps they would be rewarded when they brought Ishbosheth's head to David and said, "The Lord has taken this revenge for your enemy Saul and his family." But David was angry at these wicked men for killing an innocent man in his own bed. Taking a person's life is very bad; taking a person's life in order to impress someone else is even worse. King David made these two assassins pay for this terrible deed with their own lives.

The leaders of all the tribes came to David at Hebron and said, "We are all of the same flesh and bone. Before, when Saul was king, you led us out and brought us back in. The Lord said, 'You shall shepherd My people and be a prince over Israel.'" David made a sacred covenant with these leaders and they officially anointed David king over all the Children of Israel.

The women, now led by David's seven wives, held hands and danced in a big circle, taking tiny cross-steps before kicking up their feet and meeting in the middle. After a children's choir sang a new song to the Lord, a band of fine musicians marched before David and, on harps, flutes, bells, trumpets, and goatskin drums, played "Hail to the King."

Jerusalem

The city of Jerusalem sat like a golden crown upon a rocky throne. Purple and white grapes tumbled over the steep slopes of three surrounding valleys. With their full branches bowing to God, olive trees offered up their tangy fruit. The city's sun bleached walls were strong; two clear springs running under these walls ensured a dependable water supply. The Jebusites, an unconquered Canaanite tribe that occupied Jerusalem, had built a water tunnel under the walls. Women with water jars on their shoulders walked down the many steps carved into the rock and lowered buckets into the dark well. Their jars filled, they climbed back up the steep steps till the small blue patch at the top of the tunnel again became the sky.

When King David finally chased away the last Philistine, he set about claiming Jerusalem as his own city. While the Jebusites stood on their corner towers and taunted David, part of his army attacked the walls. This kept the Jebusites occupied while the other soldiers made their way down the water shaft and into the city. Jerusalem was quickly conquered and from then on was called "The City of David." Its fine location was easy to reach from all directions. And since no Israelite had ever called this city home, no person would feel more close to it than another. Finally there was a place where all the tribes could meet for worship, conferences, celebrations, and private conversations with the king.

As a goodwill gift, the Phoenicians, fine craftspeople who lived on the seacoast, sent cedarwood, carpenters, and stonemasons to build David a big house. While David lived in Hebron, he added four more wives to his family.

With Michal back, David now had seven wives, and they were all complaining: there was no room to hang their lovely linen dresses, no safe place to store their jewelry, not enough bathtubs, plus all the children were getting in each other's hair. A little privacy was needed. David told the architect who designed the house to make sure that there were plenty of built-in closets and several bathrooms with tubs, footbaths, and shelves for the sweet-scented oils that everyone used for cleaning themselves. Plenty of bedrooms with double-decker sleeping platforms would also be needed. David wanted to plan ahead; as king, he expected to have more wives, some substitute wives, and many more children.

When the Philistines learned that David had been anointed king over all Israel, they once again threatened to attack. They spread themselves out in a valley three miles southwest of Jerusalem. David consulted the Lord and got the go-ahead to attack: God would deliver the Philistines into David's hand.

The Philistines had no idea that the Israelites, after many victories, had finally learned the art of iron making. With God's help and some new, strong weapons, David won this battle and then declared, "The Lord has made my enemies break before me like the waters of a dam."

The Philistines, like ants after cookie crumbs, returned once again. "Shall I go after them?" David asked the Lord.

"No," answered the Lord. "Go behind them and wait by the balsam trees. When you hear rustling in the treetops, like the sound of an army marching, then move; you will know that the Lord has gone before you. The noise from the trees will hide your footsteps."

David did as God commanded. As the leaves rustled in the wind, David moved swiftly and the Philistines were finished!

As he did after every victory, David thanked God with a psalm:

The Lord is my guiding light and my hope;
Whom else should I revere?
The Lord keeps me safe;
Of whom shall I be afraid?
When evildoers attacked me,
They stumbled and fell.
If an army waits for me,
My heart shall not fear;
If war rises up against me,
I will have confidence.

My head shall be lifted up
Above my enemies who surround me.
And, in God's tabernacle, I will offer
Sacrifices and the sound of the trumpet.
I will sing,
Yes I will sing praises to the Lord.

David gathered thirty thousand Israelites and retrieved the Ark of the Lord, which had been resting in Kiriath-Jearim. It was carefully placed on a new cart pulled by two spotless oxen. Crowds of people followed the Ark as it made its bumpy way across the hills. In honor of this most wonderful day, all the birds sang their sweetest melodies; though it was not yet night,

185

crickets chirped and owls hooted. Buds opened on wild roses, sunflowers raised their heads, and red and orange poppies unfolded their petals, making the world even more beautiful to behold.

David changed from his king's robes into a priest's ephod, a linen garment tied at the waist. When the Ark reached Jerusalem, David, in his great joy, whirled around and around, dancing before the Lord with all his might.

All Israel sang and cheered as the wail of the ram's horn announced the Ark's arrival. David had erected a special tent for the Ark. After the gold-covered Ark was put in its sacred place, David offered sacrifices, blessed the people in God's name, and gave everyone a loaf of bread, some meat, and a sweet date cake.

When the festivities were over, everyone left for their homes with happiness in their hearts. Only one person tried to spoil this great day: David's first wife, Michal, came to David scowling with disapproval and said, "Such a dignified king of Israel, taking off your robes in front of servants and whirling around like a spinning top!"

David thought to himself, "Oh, well. You can't please everybody all the time." To Michal he answered, "I danced only before the Lord, Who chose me to be the leader of Israel. I will happily repeat what I have done. My people will have the good sense to appreciate my enthusiasm. Don't worry, they'll still honor me."

From that day on, David and his first wife, Michal, never again saw eye to eye. This was sad. It's always good when grown-ups can work out their problems. However, sometimes people change too much for the good or for the bad. This may confuse their partners, who, not knowing what to do, begin worrying too much about what others think.

The world also whirls around in its own dance of time. People change, day becomes night, and happy memories are sometimes like a dream.

BEFORE AND AFTER

Before we were me and you
Time, as we know it,
Was moving by swiftly
Though we never knew it.
Days, weeks, and months,
Years and centuries passed
On their way to the future,
Our time, as we know it.
Where were we when
We were not here at all?
Were we sunspots in space?
Were we stars
That would someday fall
Filling the skies
With streaks of farewell
As the earth took us
Into its heart?
Where did we start,
And where will we go
After we're finished
With saying hello
To life and to love?
After we're me and you
Time, as we knew it,
Will keep moving swiftly
Though we'll never know it.

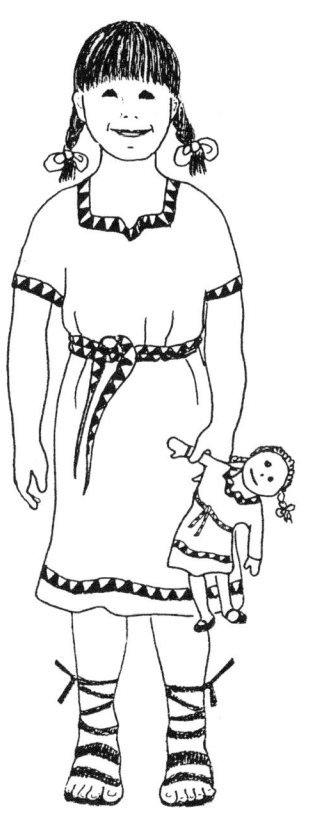

The House of David

King David enjoyed his new house. It was relaxing for him to lie back on his goose-down pillows, drink a cup of pomegranate juice, and read the business news on the weekly papyrus scroll. He loved playing games with his children, especially a board game called "Hounds and Jackals." This game used two sets of five pegs; one set had dog heads, and the other, jackal heads. These pegs were moved to various positions on a board with rows of holes. David was very good at rolling sheep-knuckle bones to determine who went first. "That's not fair. Father always goes first!" cried the children, who sat on straw mats around the board.

"Naturally," said David, smile lines crinkling the corners of his soft eyes. "Fathers go first because they're the fathers. I made that rule."

When the children weren't bothering their parents, they had plenty of other things to do:

They played hide-and-seek,
Leapfrog, hopscotch in sand.
There were lessons in writing,
Quill pens in hand,
On rolls of papyrus

Or on broken pot shards.
History lessons were not very hard
Because civilization
Was still rather new.
At art school they learned
To throw pots on a wheel,
And color them purple,
Bright red, and sky blue.
Gymnastics was fun,
They learned wrestling and tumbling,
But cut out the noise
When grown-ups were grumbling.
They took cooking lessons
And learned how to make
Lentil stew, chicken soup,
Brisket, and cake.
The best time of all
Was when their father, David,
Opened a music school
Right in their home.
Students came from all over
To sit at his feet.
They learned to sing psalms
And play music as sweet
As bird songs and whistles,
As wind through the trees.
These lessons were lovely,
And it was a treat
To hear King David's students,
Out on the street corners
Sing a cappella,
Without help from instruments,
Drum, horn, or lyre.
The best students learned
To conduct their own choir.
Others formed bands,

But when they made a racket
And grown-ups complained,
Saying, "Pack it up. Out!"
They went up to the hills
With the goats and the sheep
Who could not get to sleep.
They would rather be sheared
Than hear all this noise
Called "new music,"
And so the poor dears
Lay down on the ground,
Hoofs over their ears.

The Lord had given David a rest from all his enemies. Now that he had time to think, David said to Nathan, the prophet who was his personal adviser, "I live in a beautiful, big cedar house; but the Ark of the Lord lives in a goatskin tent. That doesn't seem right. The Ark should also have a house."

Nathan advised, "Do what is in your heart. God is with you."

Prophets were men who were privileged to hear the word of God. That night, the word of the Lord came to Nathan, saying, "Tell this to David: Do not build a house for Me. I have always lived in a tent. Have I ever asked, 'Why haven't you built Me a cedar house?'

"I took you from being a shepherd to rule over My people. I have been with you wherever you went and have cut your enemies down before you. I will make your name great like the names of your ancestors.

"My people, Israel, will someday have a safe place to live; wicked people shall not hurt them anymore. I, the Lord, will make you a house; your descendants will continue forever.

"When your days are over I will create a kingdom for your son. He shall build a house for My name. I shall be like a father to him; he shall be like a son to Me. If he does wrong, I will punish him the same way other men are punished. But I will always forgive him. The house of David shall be yours forever."

After hearing these words, David the king went into the Tabernacle of the Lord and prayed:

"Who am I, O Lord God, that You have chosen me and my family for this honor? As if what You have already given me isn't enough, now You promise that my descendants will continue to be honored.

"What can I say? You have told me about all this greatness to come. Therefore, You are great, O Lord God; there is none like You, as we have heard through the years. You brought us out of Egypt and made Israel Your people forever.

"And now, O Lord God, may the words You have spoken concerning me and my family come to pass. May your Name be praised. For You, God of Israel, have said, 'I will build you a house.' This is why I have been bold enough to pray these words to You.

"O Lord God, You alone are God and Your words are truth. You have revealed Your plans to me. Please bless my family so that its name will be blessed forever."

With his prayer to God ended, David, the king of Israel, left the Tabernacle of the Lord and walked carefully, with grateful thanks, into his blessed future.

David and Bathsheba

When pink and white almond blossoms fall in God's Promised Land, their gentle touch awakens the spring flowers sleeping under winter's brown quilt. Lilies and jasmine, narcissus and anemones soon add sweetness to the warm fresh air. Pink and red poppies, purple loosestrife, and yellow daisies turn their heads up for the sun's blessing. The winter rains move on to water other flowers in other lands. The roads littered with rocks and boulders are cleared; soggy mud dries quickly under the sun's steady glare. With the melting of mountain snows, trickles of cool water soon become torrents, racing each other down waterfalls into streams and rivers. With bird songs announcing its presence, spring unveils itself, filling the earth with hope.

King David had a lovely rooftop garden. Tubs of dill, rosemary, oregano, and coriander competed for use in the kitchen. Roses, planted in deep clay pots, spilled over the roof's edges, blending together into splendid jumbles of color.

In David's day, spring was the time of year when kings went out to battle. One particularly nice day, the perfumed air gave King David a good case of spring fever. He decided to stay home from the current battle and let his captain, Joab, lead the troops. "I'll deadhead the roses when the sun

goes down," he thought happily to himself. "Deadheading" means cutting off the faded blossoms; this makes room for more flowers to bloom.

At dusk, David woke from his afternoon nap and went up to his garden. Through the tangle of roses he saw, on another roof, a beautiful woman taking a bath. As one handmaid washed her back with fragrant oils, another combed out her long, shiny hair, which glimmered, like golden threads, in the last streaks of sunlight. "I am definitely in love," said David to himself, and he asked a servant if he knew the woman's identity.

"Her name is Bathsheba," David was told. "And she is the wife of one of your soldiers, Uriah the Hittite."

Because David was king, he allowed himself to do whatever he wanted. Most of the time, King David followed God's rules. This time, however, entranced with the perfume of roses, and enchanted by the woman bathing in the twilight, his heart governed his head. He sent for Bathsheba and she too fell under the spell of this magical spring evening. "I am truly in love," she thought and, as sometimes happens, she soon had news for David: a baby was on the way.

David ordered Bathsheba's husband to return from the battle. "How is the war going?" the king asked. "You need a break. Why don't you go home to your wife for the night?" David thought that in this way, Uriah would think he was the baby's father.

But Uriah was loyal to the king. He slept outside David's house instead of going home. "Why didn't you go to see your wife?" questioned David.

Uriah explained, "The Ark of the Lord and all of Israel's army are sleeping in tents. It would be wrong for me to be comfortable with my wife while they are in the fields."

David thought his next plan would work. "Stay with me one more day, Uriah; I like your company. Come for dinner tonight."

Uriah came to dinner, sat on piles of plump pillows, ate a wonderful meal, and drank every glass of strong wine that David offered. The king hoped Uriah would get tired, forget about his army, and go home to sleep with his wife. But it was no go. Uriah said goodnight and again went to sleep outside.

In the morning, King David, who was usually kind and thoughtful, did something awful. He wrote a note to Joab telling him to send Uriah to the front of the hottest battle. In this way, he would surely be killed!

Joab did as David ordered, and Uriah died as David had planned.

When Bathsheba heard that her husband was dead, she mourned for seven days. Then David brought her to his house and she became his wife. In time, a little boy was born to David and Bathsheba. All babies are wonderful to God. But what King David had done was so sinful that God had to create a terrible punishment. He sent Nathan the prophet to David with this message:

There once were two men who lived in one city;
One man was rich, the other man, poor.
The rich man had flocks of sheep, goat herds, and cattle;
The poor man had nothing but one little ewe lamb,

All curly and cuddly.
She grew up together with him and his children,
Drank from his cup, and lay in his arms
Like a sweet baby daughter,
Not a lamb raised for slaughter.

One day, a traveler came to the rich man
Who, needing to feed his guest, looked from his rooftop
And watched as the children played with the lamb.
"She's just what I need to feed my fine guest,"
Said the rich man, a big greedy smile on his face.
He took the sweet lamb from the children and cooked it
To eat that same night, in the sight of the man
And his children, who went to bed crying.
Their dear little friend ended up in a pot!

King David yelled, "Stop! That rich man should die!
And give four baby lambs for the pretty ewe lamb.
That man has no pity!"
Nathan the prophet said, "You are that man.
Here's what the Lord has to say about this:
'I anointed you king, brought you safely from Saul,
You have wives and a house plus all Israel.
If this were too little, I'd give you much more.
So why have you broken the Lord's sacred laws?
You caused Uriah to fall by the sword!
You desired his wife, and you took his life from him!
Therefore, David, the sword shall not leave your house.
Evil will come to you, from your own home.'"

David tried to atone, and said sadly to Nathan,
"I have sinned against God and done what is evil."
"The Lord will forgive you, and you shall not die,"
Answered Nathan the prophet.
"But because of these sins you have angered the Lord.
Your new little baby boy surely will die!"

196

With a cry, David heard these last words of the prophet.
And just as the Lord said, the baby got sick.
David prayed, asking God to please help his new son.
He lay on the ground, he refused to eat bread
For seven dark days, till he saw servants whispering.
"Is my child dead?" David asked.
"He is dead."

David arose, washed himself, changed his clothes,
Went into the tent, and worshiped the Lord.
He ate bread, and when asked why he no longer fasted,
Said, "While my son was alive I did not know
If God would be gracious and let him survive.
But now he is dead, and I can't bring him back.
I'll be with him someday but he'll never return."

Life keeps going on after death takes a dear one;
The moon comes and goes, the sun sets and rises.
When yesterday's gone, there is always tomorrow.
Each turn of God's world is full of surprises.

Although full of sorrow, David and his Bathsheba
Soon had another son,
Called Solomon,
Which means "peaceful";
He would not be struck by the sword.
God told Nathan the prophet
To give the new child
One more name,
Jididiah,
"Beloved by the Lord."

198

Absalom, My Son

In all Israel, no man was more praised for his good looks than Absalom, King David's thirdborn son. From the soles of his feet to the top of his head, he was perfect. At the end of each year, Absalom had the barber cut his long, curly hair; it weighed at least four pounds! Young ladies sent their little brothers and sisters into the barber shop to collect a silky curl or two. They pressed these souvenirs between sheets of parchment as keepsakes.

Absalom liked to show off in public. He had a comfortable chariot pulled by two sleek black horses, and fifty men running before it, clearing the streets. This was the sign of an important man. Absalom went to the city gate every day and greeted people as though they were his closest friends. He hugged and kissed them and would not let anyone bow down to him.

"Tell me your troubles," he would say sympathetically. "Oh my, they are terrible. You have great cause to be upset. Too bad there is no one to hear your problems. The king is too busy with business to be concerned about his people. If I were king in this land, I would make sure every man received justice!"

With this kind of behavior, Absalom deceived the men of Israel and stole their hearts away from his father, David. He wanted to overthrow his own father and become king. This was a very sneaky thing to do!

For a few years, Absalom continued his secret revolt against David. Then, one day he asked his father to allow him to go to Hebron, his birthplace, to fulfill a promise to the Lord.

David did not suspect his son of plotting against him. To David, all his children were perfect; he forgave them their sins and supported them in whatever they chose to do. However, David was very busy being king; like many parents, he was sometimes unaware of what his children were doing in their spare time.

Absalom took two hundred men with him to Hebron. He sent this message to Israel's tribes: "When you hear the sound of the ram's horn, you will know that Absalom is now king in Hebron." He sent for Ahithophel, David's chief adviser, who decided to join the many men now siding with David's devious son.

When David finally learned of his son's plot, he was forced to flee Jerusalem. Several hundred loyal people went with him. As they prepared to cross over the ravine separating the city from the Mount of Olives, the Levites arrived, carrying the Ark with them. King David told Zadok the priest, "Take the Ark back to Jerusalem. If God is good to me, He will bring me back to see the Ark and its home. If He is angry with me, let Him do what seems right."

King David was not as dumb as Absalom thought. He also told the high priests that they were to send him reports of what Absalom was doing.

David wept as he climbed to the top of the Mount of Olives. Looking around, he saw that all his servants and friends were also weeping, their heads covered, their feet bare as if in mourning. One person told him, "Your trusted adviser is among the conspirators with Absalom."

This news brought David out of his depression, and he allowed his hidden anger to come to the surface. "O Lord," he prayed. "Let Ahithophel's suggestions turn into foolishness!"

This mountaintop was a special place to worship God. As David reached the top, his good friend Hushai came to meet him. David had a plan for him. "Go back to Absalom and offer to be his servant. This way you can help defeat any advice given by Ahithophel. The high priests are already there spying for me. Tell what you know to their two sons. They will deliver the messages to me."

David felt like his old, proud self again and recited this new psalm:

Lord, I have so many enemies!
People say that God will not help me.
But You, O Lord, are my protector.
You will enable me to hold my head high again.
I call to the Lord and He answers me from Jerusalem.
I can sleep in peace and awaken
Because God protects me.
I am not afraid of my enemies.

As ordered, Hushai went to Absalom and cried: "Long live the king! Long live the king!"

"Is this how you treat your good friend David?" asked Absalom in a mocking voice. "Why didn't you leave with him?"

"I will serve whomever the Lord and the men of Israel choose. I served your father; I will serve his son," answered Hushai, pretending to be sincere.

Absalom turned to David's former adviser and asked, "Tell me, what should we do next?"

"Let me take twelve thousand men and go after David tonight. We'll come upon him when he's weak and discouraged. Everyone will panic. I'll kill the king and bring his people to you," said the disloyal man.

As all the men around him nodded their heads in agreement, Absalom smiled at this terrible plan to kill his father. "Now let's hear what Hushai has to say," he said, enjoying being in charge.

Hushai was thinking fast. "Your adviser's suggestions are bad. Your father and his men are mighty warriors; they are as angry as bears robbed of their cubs. David won't stay exposed among people. He'll hide himself in a pit or cave. When some of your inexperienced men fall at the first attack, others will think there's been a slaughter and run away. Even a brave man's heart will melt. I think you should gather a really big army from all over the country. With so many fighting against David, I'm sure we will win. If he goes into a city, we'll tie ropes around the whole place and drag it into the river. Not a single pebble will be found!" Hushai thought that these plans would take some time and give David a better chance to escape.

Absalom like this idea, especially the rope-tying part. "The counsel of Hushai is better than that of Ahithophel," he announced, not knowing, of course, that God had planned this all along!

The high priest's sons were waiting by a spring outside Jerusalem when a woman brought this message from Hushai for David: "Don't stay out in the wilderness. Cross the Jordan River before you are swallowed up by Absalom and his people."

Unfortunately, as they were leaving, someone saw the messengers and reported them to Absalom. The woman hid the boys in a well; a cloth spread with drying fruit covered it.

Absalom's men came as fast as their donkeys would trot. "Where are the two messengers?" they demanded.

"They've crossed that brook over there," the woman replied, pointing in the opposite direction from the well.

The searchers rode off on this wild goose chase, returning empty-handed to Jerusalem. The boys climbed out of the well, found King David in the wilderness, and delivered the message. David and his people crossed over the Jordan and were lucky to find a friendly town. The kind towns-people brought

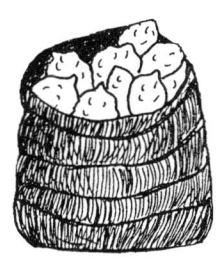

Beds, blankets, pots and pans,
Mixing bowls for bread.
David's people left so fast,
They couldn't plan ahead.
Yogurt, beans, lentils, cheese,
Fresh vegetables, and goat's milk,
And just a little meat
For those who weren't vegetarians.
King David and his people
All had healthy food to eat.

After a short rest, David organized his army. He wanted to join them in battle, but his people would not allow this. "You are worth ten thousand of us," they said. "It will be safer for you to help us from the city."

David listened to this good advice and agreed. Standing at the city gate, the king waved good-bye to the troops and commanded his generals, "Deal gently for my sake with my son Absalom."

Soon David's loyal followers were battling against the rest of Israel. In the forest of Ephraim, Absalom's untrained men fell into pits, got tangled in vines, and were easily defeated. And as Absalom rode his donkey under a great oak tree, his beautiful head of curls got caught in some overhanging branches. Happy to be rid of its passenger, the donkey trotted off, leaving Absalom hanging between heaven and earth!

A soldier reported this to Joab. "Why didn't you kill him?" demanded the general. "I would have rewarded you with money."

"Even if I had a thousand coins, I would not hurt the king's son," replied the man. "We all heard King David tell you to deal gently with Absalom."

Joab said angrily, "I have no time to waste with you!" He found out where Absalom was hanging and punished him with death for his plot against David. Joab then blew the ram's horn; his army ceased their attack and Absalom's cowardly men ran away.

Telling David the good news of victory and the bad news about Absalom was going to be a delicate job. "Is it well with my son Absalom?" David asked the man who came running with news.

The runner answered, "Let all your enemies and all who plan evil against you be like your son Absalom."

The king was grief-stricken. He went up to his room in tears, crying: "O my son Absalom, my son, my son Absalom! If only I could have died instead of you, O Absalom, my son, my son Absalom!"

The victory turned into mourning when his people heard how David was grieving. His wails grew louder and louder: "O my son Absalom, O Absalom, my son, my son!" King David still loved his children, no matter what they did to him!

Joab had had quite enough! He stormed into the king's bedroom and gave him a tongue-lashing: "You have shamed the people who saved your life and the lives of your family. You love those who hate you and hate those who love you! Your generals and your servants mean nothing to you! If Absalom were alive today and all of us dead, you would be pleased! Now get up and go out and speak to your people! If you don't do as I say, not one man will stay with you tonight!"

Shamed by the truth of Joab's words, David pulled himself together and went out to greet his followers. Although there were still to be problems with difficult people and many hard wars to be won, the Children of Israel eventually returned to David, their anointed king.

For the rest of his long life, King David continued to write beautiful psalms for his people. These psalms were gifts that would last forever.

I Kings

King Solomon

In King David's time, people did not live very long. Good health was the result of good luck, although the Hebrew laws of hygiene and sanitation helped prevent certain diseases. Doctors treated patients with special herbs and potions; some even used magic, which occasionally worked if the patient really wanted it to. Thinking good thoughts helps your body to get well. This is called "positive thinking." Praying to God is another form of healing; one way or another, it makes a person feel better!

At seventy, King David was considered a very old man. In our time, people in their seventies run marathons, do aerobics, and climb mountains. But poor King David had to wear warm pajamas and stay in bed. He was always cold and it was hard for him to walk. When he wasn't sleeping, he conducted his business from his bedroom. One day, his favorite wife, Bathsheba, burst into his room. "Wake up, David!" she cried. "Adonijah, your eldest son, has anointed himself king! You promised me that our son Solomon would be the next king. What do you intend to do about this?"

King David shook the dreams out of his head and sat up. "A promise is a promise, dear," he answered soothingly. "I'll take care of it."

An interesting project or challenge helps you forget your aches and pains. Beginning to feel like his old, strong self, David ordered Zadok the high priest to have Solomon come to the beautiful spring of Gihon, opposite the palace. There, surrounded by God's wonders, Solomon would be anointed king. He was to ride King David's own mule to the ceremony. These rare animals were half-donkey, half-horse, and riding one was a great honor.

A long procession of people followed Solomon as he made his way to Gihon. After Zadok the priest anointed Solomon with holy oil from the Tabernacle, he blew the ram's horn. Hearing this loud wail, King David was so happy that he wished that his tired legs would let him dance once again. You can do almost anything you want if you try hard enough. With strength that he hadn't known he had, King David climbed the stairs to his rooftop rose garden. The piping of flutes and cheers of "Long live King Solomon!" filled the air; this was music to King David's ears. Clapping his hands in rhythm with the sounds, the old king let his wool shawl drop from his shoulders. With his arms reaching up toward heaven, King David slowly began to dance round and round in a circle until, once again, he was whirling with joy.

Making sure that Solomon became king was David's last great achievement. After going over the building plans for the future temple, King David gave King Solomon these final instructions:

"I am about to die, as all human beings must. Remember to follow God's ways, His rules, and His Ten Commandments."

210

Then King David, who had reigned for forty years, kissed his son Solomon good-bye. Feeling nice and warm, and with a contented smile on his lips, David, the shepherd who became king, fell asleep forever.

When the mourning period for King David ended, King Solomon began the big job of running his country. He was determined to make friends with the different people living near the kingdom. This would be very good for future business ventures. He even asked the beautiful daughter of Egypt's pharaoh to be his first wife. She agreed and began making plans for the seven-day wedding celebration. After selecting bridesmaids and having them fitted for matching gowns, the bride went over the menu with the caterers and gave the musicians a list of her favorite songs.

The night before the wedding
There was a bachelor party
Given by his childhood friends
For Solomon, the groom.
They drank cups and cups of wine;
They ate fruit and cakes and pies.
They told lots of funny stories,
And laughed till tears came to their eyes.

On the day of the wedding,
The bridesmaids helped the bride
To fix her hair, put on makeup,
And her lovely gown and veils.
They tied her sash, and she was ready
To say farewell to her room.
With torches lighting up the night
The bride went out to greet her groom.

At their wedding, the royal singers sang them a marriage song. After praising the bridegroom's good looks, they described how he had been blessed by God and reminded him of his duties: to be faithful, fair, and kind.

Solomon had inherited his father's good singing voice. As his bride entered the room, he sang this part of the song:

"My heart overflows with beautiful words;
How lovely is my bride, the king's daughter,
In her bridal clothes
Woven with gold threads
And colorful embroideries.
Her bridesmaids follow behind her.
Music and dancing accompany her
As she enters the king's palace."

The marriage song ended with the choir singing to the king:

"With this song of praise your name will be remembered
throughout all generations.
And the people shall praise you forever and ever."

212

After his wedding celebration, King Solomon went to the altar at Gibeon. Until the temple was built, people were still allowed to worship the Lord in special high places. At this holy site, Solomon sacrificed one thousand burnt offerings to God. He spent the night outside, under the great blanket of stars. While he was sleeping, the Lord came to Solomon in a dream.

"What shall I give you?" asked God in the dream.
Solomon answered, "You've now made me king
And I'm barely eighteen.
I don't know how to manage this country.
Therefore, give me a heart that can hear the Lord's voice,
And give me wisdom,
When faced with the choice between good and evil,
To judge Your great people."

God was pleased that His new king
Asked only for one thing.
"Because you have not asked for long life or riches
Or your enemy's deaths,
I have given to you a wise heart
And a mind that will know right from wrong.
Along with this you shall have riches and honor
For which you have not asked.
For all of your life there won't be a king like you.
So walk in My ways;
Keep My rules and commandments.
Like David, your father,
I'll lengthen your days."

As the fingers of daylight brushed against Solomon's cheek, the dream disappeared. The new king sat up in wonder; had the Lord really come to him? Quickly, he returned to Jerusalem, stood by the Ark, and thanked God for His gifts of kindness and wisdom. Then, with his shoulders back and his head held high, King Solomon began the first day of the rest of his life.

The Judgment of Solomon

Two women innkeepers came to the king:
"My lord," one said softly,
"This woman and I live in the same house.
I gave birth to a child; he gave me great joy.
Three days later, she too gave birth to a boy.
We were all alone;
No one witnessed this deed that I bring to your ear.
Please hear me," she pleaded, her eyes red from tears.
"While sleeping that night she rolled over in bed
And lay on her child.
When she awoke, her new baby was dead.

"The following night, there was no moon in sight.
I was sleeping a deep sleep, my son by my side.
This very same woman came into my room.
She took my son from me,
Laid her son beside me, the one who was dead,
And went back to her bed.

"The next morning I tried to nurse my new child,
The one who had smiled at me, my newborn son,
I found beside me a dead little boy.
I looked at him closely and saw that he wasn't
My dear newborn son whose birth gave me such joy."

The other woman said, "No, he who lives is my son.
The dead one is your son."
"No way," said the first.
"The dead one is your son, and my son is living!"
The king listened closely to all of this arguing,
Giving much thought to this difficult chore.

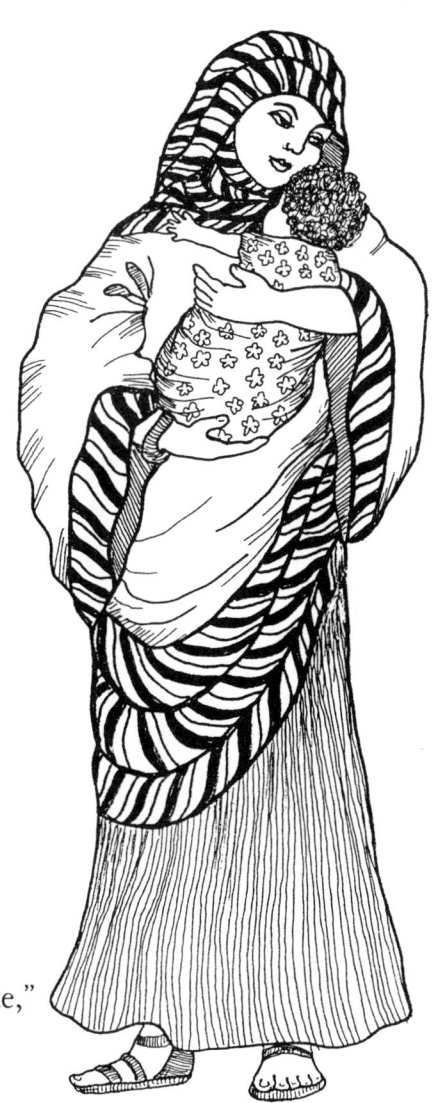

"I'll work this out," he said. "Fetch me my sword!
I'll give both of these women their proper reward!
Cut the child who is living in two equal pieces.
Give one half to one, and one half to the other."
The true mother spoke, "O my lord, please,
Give that woman my son!
Do not let him die!"
The other one cried,
"He shall not be mine!
He shall not be yours!
Split him in two!
That's the right thing to do!"

The king gave his judgment:
"The baby's true mother begged that her child
Not be cut in two pieces.
Give her the baby, whose life was too precious
For her to let die."
The true mother held on to her newborn son.
"I thank you, my lord, from myself and my little one,"
"You're welcome," the king said,
"Your child seems content."

All Israel heard about Solomon's judgment.
They honored his wisdom, respected his name.
When faced with the choice between good and evil
He listened to God's voice and judged His great people.

216

The Wisdom of Solomon

During King Solomon's reign, the tribes of Israel lived in safety, each person under his own grapevine or fig tree. Unlike his father, David, Solomon was not a military man. Like a president, he was a good leader and diplomat. He devoted himself to improving his kingdom, and he knew how to get along with other kings and rulers.

King Solomon appointed twelve governors to help him run the country. Once a year, each one had to provide food for the kingdom's forty thousand sleek horses and the twelve hundred chariot riders. He took good care of whoever worked for him, be it man or animal. Big farms were created to help feed the growing population; ships were built in order to trade these food products for luxury items.

Solomon's ships sailed for three years or more,
Bringing back wonders from exotic shores such as:
Peacocks and chimpanzees, ivory and trees
To be planted, silk to be made
Into beautiful dresses, and all kinds of wood
For building and carving.
King Solomon traded whatever he grew

To people with money to pay for such things.
He was honest and smart;
His brain kept on thinking.
King Solomon was the wisest of kings.

King Solomon was famous for his wisdom. He wrote three thousand proverbs and one thousand and five psalms. He knew all about trees and plants, from the tall cedars to the tiny hyssop that pushes its head through cracks in the walls. He knew the secret language of animals and birds, insects and fishes. King Solomon was a terrific storyteller; he made learning fun. Once a week he held classes outside, on a shady hill. People came from all around to hear him speak:

"Good morning dear friends," he would say.
"Now today I'll first tell you of one special tree.
The cedar of Lebanon grows very tall.
It's the strongest of all,
And it lasts the longest when used for ship masts.
It smells good
And makes lovely harps and toy chests.
For building a temple,
Cedarwood is the best.
When you need a small plant for special occasions
Like sacrifices or purifications,
Pick some hyssop right out of the cracks in the wall.
The caper's another plant found in a tight place;
When pickled, its fruit gives a salad great taste.
Be careful, my friends, do not eat wild gourds.
Though they look good to you,
If you put them in stew
They will make you quite sick.
And if you do get sick, try coriander,
Or mint for your stomach and chamomile tea.

"Be careful whenever you go to En-Gedi;
Lions hide in the caves and you'd better be ready

To run away quickly or climb a big tree.
Here are some creatures that you may not know:
A behemoth is most likely a hippopotamus.
A leviathan is a crocodile.

Oryxes are antelopes,

Ibexes are goats,

Please note,
Aurochs are oxen,

Coneys are badgers,

And though I've not seen this beast with one horn,
Someplace, somewhere,
There's a blue unicorn!

"Here in our land there are three hundred birds,
Big ones like ostriches,
Small ones like quails.
When the hen ostrich lays her eggs, she never fails
To make sure the father bird shares the egg sitting.
When she feels like quitting,
He waits for the first peep
While she gets some sleep!

The spotted quail eggs are so tiny you'd have to use
Twelve
Just to scramble enough for a meal.
It's very unkind to steal eggs from a nest;
Wait and see if they've been left behind
Or knocked down to the ground with no crack.
Most likely, the adult birds will not be back.

"If you're lazy, consider the way of the ant;
Nobody tells her what she has to do
To feed her large brood.
In summer she scurries around, finding bread,
And when harvesttime comes she stocks up on food.
That's using her head!

"My last talk today will be about something
That swims in the waters,
Not fish you can eat
Like the bream, loach, and bleak,
Which swim in the Jordan and have fins and scales,
But about the sea monsters,

The wonderful
Whales,

Which really are mammals like people and camels.
Whales have their own songs that they sing to each other
From faraway places under the sea.
No one knows what they're saying.
Perhaps they are praying
To God Who created them on the sixth day."

King Solomon's lessons came to a close.
As he rose from his chair, everybody was clapping
Except for two grown-ups who'd spent the time napping.
His people said, "Thank you, your lessons were fine.
May we come back soon?"
"Next week at noon," he said.
"Same place, same time."

King Solomon's Temple

The Phoenicians lived on the fertile coast between the mountains of Lebanon and the Mediterranean Sea. The giant cedars of Lebanon grew in their forests; from their mountains came marble, iron, and the fine sand used in glassmaking. The Phoenicians were skilled artists and craftspeople; they carved wood and ivory, worked with all kinds of metal, including gold and silver, and were fine carpenters and stonecutters. In their great sailing ships, the Phoenicians brought all sorts of wonderful goods back from foreign lands:

 *There was linen from Egypt,*
Copper from Cyprus,
Horses from Turkey,
And iron from Spain.
There were peacocks from Africa,
Also monkeys and apes,
Ivory from India,
And jewels of all shapes,

Colors, and sizes.
Phoenician ships
Were filled with surprises!

Hiram, the Phoenician king of Tyre, had been good friends with King David. Now that Solomon was king, he sent his congratulations. As part of his schooling, Solomon had learned the Phoenician alphabet. He sent a letter back to King Hiram, written on a parchment scroll.

Dear Hiram,
Thank you very much for your good wishes. I have some business to discuss with you:
The Lord has given my country peace and I can now build a great house to honor Him. My father gave me the architect's plans. I need an expert contractor like you to get the job done right. I need a large amount of cedar

paneling cut to size and decorated with carved palm trees, open flowers, and cherubim. Since there are no better carpenters than your people, I'll send them as many helpers as they need and pay you whatever you ask.

Also, I'd like to commission some very large bronze bowls and ladles, plus some iron meat forks. My father left me all the gold he acquired during different wars. I want this to be melted down and made into special objects for the Lord's temple. By the way, I may have to buy or trade for more gold to be hammered into thin sheets to cover the wood. Could you supply some of your famous artists and craftspeople to do this delicate work?

I'm hoping to hear from you soon. Say hello to your family for me.

Yours truly,

Solomon

Hiram was delighted to receive this big order! "Blessed be the Lord who gave David such a wise son!" he exclaimed as he signed a work agreement and had it delivered to Jerusalem by his swiftest horseman.

Dear Solomon,

No problem. I can get you anything you want at a very good price. Just say the word and I'll find it. Since you're such a good customer, along with the cedar I'll throw in some cypress wood, free of charge. My men will make the logs into rafts, float them to your harbor, and your men can haul them up to Jerusalem.

In exchange, for each year of work, I would like one hundred and twenty-five thousand bushels of wheat and one million, one hundred and sixty-two thousand gallons of oil.

It's a pleasure doing business with you. Regards to your wives.

Sincerely,

Hiram

Because the Lord had given Solomon the wisdom to deal with other kings, a good business partnership developed. Solomon made plans to grow more wheat and olive trees on even larger farms. Then, he found thirty thousand men to work with King Hiram in shifts, one month on and two months off. By putting more people to work, King Solomon was improving his country's economy. Between the two countries there were

Log cutters, log carriers,
Stone quarriers, stonecutters,
Porters and measurers,
And a decorator or two.
There were goldsmiths and silversmiths,
Blacksmiths, engravers,
And weavers weaving threads of
Red, purple, and blue.

Solomon's temple sat on a high hill, its entrance facing the rising sun. It was one hundred five feet long, thirty-five feet wide, and fifty-two feet high. Because Solomon wanted it to be a symbol of peace, no iron tools were to be used in putting it together. All the limestone for the walls was cut to size at the quarry, and each piece fit perfectly. This is called "prefabrication." The walls were paneled with sweet-smelling cedar boards carved with palm trees, open flowers, and cherubim, imaginary heavenly creatures with great wings. The floor was made of strong cypress planks and, like everything else in this sacred house, was covered with gold. The windows were wide indoors but thin slits outside. This kept the temple cool and mysterious looking; the light was to come from God.

In the innermost chamber, called the "Holy of Holies," were two big cherubim made of old olive wood; using wood from any tree that still bore fruit was not allowed. These were covered in gold; their giant wings touched the walls and each other. They would help protect the Ark of the Lord. The high priest could enter this room only on the Day of Atonement; for the rest of the year, it was the Lord's private home.

225

Outside the temple was a gigantic bronze basin so big it was called "The Sea." It sat on twelve statues of oxen facing north, south, east, and west. Here, the priests purified themselves and ladled water into ten basins on wheels, which were used to wash sacrifices. Only perfect male bulls, rams, goats, doves, and some farm products were allowed to be sacrificed on the huge outdoor altar. Personal peace and sin offerings, as well as offerings on behalf of everyone, took place each morning and evening, with additional ones on the Sabbath and holidays. (Many years later, morning, afternoon, evening, and holiday prayer services would take the place of sacrifices.)

After seven years, the temple was finished. Solomon arranged all the new golden objects in their proper places.

There was a golden altar and a golden table,
Which held the gold container for the special bread.
Golden flowers decorated the golden candelabra
That stood five on each side of the tall, gold-plated doors.
More gold was used for candlesnuffers,
Basins, cups, and pans.
The temple gleamed as though the sun shone
From within God's earthly home.

Important people from all over came to celebrate the temple's completion. They lined the streets as the Levites and priests carried the Ark holding Moses' two tablets and its tent and special dishes to the beautiful building. The priests entered the Holy of Holies and gently set down the Ark. And the Ark rested safely under the giant wings of the cherubim.

When the priests came out of this holy room, a choir of Levite singers carrying cymbals, flutes, and harps waited at the altar. One hundred twenty men with trumpets stood with them. Together, as one mighty voice, the choir and musicians gave thanks to the Lord, singing,

"He is good;
His mercy will live forever!"

227

At that very moment, a great cloud filled God's house. This was the Glory of the Lord!

"I have built You a house," said King Solomon, holding out his arms toward the billowing cloud. "It is a place for You to live forever. With reverence I will worship You in Your holy place."

The king turned around and blessed the Children of Israel:

"Blessed be the Lord Who told my father, David, that his son would build Him a house. The Lord's words have now come true."

Solomon stood before the altar, raised his hands toward heaven, and prayed:

"Keep watch over this house so that You may hear Your people's prayers.

Judge Your people's sins; punish the wicked and reward the good.

Please help us when no rain falls or when insects and diseases invade our land.

When Your people pray to You, listen and forgive them. You alone know what is truly in their hearts.

Please listen to the prayers of strangers who come into Your home. This way all the people on earth will know that You alone are the Lord."

When King Solomon finished praying he blessed his people saying:

"Blessed be the Lord Who has given peace to His people. May You be with us as You were with our ancestors; may You never forsake us.

Let your heart be with the Lord; walk in His ways and keep His commandments."

The Children of Israel offered thousands of sacrifices to the Lord and had a great feast. After many joyous days, they left for their homes, their hearts filled with the Lord's goodness.

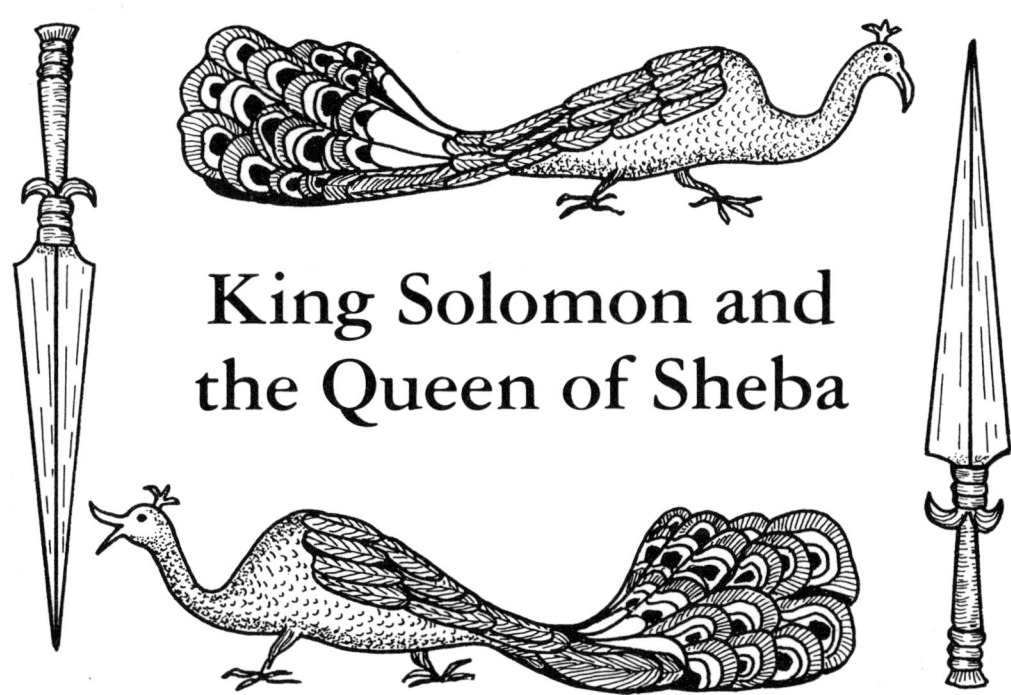

King Solomon and the Queen of Sheba

News of King Solomon's ventures seemed to travel with the desert winds. When the Queen of Sheba heard some of these stories, she decided to visit him and test his wisdom with difficult questions.

Great caravans bound for distant lands passed through the queen's country. These provided a good market for her unusual spices and the precious jewels found in nearby mountains. She remembered hearing that Solomon used special spices for his temple's incense. Being a smart businesswoman, she thought: "Well, I've got those spices and I'll bet his new sailing ships have brought back wonderful treasures. Maybe we can do business together."

The queen ordered a large camel caravan to be ready in the morning. As the sun peeked around the hills, the Queen of Sheba's royal camel sat waiting, his feet tucked under him. A cushioned seat with sunshade was perched on his hump. The queen climbed aboard and took out some knitting to work on during the long trip. The camel handlers made a "chkk, chkk" noise. With a snort, the big animal unfolded himself, lumbered to his feet, and started moving. Riding on top of a swaying camel can make you feel seasick; that's why camels are called the "ships of the desert."

A long line of camels followed behind the queen, carrying, in camel-hair saddle bags, two hundred pounds of gold, straw baskets filled with spices, and sandalwood boxes filled with precious stones. Along with blue lapis lazuli, green emeralds, and fiery opals, there were boxes of reddish-brown amber stones. Wearing amber near your neck is supposed to keep sore throats away; the queen thought that Solomon's choir might find these useful.

As she approached Jerusalem, the queen saw Solomon's temple, its white limestone walls gleaming in the noonday sun. Alongside it stood King Solomon's palace buildings. One of these, a great hall with forty-five cedar columns supporting its roof, was called the "House of the Forest of Lebanon." Solomon loved trees and was happy to have his own private forest to walk through as he thought up new proverbs.

As the Queen of Sheba entered the city gates, she saw other foreign caravans resting at the city's wells, their wares spread out on blankets. The queen loved flea markets; sometimes, she found antique Greek jewelry and soft Egyptian cotton bed sheets. She liked collecting tortoiseshell combs and mother-of-pearl wine goblets. Being a good bargain hunter, she had the camel handler lower her down so that she could look around. She'd never seen so many colorful fabrics, ankle bracelets, and long, jangling earrings. Someone

was even selling Syrian beauty creams guaranteed to make wrinkles disappear or your money back.

The queen wandered down Jerusalem's narrow streets; its one- and two-story mud-brick houses looked like a jumble of toy blocks. Everywhere she turned there was something for sale. Pyramids of fruit were stacked in wooden carts: red pomegranates, fuzzy orange apricots, and the large yellow citrons called "etrogs." The queen had heard that this tart fruit was especially good for stomachaches and bad breath; it made the best mouthwash around. Striped awnings shaded bunches of leeks, strings of garlic, hills of lentils, baskets of dried and smoked fish, and jars of honey. Hooks on shop walls held curly sheepskin cloaks and soft goatskin boots.

There was so much to buy! She definitely needed new copper pots and some extra-virgin olive oil, and it was hard to resist buying one of those fur cloaks, especially when the shopkeeper began reducing his price. Walking by a pet store, she heard a green African parakeet calling, "Hello queen, hello queen," and laughed when a big-mouthed macaw screeched, "Have a nice day!"

"I'd better get going," she thought, reluctantly leaving the tempting stores. Her servants brought her portable chariot and, sitting regally on a sheepskin seat, she was pulled up the hill to Solomon's palace.

A great trumpet fanfare announced the arrival of the Queen of Sheba. Followed by her servants, the queen walked through the cedar-pillared hall toward the king's throne in the Hall of Judgment. The throne had six steps, a golden footrest, two carved lions standing beside the arms, and twelve lions on either side of the steps. "Welcome," said the king. "What can I do for you?"

"I have heard of your great wisdom," replied the queen. "How much better it is to get wisdom than gold. Learning is better than silver."

"I could not have said that as well myself!" laughed King Solomon, recognizing one of his own proverbs. "The wise of heart teaches his mouth and adds learning to his lips."

"Tell me," asked the queen, "which four small things on earth are exceptionally wise?"

"Let's see," said the king. "I think I know the answers:

1. The ants are not strong,
   Yet in the summer, they store food for the future.
2. The rock badgers are weak,
   Yet they know how to make houses in jagged rocks and cliffs.
3. The locusts have no king,
   Yet they move together like an army.
4. You can hold the spider in your hands,
   Yet she lives in kings' palaces."

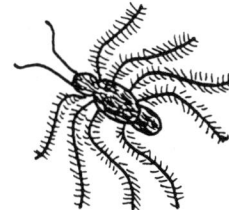

Delighted with this reply, the queen smiled at the handsome king and asked, "What are four things both wonderful and hard to understand?"

Solomon thought for a moment before saying: "There are three marvelous things; no, I take that back. There are four wonders that I do not understand:

1. How an eagle flies,
2. How a serpent moves on a rock,
3. How a ship sails,
4. And why a young woman makes a man feel the way he does."

The Queen of Sheba lowered her eyes and understood Solomon's unspoken words.

After spending a relaxing time with King Solomon, the queen's curiosity was satisfied. "I didn't believe the rumors about your wisdom and accomplishments until I saw them with my own eyes. They exceed all that I have heard, and I only knew the half of it! And all your servants seem so happy! Blessed be your Lord Who loved you enough to make you king of Israel. And now I have a gift for you," declared the queen as her servants placed hundreds of bags, boxes, and chests at the base of the throne.

"It is known that the Lord gave your great ancestor Moses a special recipe for incense to be burnt on the temple's golden altar. I happen to have with me those same hard-to-find spices: sweet stacte and onycha, pure frankincense, and galbanum. This last spice doesn't smell good. I have learned that it is included with the others just as a sinner's prayers are offered with the prayers of those who have not sinned."

"Also," she continued, "I have all the perfumed spices that you need for your anointing oils: myrrh, cinnamon, calamus, and cassia. There's enough to last several lifetimes. And please accept these chests of precious stones. I'm certain that your wives will be very interested in them. I have also brought you almost two hundred pounds of pure gold," she concluded, saving the best for last.

King Solomon could not keep his eyes off this beautiful, dark-eyed young woman, whose skin was the color of hazelnuts. Her wealth and intelligence matched his own; he had finally met someone with whom he could share his thoughts. Dismissing all the servants, Solomon took the queen on a tour of his storehouses. "Take anything you like," he offered. "My house is yours. Your pleasant words are like a honeycomb. They add sweetness to the soul and health to the bones."

"Thank you, dear Solomon," the queen said, looking up into his soft eyes. "There is gold and many rubies; but the lips of knowledge are a precious jewel."

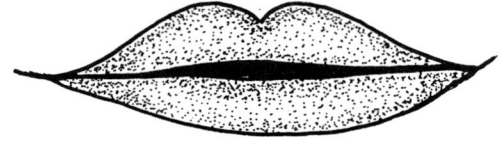

234

With that, the king escorted the queen back to her chariot. As a long line of servants carried her selection of gifts back to the caravan, King Solomon kissed the Queen of Sheba farewell. Waving good-bye, he took one last look at her beautiful smile and thought:

"A wise man knows true love when he sees it;
When it leaves him, he keeps its memory forever in his heart."

Kings

Long before Solomon's time, the Lord had warned the Children of Israel against marrying people from foreign lands. He did not want His people turning to other gods. King Solomon, however, loved many foreign women; he had seven hundred wives and three hundred substitute wives. They were called his "harem." He built small palaces for his favorites; the rest lived together with their many children in a separate building. Solomon felt that these marriages would be good for business. To help keep his wives happy, Solomon built temples and shrines to their gods, Ashtoreth, Chemosh, and Molech. As predicted, these wives turned his heart away from the Lord.

The Lord was angry with King Solomon for not keeping His commandments. "Because you have disobeyed My words, I will take your kingdom away and give it to one of your officers," said the Lord. "For your father, David's, sake, I will not do this in your lifetime. I will take the kingdom away from your son. However, in David's memory, I will give your son the tribe of Judah and My chosen city, Jerusalem."

As Solomon grew older, he began to have trouble managing the kingdom. His people complained about taxes, the money spent on the temple and palace upkeep, and the national debt. Solomon had to trade King Hiram twenty cities in return for a loan just to keep his country going.

Solomon's son Rehoboam was a hot-headed young man and a poor leader. Jeroboam, one of his officers in the north, had been hearing the northern tribes' complaints for months. One day, Ahijah the prophet came to Jeroboam with God's words: "I am about to tear the northern kingdom away from Solomon. You will be king over these ten tribes of Israel if you walk in My ways and keep My commandments."

When Solomon heard about this prophecy, he tried to have Jeroboam killed, but the man escaped to Egypt, staying with Shishak, the current pharaoh.

Solomon had been king for forty years. His accomplishments in trade and industry had helped the country become a world power. With his wise and understanding heart, there truly had not been any king like him before. In many ways, especially in his writings, the glory that was Solomon's would live forever. Unfortunately, he had been too busy to follow God's sacred rules and commandments. When Solomon died, God's words were fulfilled: his country was divided into Israel and Judah. His son Rehoboam ruled poorly over Judah. Jeroboam, whom God had chosen to rule Israel, made golden calves and appointed priests who were not Levites. Once again, the Lord was angered and declared, "I will sweep away the house of Jeroboam as one sweeps away waste!"

Jeroboam was king for twenty-two years,
His son Nadab became king for two.
He did what was evil in the sight of the Lord.
Baasa slew Nadab,
Ruled twenty-four years.
Then Elah, his son,
Became king for two years,
Until Zimri, his servant, conspired against him.
Zimri ruled seven days and then died in a fire.
Omri, the army chief, was the next king.
He ruled for twelve years,
And like Jeroboam,
He made Israel sin.

237

His son Ahab ruled after him;
The least of his sins was, he took for a wife
Jezebel, a cruel woman.
He built for this wife a temple to Baal.
Ahab angered the Lord more than others before him.
No longer would God, the Lord,
Choose to ignore him.

Rehoboam became the first king of Judah.
He ruled seventeen years in Jerusalem.
He did what was evil in the sight of the Lord.
Then Shishak, the Egyptian,
Who had helped Jeroboam,
Attacked Rehoboam
And took Solomon's treasures.
There was war all the time
Between the two kingdoms,
The north and the south.
Rehoboam died, and his son,
Abijam, was king for three years.
He fought Jeroboam and when he died
His son Asa became king for forty-one years.
Asa did what was right in the sight of the Lord:
He got rid of idols,
Brought back sacred vessels to Solomon's temple,
And successfully fought against
Baasa of Israel,
And Baasa's son Elah,
And his servant Zimri
Who ruled after him.
Omri followed Zimri,
And while Asa of Judah continued his ruling,
Ahab, Omri's son, became Israel's king.

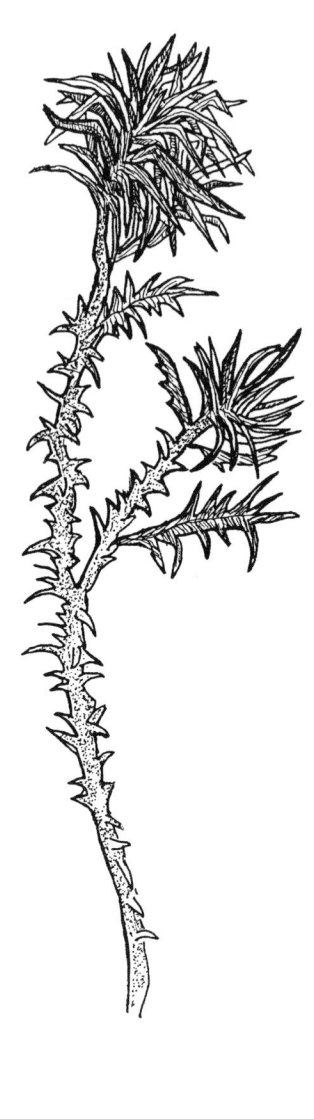

Elijah the Prophet

Elijah the prophet came from Tishbe
In the mountainous province of Gilead.
Mountain streams watered the fertile green land,
Fields of wheat leaned toward the warm summer breezes,
And farmers grew onions, beans, leeks, and red lentils.
The hills and the valleys held orchards
Of olive and apricot trees.
There were groves of tall oaks,
Vineyards covered the slopes,
And herbs, like the sweet balm of Gilead, were found
In the pretty herb gardens of Elijah's town.

Elijah was holy, a prophet of God.
Clothes meant nothing to him.
He looked rather odd, in leather loincloth
And rough, hairy cloak,
Whatever the weather.
One day, Elijah came to King Ahab
Who did not expect him,

239

Although he suspected to hear the worst from him.
The prophet spoke clearly, his voice loud and strong:
"For many long years you shall suffer from thirst.
No rain shall fall here
Until I say so."

Elijah heard God say, "Leave and go hide
By the brook that is found on the Jordan's east side.
Ahab and Jezebel, his wicked wife,
Will be looking for you.
Now run for your life.
Drink from the brook and My ravens will feed you."

He did as God said and the birds brought him bread
And meat in the morning and the same food at night.
The river dried up and God spoke once again,
"Go to Zidon; you'll be fed by a widow."

Elijah came up to the gate of the city.
He said to a poor widow gathering sticks,
"Bring me, I beg you, a cup of cool water,
And bring me, I beg you, a morsel of bread."
The widow replied with a tear in her eye,
"I have no bread, just a handful of meal
And a small bit of oil
For me and my son to eat before we die."

"Fear not," said Elijah. "Bring me a bread cake.
Make one for yourself and one for your child.
The Lord said the meal in your jar will stay full,
And the oil won't give out
Till the Lord ends this drought."

The woman invited him into her home,
Took some meal and some oil, made a pancake-shaped cake,
Which she baked on the coals of her small, outdoor oven.
Day after day, the jar remained full;
The oil did not fail.
God's words, through Elijah the prophet, prevailed.

One day, the widow's son took sick and died.
"What have you against me?" the poor woman cried.
"O man of God, you have caused my son's death!"
"Give him to me; I shall pray for his breath
To return," said Elijah, and carried the limp child
Upstairs to his room, where he placed him
Upon his own bed.
Stretching over the boy he prayed,
"Lord, let this child's soul come back into him."
The child opened his eyes!
His soul had come back!
He smiled at Elijah!
The child was alive!

Elijah then brought the boy down to his mother,
Who hugged him and kissed him as mothers will do.
She looked at Elijah and said with a smile,
"I know now that you are a prophet of God;
The words of the Lord from your mouth
All come true."

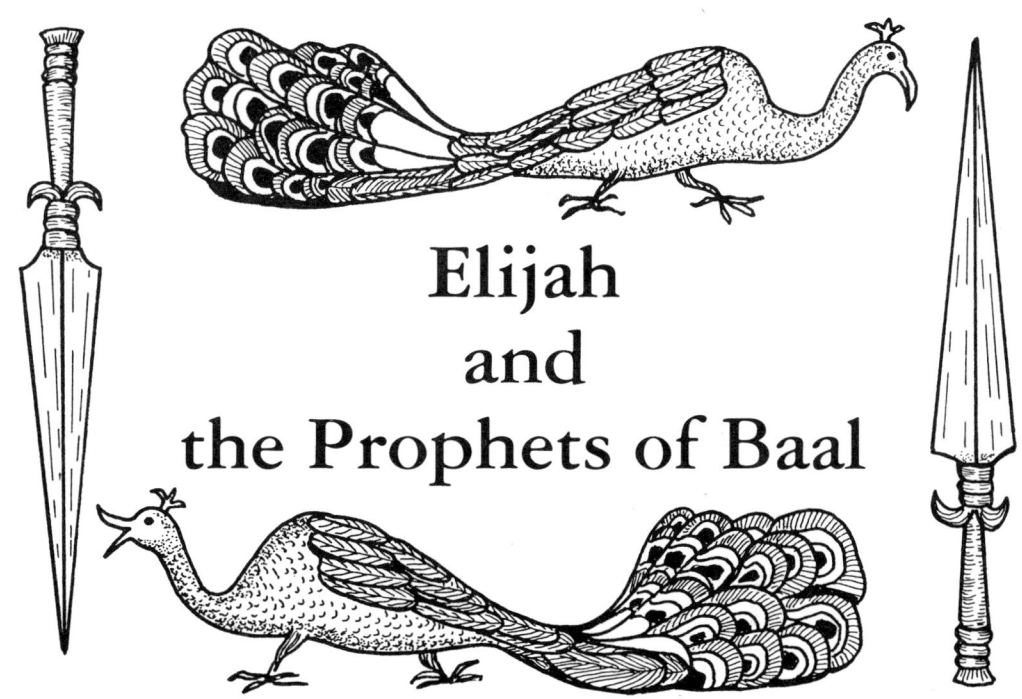

Elijah
and
the Prophets of Baal

Elijah the prophet heard the Lord's words,
"Show yourself to King Ahab; I'll bring rain to the land."
When King Ahab saw him, he asked,
"Is it you again, troubler of Israel?"
"It isn't I who has troubled this land," said the prophet,
"It's you and your family.
This worship of idols is way out of hand!
Have the people of Israel who worship Baalim
Come to Mount Carmel, as soon as they're able.
Bring the prophets of Baal,
And the four hundred prophets of the Asherah
Who eat with your wife Jezebel at her table."

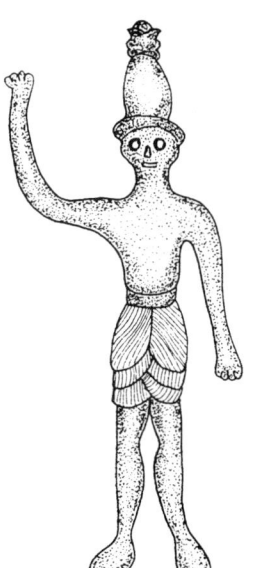

As dawn placed its kiss on the oaks and the willows,
Hundreds of people came through the woods,
Climbed up the mountain, and there they stood waiting
To hear what Elijah would say.
As he came near he asked them:

243

"How long will you waver between two opinions?
If the Lord is God, follow Him;
But if Baal is god, follow him.
Today I am God's only prophet,
While the prophets of Baal are many.
Let us each prepare bulls and lay them on logs,
Then you call to Baal; I will call to the Lord.
And who answers by fire, he shall be God!"

The prophets of Baal called out,
"Baal, answer us!"
From morning till noon they called;
Still, no voice answered
As dancers danced round the altar.
Elijah was mocking them, "Has your god faltered?
Is he meditating?
Perhaps he's away.
Maybe he's sleeping and has to be shaken
Until he awakens!"
Weeping and wailing, they slashed themselves bloody.
Would Baal take pity on them in their plight?
Where was Baal when they needed him?
Day turned to night;
Their god still hadn't heeded them.

Elijah the prophet called to the people
To gather around him as he built an altar
Of twelve stones for Israel's twelve tribes.
The altar was piled high with logs and the bull;
A wide trench ran around its four sides.
Elijah ordered that four jars of water
Be poured on the offering and on the wood.
Three times they poured water over the bull.
The trench was now full when the prophet Elijah said,
"Lord God of Abraham, Isaac, and Jacob,
Let it be known today that You are God."

The Lord's fire came like a bolt from the sky.
The bull and the wood and the altar were gone!
All the people bowed down to the ground and cried,
"The Lord He is God, the Lord He is God!"
"Seize the prophets of Baal; let no one get by!"
Said Elijah in triumph.
Soon the prophets all died.

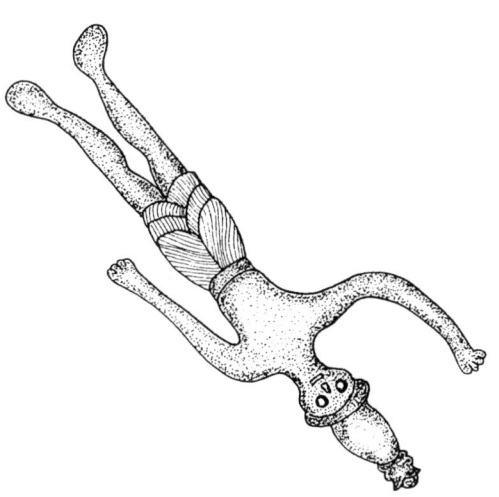

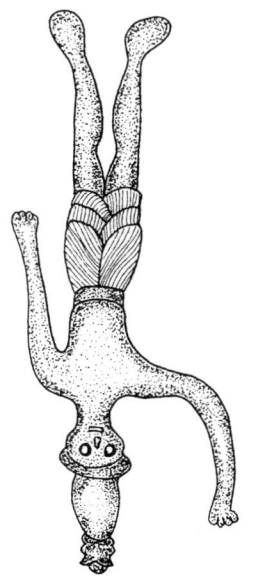

Elijah told King Ahab very good news:
"I feel in my bones it will rain."
He climbed to the mountaintop wrapped in his cloak
And sat, head on his knees,
Then said to his servant, "Please look toward the sea."
"There is nothing to see," the servant replied.
"Look seven times," said Elijah the prophet.
The man looked seven times,
Then saw something surprising.
"I see arising a cloud from the sea.
It's as small as the palm of a hand."
"Tell King Ahab to leave for his land," said Elijah,
"Before this great storm holds him back."
The sky soon grew black;
There was wind and a downpour!

Elijah, ecstatic, ran before the king's chariot,
Laughing and singing as rain turned to flood.
Through puddles and pools, Elijah the prophet
Was dashing and splashing and covered with mud!

Ahab told his wife what Elijah had done.
Jezebel sent the prophet a message:
"May the gods do to me what you've done to my priests
If I don't have you dead by tomorrow!"
With this threat, all his happiness turned to great sorrow.
Ahab's wicked wife would soon take his life.

Elijah went to Beersheba to pick up some water,
Then to the desert and found a wide broom tree
Clinging to life in a dry plot of earth.
He got off his feet and lay down in defeat.
"O Lord, take my life," he wept, sad and depressed.
As he slept there, Elijah was touched by an angel.
"Arise now and eat," he was told.
By his head on some hot stones he found some bread baking;
A cold jar of water was left for the taking.
He ate and he drank and once more fell asleep.

God's angel awoke him, "Arise now and eat.
The journey is long, and you must be strong."

After eating, Elijah took off for Mount Horeb,
The mountain where Moses received the Lord's word.
He soon found a cave, the same cleft in the rock
In which Moses had stood as God's Glory passed by.
High on this mountain, no sound would be heard,
Not a jackal's cry, dove call, or raven's rejoice,
The only sound heard would be God, the Lord's, Voice.

Elijah then covered his head with his cloak.
The Lord spoke, "Elijah, why are you here?"
Without fear he replied, "The Children of Israel
Have broken their promise.
They've thrown down Your altars.
With daggers and swords they have slain the Lord's prophets.
I, only I, am left living today.
And they now seek my life to take it away."

Then God said, "Go outside and stand before Me."
Wind tore through the mountain;
Rocks broke into pieces.
But the Lord was not in the wind.

He felt the earth shake and a mighty earthquake
Rumbled over the ground.
But the Lord was not found in the earthquake.

After the earthquake a fire erupted.
The cool mountain streams became hot.
But the Lord was not in the fire.

Then after the fire,
A small voice,
A whisper,
Interrupted the stillness.
"Go home," said the Lord, "and continue your work.
Find young Elisha.
Anoint him in your place.
I will punish all Israel
Except those who've not turned their face
And kissed Baal."

Elijah departed and found young Elisha
Plowing his field with oxen before him.
He took off his cloak,
Placed it on young Elisha, who knew that this meant
He must answer the call of Elijah the prophet.
"Let me say good-bye to my mother and father,"
Said young Elisha. "Then I'll follow you."
Elijah was cranky, "Don't come at all
If you delay in answering the call."
After cooking two oxen and burning his plow,
Elisha gave everyone portions of meat.
He said his farewells and promised he'd never forget
All his friends.
Then he answered the call of Elijah the prophet.

II Kings

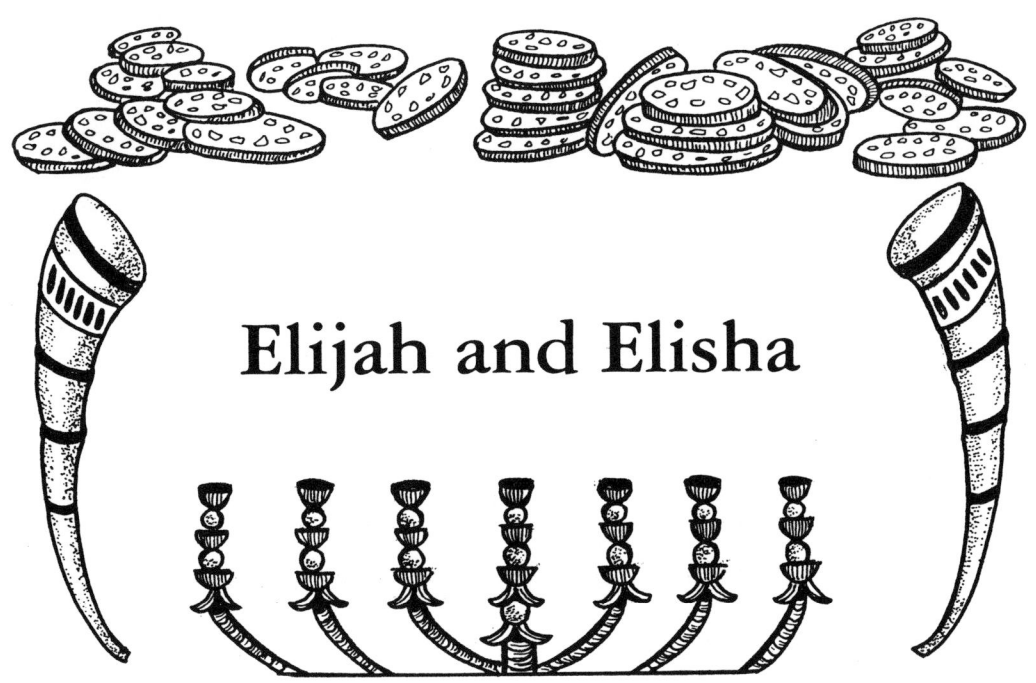

Elijah and Elisha

Elijah the prophet spent his days bringing God's word to the Children of Israel. Sometimes the people were stubborn and unfriendly. And sometimes they listened to him and began changing their ways. Being a prophet was a hard job, especially for a man wearing nothing but a hairy cloak and leather loincloth. Elijah knew that no matter how he looked, it was what he said that mattered. And he kept saying and praying and teaching until he grew very old.

Elisha traveled everywhere with Elijah. Unlike Elijah, he dressed normally and was soft-spoken and friendly. Although Elisha learned how to be a prophet from Elijah, he had his own way of teaching people.

TEACHERS

There are all kinds of teachers,
All shapes and all sizes,
Some teach by the book,
Some are full of surprises.
Some teachers are fun,

253

Some are quite serious,
Some laugh when we laugh,
Some holler and scream at us.
Some teachers are easy,
Some teachers are firm.
If you listen there'll always be
Something to learn!

The time came for Elijah to join the Lord in heaven. Before he left forever, the old prophet wanted to say farewell to the Sons of the Prophets. These groups of men lived lives dedicated to God.

"Wait here," Elijah said to Elisha. "The Lord is sending me to Beth-El to say my farewell."

"I will not leave you," stated Elisha.

And so, the old man with the hairy cloak and the white-robed young man went down to Beth-El.

The Sons of the Prophets asked Elisha, "Do you know that the Lord will take Elijah away today?"

"I am aware of it," answered Elisha sharply. "Now you be quiet!"

254

Once again, Elijah asked Elisha to stay behind while he visited the Sons of the Prophets in Jericho.

"I will not leave you," said the younger man, climbing on his donkey.

Spending all their days in prayer seemed to help the Sons of the Prophets know the will of God. They also told Elisha about Elijah's coming departure.

"I am already aware of it," he answered, not willing to accept the future. "Now you be quiet!"

ACCEPTING THE TRUTH

Knowing the truth and accepting it
Is sometimes a hard thing to do,
Especially when you don't want to know
That someone is leaving you
For a long time
Or maybe for good.
It would be nice if everyone stayed
Where they are in this world.
But if nobody left,
And each stayed in their place,
The world would eventually
Run out of space!

"Stay here, young friend," ordered Elijah. "The Lord wants me to go down to the Jordan River."

"As the Lord lives and as your soul lives, I will not leave you," Elisha declared, turning his nibbling donkey away from some hanging vines.

As the two men stood by the Jordan, Elijah took off his hairy cloak, rolled it up, and struck the river. The water parted in two gigantic waves and the men crossed over on dry ground.

When they reached the other side, Elijah asked Elisha, "What shall I do for you before I am taken away?"

Elisha replied, "Please leave me a double portion of your gift of prophecy."

255

"You have asked a hard thing," said Elijah. "Yet, I'll tell you what: If you see me as I am taken, then your wish shall be granted. If you do not see me, then it shall not."

As they walked and talked, a chariot of fire pulled by flaming horses came between them. The astonished Elisha watched as a great whirlwind drew Elijah up into God's heaven.

"My father, my father!" cried Elisha. "The chariots of Israel and the horsemen!"

As Elisha described the power of this scene, Elijah the prophet disappeared.

The young man lifted his teacher's old, hairy cloak, went back to the river, and called, "Where is the God of Elijah?"

He touched the waters with the cloak and once again they rolled back to the right and to the left. Elisha, the new prophet, walked across the Jordan on dry ground. The Sons of the Prophets of Jericho, watching from afar, proclaimed, "The spirit of Elijah rests on Elisha!"

256

The Wonderful Miracles of Elisha the Prophet

Elisha the prophet was a kind man. He traveled across the land, giving help to the poor and the sick. Elisha was a good listener and problem solver. Most importantly, he knew the word of God.

The Poor Widow

One day, the grief-stricken widow of a holy prophet came to Elisha. "My husband is dead, I cannot pay his debts, and the creditor is about to take my sons as slaves."

"What shall I do for you?" asked the prophet. "Let's see. What do you have in your house?"

The woman had nothing but a small jar of olive oil. Elisha told her to borrow as many jars as she could and begin pouring the oil from her jar into them. To her amazement, the oil flowed and filled all the borrowed jars.

The woman came running to Elisha with this unbelievable news. "Go sell the oil and pay your debt. You and your sons can live on the rest," said Elisha the prophet, silently thanking the Lord as the grateful woman went home.

The Kiss of Life

The village of Shunem lay snuggled in a green valley between mountains and hills. Every time Elisha and his servant Gehazi came to this pretty place, they were invited in by a lonely, childless couple. After a while, these nice people built a rooftop room for Elisha, complete with bed, table, stool, and candlestick. "When he comes to visit, he can rest here," said the wife.

One hot day, Elisha accepted their invitation, thankful for a place to rest his sore bones. Traveling by donkey is a bumpy experience; your poor body feels every rock and pebble. And when the animal stumbles, you bounce up and down like a rubber ball. "Find out what I can do for this good woman to show my gratitude," Elisha ordered his servant.

"Her husband is old and she dearly wants to have a child," was the reply.

"Call her," directed the man of God.

The woman stood by the door to the little room. Her eyes widened in disbelief as Elisha said, "Next spring, you shall have a son." And so she did.

Some years later, the child was working in the fields under a blazing sun. "My head, my head!" he cried to his father before fainting from sunstroke. Sunstroke happens when your body gets too hot. Wearing a big hat and drinking lots and lots of water on hot days help keep your body temperature down.

The mother held her child until he breathed no more, then laid him gently on Elisha's bed and closed the door. Frantically, she ordered a servant to saddle a donkey and take her the twenty miles to Mount Carmel where Elisha was working. Finding the man of God, she took hold of his feet. The servant tried to pry her away but Elisha, suddenly understanding the problem, said, "Leave her be; she is upset. The Lord hid this news from me. Be quick! Take my staff, go straight to her home, and lay it on the child's face."

The mother insisted that Elisha come back with her. On the road, they met the sweating servant and his panting donkey. Breathlessly, he reported, "I laid the staff on the child but there was no sign of life."

When Elisha arrived, he found the dead child on his bed. He went into the room, shut the door, and prayed to the Lord. His teacher, Elijah, had done the very same thing for a child many years before. Crouching over the dead child, he put his eyes upon the boy's eyes, his hands on his hands, and his mouth upon his mouth. In this way Elisha, the man of God, gave him the kiss of life.

The child's pale skin turned pink as his body slowly came back to life. Elisha left the room, walked once around the house, returned, and once more crouched over the child. The child sneezed seven times! "Good health to you!" said the prophet, and the boy opened his eyes!

Not knowing what to expect, the mother came up to the room. "Take your son," said Elisha as the woman bowed down to him, thanking him a million times.

The grateful mother left the little room and, shaking her head, smiled as she watched her healthy son slide down the stairs in front of her.

The Magic Gourds

One day, Elisha came to Gilgal, where there was a terrible famine. The Sons of the Prophets had only wild roots and berries to eat. During his visit, the prophets made soup from some wild gourds. But when they tasted it, they knew right away that it was poisonous.

Never eat anything growing outdoors unless you absolutely know that it is safe. Some pretty berries are only safe for birds and animals. Certain mushrooms and fruit are only decorations for God's beautiful gardens; eating them could be very dangerous.

"O man of God," warned the prophets. "There is death in the pot. Do not taste it!"

Elisha said, "Bring me a little ground-up grain." He sprinkled the meal into the poisonous pot of soup and, to everyone's amazement, nobody became ill!

Plenty of Leftovers

Elisha was staying with another group of prophets when a farmer brought in some food. There were twenty loaves of barley bread and some freshly cut wheat. "Feed all the people with this food," Elisha directed.

"How can I feed one hundred men with this?" asked his servant.

Elisha answered, "The Lord has said that they shall eat and have some left over."

The loaves and the grain multiplied into a great big pile. Everyone was fed and there were plenty of leftovers! Once again, Elisha, the man of God, had helped the Lord with His wonderful miracles.

The Bones of Elisha

Elisha, the kind and wise prophet, had finally taken his last journey across the land. He set his trusty donkey free to roam the fields and nibble dandelions till his nose turned yellow; after all, he too was old and deserved to retire.

When Joash, the new king of Israel, came to say his farewell, Elisha tried to teach him how to wipe out the approaching Syrian army. Unfortunately, the king was not a good listener. Elisha lost what patience his old body had and gave up. Wearily, he closed his eyes and went to sleep forever.

Years later, as some men were about to dig a grave, a roving gang of Moabites appeared, ready to attack. The frantic grave-diggers tossed the dead body into the nearby tomb of Elisha and ran away. When the body touched the bones of Elisha, the most amazing thing happened: the dead man revived, jumped up on his two feet, gave a big yawn, and walked off as if nothing had happened! This was the very last, great miracle of the prophet Elisha.

MIRACLES

There are miracles happening
Every day,
Though most of the time
You don't really know
That they are what they are:
The stars in the sky,
The moon and the sun,
Rain that waters the grass,
Birds and butterflies helping
The flowers to grow.
Seeds that make food,
Even weeds have a reason
For being so pesty.
Some look the same
As the plants they protect
From nasty old bugs
Who never suspect
That they're being fooled!
Life is a miracle,
And when someone dies
We give praises to God
And thank Him
For the person He lent to us
For a short while.
A smile is a miracle
Chasing a tear.
Each day of the year,
Winter, spring, summer, fall,
Brings its own miracles,
Rainbows and shadows,
A firefly's light.
But a baby's first cry
Is the best one of all.

Jehoash
the
Boy King

There were so many kings after Solomon died,
　　It's hard to keep track of them all.
　　Some kings were good kings,
Others were bad,
Some kings were old men,
And one was a young lad of seven, Jehoash.

When King Ahaziah of Judah was killed,
His very own mother killed all his sons
So that she, herself, could be queen.
But one son, Jehoash, was saved by his aunt,
And was hidden away where he wouldn't be seen
In the temple, along with his nurse.
The high priest and his wife feared for his life.
They loved the boy dearly, gave him good care,
And taught him to love God, to pray, and to sing.
When he was seven, the priests and the Levites
Brought Jehoash out and anointed him king.

Jehoash did what was right in the sight of the Lord.
Day and night, the high priest taught him
All he should know about God and His rules.
This was his special school, made just for a king.
He also learned history, music, and writing.

While other kings spent their time screaming and fighting,
The young king, Jehoash, tried to keep peace.
For a short time, it seems, he succeeded.
One day he noticed that Solomon's temple needed repairs.
The stone walls had cracks,
Grass grew through the stairs,
Some cedar was splitting,
The roof had been leaking,
Mice had built themselves tunnels
With holes leading out to the Holy of Holies.
This had to be fixed!

It seemed, to the king, that for years all this work
Had been left undone by priests and kings busy
With all things excepting God's home.
Jehoash established the first "Building Fund."
The high priest took a chest, bored a hole in the lid,
And placed it alongside the altar.
Whoever came in dropped a coin in the chest,
Which was soon filled with gold and with silver.

The king's scribe and the high priest
Took charge of the counting.
They bagged all the money, the amount of it mounting.
They gave out the money to masons and builders,
To carpenters, roofers, and exterminators.
They bought new wood and stone for the cracks in God's home.
With leftover money, new vessels were made,
Basins and cups, plus some long silver trumpets.
Once again the Lord's temple gleamed in the sun.
Everyone prayed there while Jehoash ruled,
Till the king of Aram said, "Attack!"
Jehoash held him back by sending him
All the new vessels, the basins and cups,
And the wonderful, long silver trumpets.

Stripped of its finery
The temple looked odd.
Nevertheless,
It was still home to God.

The Assyrian Exile

For some time, the Children of Israel had been divided into two countries: Judah, with Jerusalem as its capital, and Israel, whose capital city was Samaria. Although the people living in Judah and Israel were the descendants of the twelve tribes Joshua had led into God's Promised Land, they had trouble getting along with each other and with different countries. Like most brothers and sisters, they fought, called each other names, and took each other's things. However, when big countries do this to each other, it becomes much more serious.

The Lord sent prophets to help His people follow His rules and commandments. But the people had turned away from God and were worshiping idols. Occasionally, one king or another tried to do what was right in the eyes of the Lord. More often, these kings did not please God. Because of their poor behavior, the Children of Israel were destined for destruction!

Assyria was a warlike country lying far to the east of Israel. For many years, its fierce soldiers would march into the surrounding countries, taking prisoners and whatever treasures they could find.

King Pekah of Israel joined the Syrian king in trying to conquer King Ahaz of Judah. King Ahaz sent an urgent message to the king of Assyria saying, "I am your servant. Please help save us from these kings." As a bribe,

King Ahaz took all the treasures in the Lord's temple and sent them to this king, who was usually an enemy.

Agreeing to help, the Assyrian king captured Damascus, Syria's main city, and killed the Syrian king. When King Ahaz went to thank him, he saw the fancy Assyrian altar. He instructed his priests to have one made just like it to use when the king returned his visit.

Solomon's great altar was moved and the new, larger altar was put in its place. Because he did not entirely trust the Assyrian king, King Ahaz took apart many of the temple's costly ornaments and hid them away.

After killing King Pekah, Hoshea became what would be the last king of Israel. He did what was evil in the eyes of the Lord, although he was not quite as bad as previous kings. Shalmaneser, the new king of Assyria, fought against Hoshea, conquered him, and accepted yearly presents. But when Hoshea missed a payment and secretly tried making friends with Egypt's king, Shalmaneser had him tied up and placed in custody.

After three years of fighting, Shalmaneser took over Samaria and made all the people of Israel go to Assyria. Twenty-seven thousand, two hundred and ninety people were exiled.

The Children of Israel had sinned against the Lord their God, Who had brought them up from Egypt, out of the hand of Pharaoh. They would not listen; they were stiff-necked and they turned aside, worshiping idols and practicing witchcraft. Like leaves falling into a fast-flowing river, they were carried away for-ever.

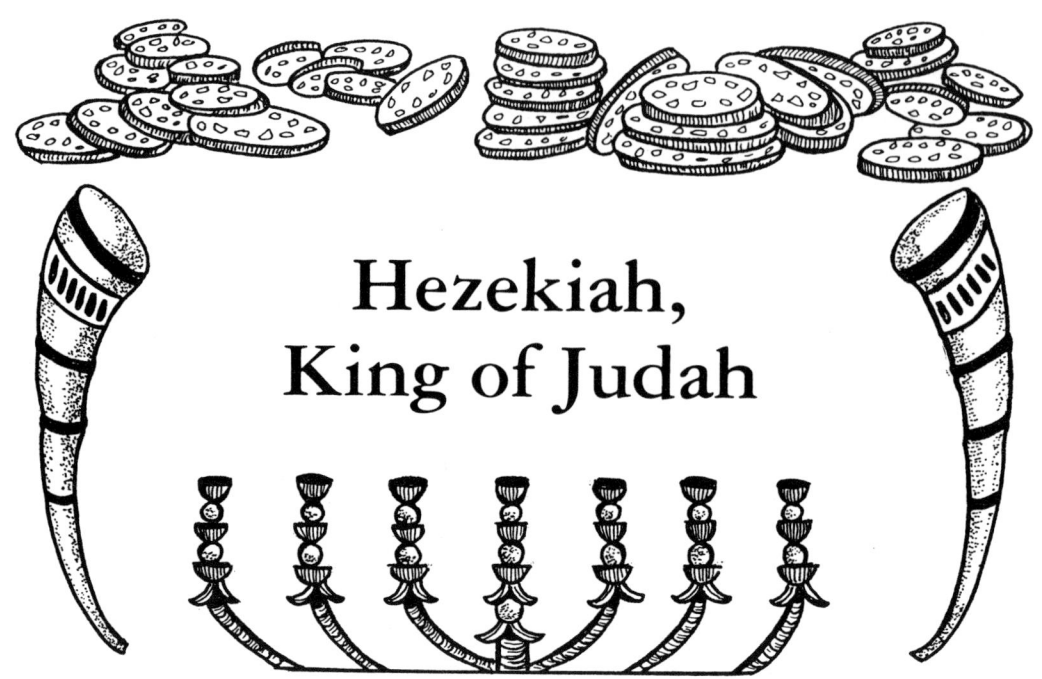

Hezekiah, King of Judah

Hezekiah, the son of Ahaz, was the thirteenth king of Judah. He did what was right in the eyes of the Lord: idols were destroyed and their altars removed. Once again, the Lord and His commandments were to be honored.

Sennacherib, the king of Assyria, was busy capturing all the cities of Judah. King Hezekiah sent him a message asking what it would take to make him go away. "Lots of silver and gold" was the answer. Hezekiah paid him with all the temple and palace silver plus the gold from the newly decorated temple doors.

Honorable people expect others to keep their word. King Hezekiah thought this big payment would keep Judah and Jerusalem safe. But Hezekiah had been tricked!

While he was busy helping his troops destroy the city of Lachish, Sennacherib sent three spokesmen and a great army to Jerusalem. When they called for the king, Eliakim, the palace chief, came to greet them.

"Hear the word of the great king of Assyria," proclaimed Sennacherib's number one cup-bearer. "Don't let Hezekiah fool you. He won't be able to save you, and neither will your Lord. Make peace with me. Stay in your homes, eat from your own vines and fig trees, and drink your own cool water until I return. Then I will take you to a land just like your own, with plenty of grain, vineyards, olive trees, and honey. Here you will live well and not die. No gods of any countries have delivered their people from my hands. So why should the Lord be able to save Jerusalem?"

The people were silent; they trusted King Hezekiah and obeyed his command: "Do not answer him!"

KEEPING QUIET

It's hard
Keeping your mouth shut
When it wants to speak up.
It's difficult holding your tongue
When somebody says something to you
That you don't believe
Or that you disagree with.
Sometimes it is better
To leave things alone;
Words unsaid can't come back
And hurt you one day.
Some people rant and rave
Just to get noticed.
They never shut up;
They never relent.
Surprise them with silence
When they taunt you or tease you,
Or call you names day after day.
While they cause a riot
It's best to be quiet.
If you ignore them,
They might go away.

269

When King Hezekiah heard the bad news about his country, he went into mourning, tearing his clothes and covering himself with sackcloth, the rough material used in making grain bags. He sent Eliakim, Shebna, the scribe, and the senior priests, all dressed in sackcloth, to see Isaiah, the prophet. Sadly, they told Isaiah: "This is a disgraceful day. Perhaps the Lord your God will hear the insulting words of the king of Assyria and take vengeance on him."

Isaiah answered: "Tell the king not to be afraid of these loud-mouthed boys from Assyria. Fear shall be put into their king. He will hear a rumor about war, return to his country, and then die by the sword."

When Sennacherib heard a rumor that the king of Ethiopia was coming to fight him, he sent another taunting message about the Lord to Hezekiah. If he could get this king to surrender Judah, it would be easier for him to win the coming war.

Hezekiah went to the temple and placed the letter before God. "Save us, please," he prayed "so that all the kings on earth will know that You are the Lord."

Isaiah the prophet gave the king God's answer concerning Sennacherib and his attempt to capture Jerusalem:

"Jerusalem has never been conquered,
She laughs at you, shaking her head.
You've raised your voice and insulted the Lord.
You say that your chariots have climbed to the tops
Of Lebanon's mountains,
And the soles of your soldier's feet
Dried up the rivers of Egypt.
Do you not know that long ago I decided your destiny?
I will put My hook in your nose,
My bridle in your lips,
And turn you back the way that you came."

The Lord promised that Sennacherib would not attack Jerusalem, and that He, the Lord, would defend it.

That night, as Sennacherib's army lay in wait by Jerusalem's gates, the angel of the Lord came into the camp and took the lives of one hundred and eighty-five thousand men! Sennacherib went back to Nineveh, his own city, and as he was worshiping one of his idols, he was killed by his own sons!

King Hezekiah became very sick. "Set your house in order," said Isaiah, the prophet. "You are going to die soon."

With tears, King Hezekiah prayed to the Lord. The Lord's words came to Isaiah and he repeated them to the sad king:

"I will add fifteen years to your life and defend this city for my own sake and for my servant David's sake."

Hezekiah recovered and regained his old strength. One day, the son of the king of Babylon sent him a get-well message and a present. Hezekiah thought this was a very nice compliment, especially from another enemy of Sennacherib. Hezekiah invited the king's messengers to the palace and showed them the treasures.

Isaiah asked Hezekiah angrily, "Who were those men and where did they come from?"

Hezekiah boasted that the men had come from Babylon to pay him honor and to seek his friendship.

"What did they see in your house?" asked the prophet, barely controlling himself. He could not believe that Hezekiah would be dumb enough

to make friends with these people and that he didn't trust God to keep him safe from the Assyrians.

"I showed them everything in my house; there are no treasures that they haven't seen. They really liked my new couches and armchairs with the ivory trim and they said they had never seen such beautiful wine glasses and gold dishes. When I showed them my water clock, they put in an order for ten of them. I had to explain that our bathtubs were not horse's drinking troughs; they laughed when I told them how our people like to bathe with sweet-smelling bath oils. They were very interested to see our army equipment, the leather shields, long spears, and metal armor, and they were

272

impressed with those new three-man chariots. I also showed them the grain storage rooms and gave them some wine from our best vineyard," answered King Hezekiah, happily remembering the impression he'd made.

But he had not taken the time to think what he was doing. Everyone makes mistakes; however, God was keeping a careful watch over the king and over His city. Although Hezekiah tried very hard to do most things right, God finally made a terrible decision. Because of this one incident of arrogance and lack of faith, Isaiah gave King Hezekiah this terrible message from God:

"In the future, everything in your house shall be carried to Babylon. Your sons will be taken captive and work for Babylon's king."

"I have made a mistake," admitted the king. "God has been merciful not to let this tragedy happen in my lifetime."

Despite his weaknesses, King Hezekiah was a good man and a fine king. His people loved him and, when he died, they carved this verse over his tomb:

Here lies Hezekiah of Judah, the king,
Who, to the Lord, devotion did bring.
Before death, gold and silver and all treasures flee.
What is left of this man?
His good name and charity.

Manasseh the Evil King

Hezekiah's son Manasseh was twelve years old when he became king. Since most people did not live very long in those days, a twelve-year-old king was not so unusual. Manasseh reigned for fifty-five years, longer than any other king of Judah or Israel.

No matter how hard parents try, some children do not grow up as well as expected. Manasseh, the son of a good king, did a great amount of evil in the eyes of the Lord.

He built altars in the high places for idols like Baal
And the moon, stars, and sun.
He depended on sorcerers, magicians, and witchcraft,
And on anyone speaking with ghosts and with spirits.
He killed many prophets and did much more evil than all evildoers
Whom God had already destroyed.
This time the Lord wasn't sad or annoyed.
He was furious with His own people!
"I will wipe out Jerusalem as one wipes a dish!
I will turn the whole town upside down.
Whoever is left of My people I'll place in the hands of their enemies!
They're a disgrace!"

King Josiah
and
the Great Discovery

King Josiah was the grandson of Manasseh, the evil king. His father, King Amon, did not walk in the way of the Lord. After two years as king, he was killed by his servants. This made eight-year-old Josiah king of Judah.

Unlike the seven-year-old king Jehoash, Josiah had no high priest to teach him right from wrong. And he did not have Moses' holy writings; they had been lost during his grandfather's terrible reign. Despite these obstacles, Josiah managed to do what was right in the eyes of the Lord. Somehow his good character was stronger than any bad traits passed on by his ancestors.

When Josiah was having the temple repaired, he asked the new high priest to count the money collected to pay the workmen. Hidden in the bottom of the money chest was a parchment scroll. "I have found the Book of the Law in the house of the Lord!" cried the excited priest, taking the scrolls to a scribe. After the scribe read the scroll to Josiah, the king realized that he and his people were not living as God had commanded. Josiah was determined to do things correctly. "Go to Huldah the prophet and ask her to ask God what we should do," he ordered his closest advisers.

Closing her eyes, Huldah the prophet prayed silently to God. Huldah

275

was a tenderhearted person. Although most of the words she related were frightening, she knew how to give some good news along with the bad. "Here are the words of the Lord: 'A great calamity will befall Judah because for many years they have broken My commandments. My anger shall be like a fire that will not be put out. However, King Josiah's heart is good, filled with desire to follow Me. Therefore, he shall go to his grave in peace; his eyes will not see the evil which I intend to do.'"

Josiah went to the temple and read the word of the Lord to all the people of Judah. He made a covenant with God to keep His commandments with all his heart, his soul, and his might. And everyone said, "Amen."

The king ordered the priests to get rid of everything having to do with idol worship. This included the priests who sacrificed to Baal, the moon, the stars, and the sun. All practices that offended the Lord were utterly destroyed.

And when each and every idol, altar, and evil priest was gone, scattered as dust over the land, King Josiah announced that the great Passover would be celebrated. In the whole history of the judges and kings of Judah and Israel, there had not been such a Passover as this one!

At twilight, each family was instructed to bring an unblemished male lamb or goat. After the high priests performed the proper rituals, they read

everyone the story of the first Passover. Little children sat spellbound hearing how at midnight, the Lord destroyed all the firstborn in the land of Egypt except for His people, whose doorposts were smeared with the blood of lambs and goats. When the story was over, the animals were placed on spits and roasted in ovens dug into the ground. For six hours, the wonderful smell of meat cooking made the people's mouths water! At midnight, when the meat was done, each family took their portion home. They were reminded to eat it all up quickly, with unleavened bread and bitter herbs. When the children asked, "Why is this night different from all other nights?" they were told that this was to remind them how the Lord passed over the houses of the Children of Israel and brought His people out of Egypt.

Josiah had been a faithful king for thirty-one years when he was killed in a battle against the Egyptian pharaoh, Neco. There was no king before or after Josiah that turned to the Lord, as Moses had commanded, with all his heart, his soul, and his might.

Why

We don't know why some people die
While others live on to do good or bad.
We're sad when the good people
Leave us too soon,
With work left undone
And days in the sun yet to be.
It's hard to see past the unhappy part,
When the person who leaves
Takes a piece of your heart.
But the Lord has His plan,
And He made us with heads to hold
Sweet memories of those who have gone.
When we remember them,
After a while,
Tears will disappear;
Once again we will smile.

277

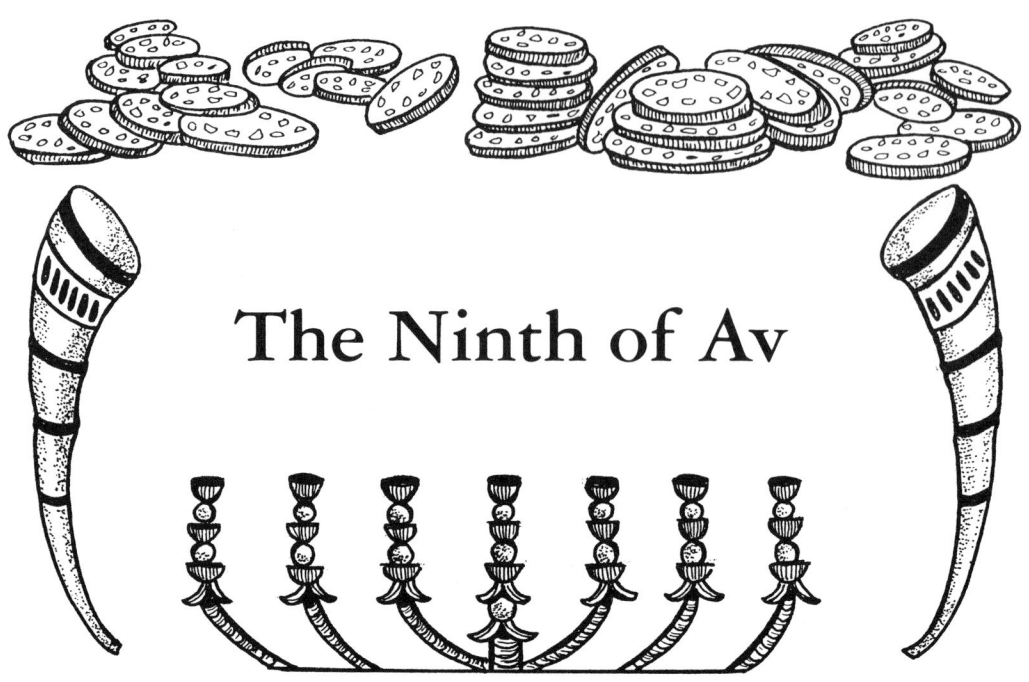

The Ninth of Av

The two sons of Josiah, Jehoahaz and Jehoiakim,
Did what was wrong in the sight of the Lord.
The first died in Egypt; the second was captured
By Nebuchadnezzar, Babylon's king.
Jehoiakim's son Jehoiachin
Became the next king of Judah.
He did everything wrong in the sight of the Lord.
And ruled for three months till King Nebuchadnezzar
Came up to the city,
And without any pity,
Took everyone captive:
His mother, his servants,
Princes and princesses,
Craftsmen and warriors,
All of the chiefs.
Only the poorest had any relief;
They were no threat to Babylon's soldiers.

Nebuchadnezzar made Jehoiachin's uncle
Zedekiah the next king of Judah.
Jeremiah, the prophet, told this stubborn king
To do the right thing in the eyes of the Lord
And not fight against Nebuchadnezzar.
But Zedekiah sinned greatly,
Polluted the temple,
And made fun of God's prophets
Till God's anger rose like a thunderstorm
Waiting to pour tons of water and flood the dry land.

There would be no remedy!
God cast from His sight
The Children of Israel.
They soon would be gone
As light becomes night
With no hope of a dawn.

On the seventh and eighth days of the fifth month,
King Nebuchadnezzar's army began
Destroying Jerusalem.
And on the ninth day of the fifth month of Av,
They burned the Lord's house,
And took all that was left,
The bronze, silver, and gold,
And took everyone captive,
The young and the old.

With sword and a cruel hand,
The Lord's chosen people
Were sent into exile
From His Promised Land.

Isaiah

Isaiah the Prophet

When Isaiah the prophet was born in Jerusalem,
His father, Amoz, gave him his name, which means
"Help of God."
Who would have known that someday this same boy
Would do all he could to save Israel's people
From being destroyed by their own faithless ways.

In those days, when Isaiah the prophet was young,
There was peace and prosperity;
Houses were well built, the people well dressed.
No one would have guessed that within this boy's lifetime,
The ten tribes of Israel would be lost forever,
And that God would sever the great land of Judah
From His divine Hand.

Isaiah's father was his first teacher,
Teaching him lessons about right and wrong.
He learned that the Lord would reward those whose conduct
Was faithful and good;

283

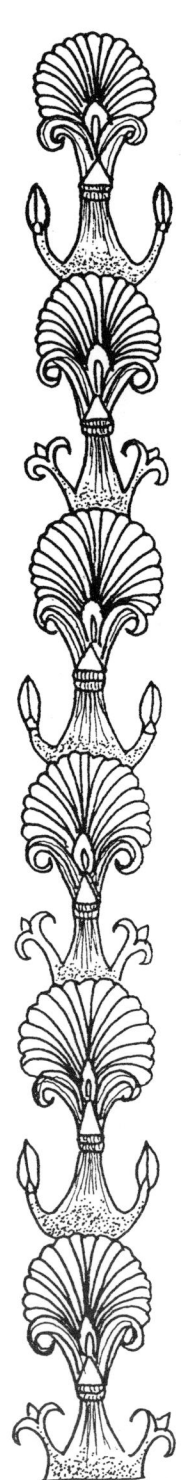

He would protect those who honored His words.
The priests taught Isaiah God's laws and rules,
Which were written by Moses,
The dos and the don'ts,
The I wills and I wont's.

Though Isaiah was always a serious boy,
He also had fun playing games with his friends:
Leapfrog, tag, tugs-of-war, and racing toy chariots
Down the hills of the town.
When he grew older, he noticed that throughout
The kingdom of Judah, the rich were content
But there was no relent for the poverty-stricken.
The poor became poorer.
Life for them was not fair;
They were filled with despair.

Isaiah gave speeches inside of the temple
On Saturday mornings, and at the time
Of the new moon and holidays.
He always warned the elders of Judah
That God soon would judge them
For their bad behavior concerning the poor.
By the time of King Jotham, Isaiah had changed from
His white linen robes to the sackcloth and sandals
That most prophets wore.

A vision came to him of God on a throne,
Seraphim above Him calling to one another,
"Holy, holy, holy
Is the Lord of Hosts;
The whole earth is full of His Glory."

284

The story is told how this vision of God
Showed Isaiah what he had to do for God's people:
To speak in God's name and to teach them God's laws,
His commandments and rules.
If they remained fools and did not obey him,
The Lord God of Israel would surely destroy them.

Isaiah spoke where the people could hear him,
Walking through the bazaars in his sackcloth and sandals,
Talking to carpenters, potters, and metalsmiths,
Shopkeepers, wine makers, bread bakers, dressmakers.
Praising God, he chastised them for turning away
In favor of riches, more money and jewels.
He didn't care what others thought of him;
He was speaking for God,
Nasty words did not touch him.

Isaiah the prophet tried teaching the people
That worshiping idols offended the Lord,
And that riches and all sorts of greedy behavior
Would someday be met with the dagger and sword.
Teaching these people was a difficult chore;
When the rich have their riches, they only want more,
And forget about others, the sick and the poor.
He said:
"Wash yourselves, become clean,
Put away the evil of your doings
From before the Lord's eyes,
Cease to do evil;
Learn to do well.
Seek justice, restrain the oppressor,
Be fair to the orphan, defend the widow,
Help those who cannot help themselves."

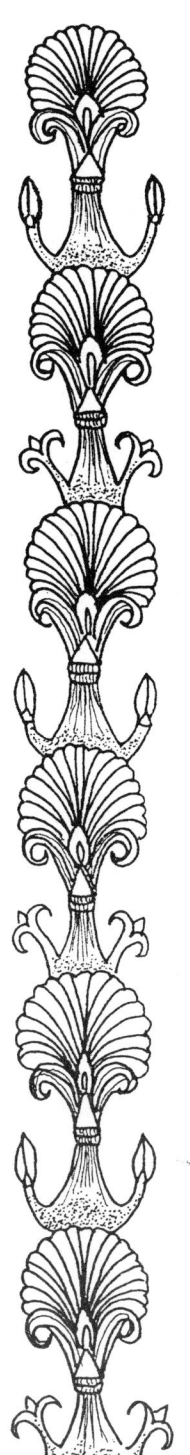

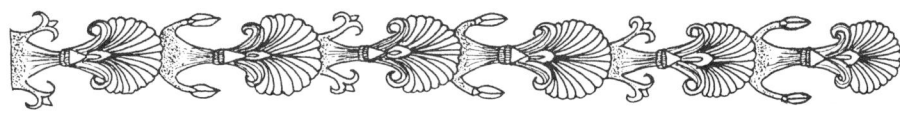

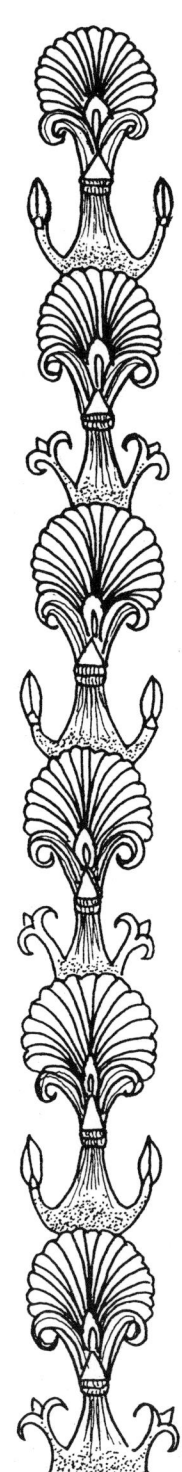

Isaiah believed with all of his heart
That people, wherever they live in God's world,
Should live lives filled with goodness, justice, and peace.
When they walk in God's light,
All wars shall cease.
He said,
"And they shall beat their swords into plowshares
And their spears into pruning hooks;
Nation shall not lift up sword against nation,
Neither shall they learn war any more."

The faithful and the foolish,
Soldiers, writers, teachers, priests,
Wealthy princes and fine dressers,
Beggars, shepherds, and wine-pressers,
Gathered in the temple's courtyard
To hear news and to exchange their different views
About the problems with Assyria, with Egypt,
And with others.
They debated about Israel, their kinsmen and their brothers,
Who, according to Isaiah the prophet,
Would be captured.

All this doom saying and praying to the Lord,
How would it help them?
After all, this fate for Israel
Could never befall Judah,
Where anything you wanted was available
To anyone with money:
Rings and bracelets for the women,
White linen robes for men,
Sturdy donkeys, golden chariots,
Spices, apricots and honey,

Copper pots and silver goblets
Made to hold the wine production.
Why was Isaiah, the great prophet,
Predicting nothing but destruction?

In his old sackcloth and sandals
Isaiah stood among these people.
The sun was not yet high
And puffy clouds in the pale sky sent breezes down
To lift his voice above the crowd.
Isaiah had decided to tell them all a fable,
A story that says one thing but really means another.
Perhaps they'd listen to him this time,
And not fight against him.
And so he spoke about a vineyard;
The meaning was not hard to grasp:
"My friend had a vineyard
On a fertile hill.
He dug it, he cleared it of stones,
And planted it with choice vines.
He made a winepress for it
And hoped that it would make good grapes.
But it yielded sour grapes."

The people stood and listened,
Shook their heads and clucked their tongues.
They felt sad for the grape farmer;
They felt bad for his bad luck.
Isaiah had their full attention,
Which was exactly his intention.
Now he could show them how God was the friend,
And Judah was the garden filled with sour grapes.
He spoke not of destruction,
Or the fate of their own nation,

287

He spoke only of God's sorrow,
His grief and His frustration.

"And now, O inhabitants of Jerusalem and Judah,
Tell me what more should I have done for my vineyard?
When I looked for it to yield grapes,
Why did it yield sour grapes?

"Now I'll tell you what I will do to my vineyard:
I will remove its thorny hedge,
And animals shall eat it;
I will take away its fence,
And it will be trampled down.
It will not be pruned or hoed,
It will grow briars and thorns;
I will tell the clouds
Not to rain upon it.
Israel is the Lord's vineyard,
Judah's people are the Lord's beloved plantings.
He looked for justice, but found violence;
He looked for righteousness, but found only a cry.

"Woe to them who drink and carry on into the night;
With music and pleasures they forget the work of the Lord
And what He has done with His Hands.
My people, therefore, will go into captivity
Because they have not thought ahead."

Throughout the reign of King Ahaz
Isaiah gave his warnings.
But no one chose to listen;
They just went about their business.
Someday other kings would capture them
And force them from their houses,

Take all their lovely things,
And make them slaves in foreign lands.
At that time God, the Lord,
Will wash the faithless from His hands.

Along with these sad predictions
Isaiah had his dreams
Of a time when God would rule a peaceful kingdom.
Kings and queens would join together,
And the people all would follow
God's commandments, laws, and rules.
There'd be no need for gold or jewels;
The light of God would shine
More brilliantly than all the stars,
Brighter than the moon or sun.
A day will come when all the earth will know
That God, the Lord, is One.

A Remnant Remaining

King Hezekiah, the son of King Ahaz,
Tried very hard to bring his people closer
To God, the Lord.
While this king understood the game of win or lose,
Isaiah the prophet only knew truth,
The truth inside the heart that yearns
For such a day when all men will be free,
A peaceful beginning,
No losing,
No winning.
He said:

"A shoot shall come from the house of David,
A twig shall grow from his roots.
The Lord's Spirit shall rest on him,
Wisdom and understanding,
Knowledge and awe of the Lord.
He shall not judge by
What He sees and hears,
But with fairness He shall rule

And help the helpless, the distressed.
He shall help the oppressed
And he shall destroy the wicked.
His strength shall come
From righteousness and faithfulness.
And the wolf shall dwell with the lamb,
And the leopard shall lie down with the kid,
And the calf and the young lion will graze together,
And a little child shall lead them.
The cow and the bear shall be friendly;
Their young shall lie down together;
And the lion shall eat straw like the ox."

Isaiah the prophet predicted that Judah,
Along with Israel,
Would be sent into exile,
Deported from homes and from farms.
They would live in harm's way
Until the day that a few might return,
A remnant remaining,
Who, with the Lord's Hand,
Would return to God's land.
"And it shall come to pass on that day,
That the Lord will set His Hand again the second time
To recover the remnant of His people.
He will send a signal to the nations
And will assemble the dispersed of Israel
And gather the scattered of Judah
From the four corners of the earth."

In his later years, the vision of Isaiah
Became one of hope and happiness,
Praising God and raising high His people,
Those returning to the Lord
And His eternal city.
Isaiah's heart was filled

With compassion, love, and pity,
And devotion to his people.
For them he felt both hope and pride,
For once again they'd carry forth
The light of knowledge, truth, and learning,
With the Lord God at their side.

Dressed in tattered sackcloth and wearing his old sandals,
Isaiah, the prophet, walked among his people,
Bringing words of comfort,
Consolation for their sorrows,
And the hope for bright tomorrows.

"Arise, shine, for your light is come,
The Lord's Glory has delivered you.
Darkness, trial, and tribulation
Cover all.
But the Lord's Glory will shine on you;
The nations will learn God's ways from you.

"Look about and see the exiles returning to Jerusalem,
Bringing gifts to beautify My house.
Violence shall no more be heard in your land.
There will be no desolation or destruction
Within your borders.

"Your sun shall no more go down,
Neither shall your moon withdraw itself;
For the Lord shall be your everlasting light,
And the days of your mourning shall be ended."

Jeremiah

Jeremiah the Prophet

Jeremiah the prophet was born in the village of Anathoth, four miles from Jerusalem. There were many priests in his family, and he was given a good religious education. Minutes from his home was the desolate wilderness, a silent place of parched grass and rounded boulders that looked like a sea made of stone. Jeremiah would often go there to think about God and the future of His people. He was a lonely child, and these thoughts and worries became his constant companions. However, when King Josiah began his drive to rid Jerusalem of idols and return it to holiness, Jeremiah's unhappy heart became a bit more hopeful.

Jeremiah was a shy young man when he first received the call to be a prophet. Imagine how sad he was when God revealed to him the coming destruction of Jerusalem.

The word of the Lord came to Jeremiah, saying:

> *"Before you were born, I made you holy.*
> *I have appointed you to be a prophet to the nations."*

Jeremiah protested this honor and said, "Lord God! I cannot speak; I am just a child!"

The Lord answered him, saying:

"Do not say 'I am a child.' You shall go to whomever I send you, and you shall say whatever I tell you to say. Do not be afraid; I will take care of you. I have put My words in your mouth.

"Evil will come from the north and Judah's people will be doomed. I will judge against them for all their wickedness in forsaking Me by worshiping idols and the works of their own hands. You will be like an armored city against the whole land of Judah. They will fight against your words but shall not win. I, the Lord, am with you to take care of you."

Jeremiah, God's newest prophet, was no longer filled with hope. As he began his work, he carried all these sad predictions inside his heart. His shoulders drooped, and he always appeared to be stooped over with a heavy burden.

One day, as the priests were counting out money to pay for temple repairs, they found the lost Book of the Law in the bottom of the money chest. This wonderful discovery made King Josiah even more determined to have his people once again accept God's covenant. He tried to set a good example with his own faithful behavior. This should have been a great help to Jeremiah as he tried to teach God's word. But the hardheaded people of Judah were not about to change their faithless ways. For fifty-five years, the previous king, Manasseh, had allowed them to worship idols and accumulate wealth. Why did this prophet keep warning them about God's anger? And what kind of threat were the Babylonians? Didn't they have enough trouble with the Assyrians and Egyptians? The people of Judah went about their business and ignored Jeremiah's words.

When Pharaoh Neco of Egypt joined with Assyria to try and hold back the approaching Babylonian army, King Josiah became worried that this aggressive team would also threaten Judah. He led his army into battle against the Egyptians and, sadly, this brave king who tried so hard was killed. His son, the new king, Jehoahaz, was taken captive by the Egyptians, who

appointed his brother, Jehoiakim, king. For a few years the land of Judah was under Egypt's control. The good religious reforms of King Josiah were forgotten. The desire for luxuries and the worship of idols once again took over the hearts and minds of Judah. Jeremiah the prophet wept for the lost King Josiah, for the terrible punishment that awaited Judah, and for the great teachings of Moses, at once rediscovered and rejected. "Why does the way of the wicked prosper?" he asked the Lord.

The Lord told Jeremiah to stand at the temple gate and proclaim these words:

"Change your ways and I will let you live here. Do not believe that this temple will help you; it is just a building. Only good deeds will help you. If you do not fight among yourselves, do not hurt those who are helpless, do not shed innocent blood or follow other gods, then I will allow you to live in this land which I gave to your ancestors. Unfortunately, no matter how many times I have warned you, you still trust in lying words and do not follow My Ten Commandments. Therefore, people of Judah, I will cast you out from My sight, the same way I cast out the people of Israel!"

The people of Judah, more interested in fancy ceremonies than true obedience to the God of their ancestors, called for Jeremiah's death. By being so wicked, Judah had given up its chances for God's protection. However, Jeremiah always kept the hope alive that if the people repented for their sins, God would once again take care of them. He gave the people a choice:

"Return to the Lord, faithless people. He will not look upon you in anger, for He is merciful. But if you take my life, you will bring destruction upon yourselves, this city, and all who live here."

Jeremiah's life was spared, and he left the temple. This incident only increased his determination to warn of God's threats of vengeance against His people. Though he was often treated cruelly, Jeremiah never gave up his job of speaking the Lord's words and proclaiming his own prophecies of impending doom:

"I will utterly consume them," said the Lord.
"There are no grapes on the vine,
Or figs on the fig tree,
And the leaf is faded;
What I have given them shall go to their enemies."

"We looked for peace and no good came;
We looked for a time of healing and found terror!
The neighing of war-horses is heard.
The whole land trembles;
They are coming and will devour the land!" warned Jeremiah.

"The enemy I send will be like serpents. They cannot be controlled and they will bite you," said the Lord.

From a far-off land the exiles will ask,
"Isn't the Lord in Zion?"
"Why have they provoked me with idols?" replied the Lord.

"I mourn for my people," cried Jeremiah.
"Is there no soothing balm in Gilead,
No prophets to heal their unhappy souls?
Oh, that my head could be turned into water
So that I might weep day and night for my people."

"I will make Jerusalem a ruin," said the Lord through Jeremiah, His prophet.
"Only jackals will live in it.

Judah's cities will be empty.
All this because they have forsaken My law,
Neither listened to My voice nor walked in My ways,
And have followed their idol-worshiping forefathers.

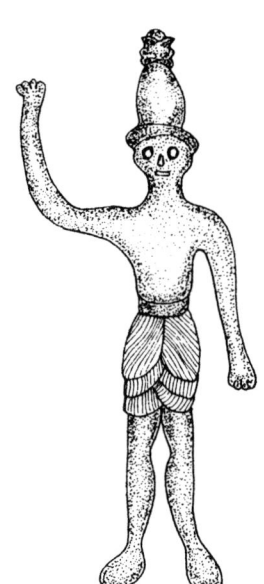

"The wise man must not glory in his wisdom,
The mighty man must not glory in his might,
The rich man must not glory in his riches;
But let those that glory, glory only in this:
Know that I am the Lord Who brings loving-kindness,
Justice, and righteousness to all the earth.
When they have learned these things,
Then I will be happy."

King Jehoiakim ignored Jeremiah's warnings and, using forced, un-paid labor, built himself another luxurious palace.

"Woe to him who builds his house dishonestly," warned the prophet.

A few years later, when the Babylonians defeated the Egyptians, this faithless king of Judah became King Nebuchadnezzar's servant, paying him whatever he wished in goods and money. When the Egyptians won the next battle, King Jehoiakim unwisely rebelled against Nebuchadnezzar, who sent new armies against Judah. For two years they demolished much of the country. Then, Nebuchadnezzar himself attacked with his own troops.

Jehoiakim's eighteen-year-old son, Jehoiachin, was now king of Judah. He fought the invaders for three months before surrendering the city. This new king and thousands of important citizens, soldiers, and craftspeople were all taken to Babylon as captives.

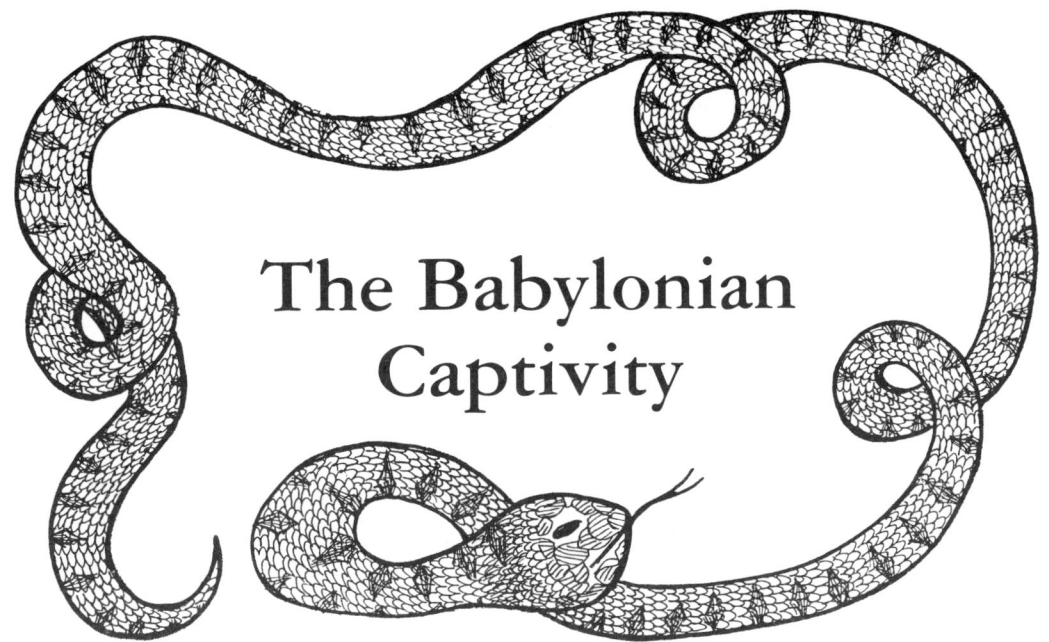

The Babylonian Captivity

Nebuchadnezzar appointed Zedekiah the next king of Judah. He did not listen when Jeremiah told him that God said to obey Babylon's king and live. At the same time, Jeremiah sent God's words in this letter to the captives in Babylon:

"Build houses, plant gardens, marry, and have many children. Live in peace in this city where I have made you captive. Pray to the Lord for peace; for in that peace you will be peaceful.

"Do not listen to anyone who preaches against peace. I have not sent them to you; they are false prophets. After seventy years I will again return you to your land."

In the seventh year of King Zedekiah's reign, he ignored Jeremiah's objections and declared independence from Babylon. Nebuchadnezzar stormed through the land of Judah, taking city after city. As the Babylonians were attacking the walls of Jerusalem, Zedekiah pleaded with Jeremiah to ask the Lord for help.

The Lord answered with these words:

"Those who stay in this city shall die; those who surrender will have their lives as their prize. This city shall be given into the hand of the king of Babylon and he will burn it down."

Lamenting this prophecy, Jeremiah cried:

"I writhe in pain. Disaster follows disaster. Judah will be destroyed!"

When Egypt suddenly began an invasion into Judah, the Babylonians stopped their siege and went to fight them. Jeremiah tried to tell the king that the enemy would return and that he should be ready to surrender. As Jeremiah left the city to visit his birthplace, he was arrested, beaten, and thrown into a dungeon. When he finally was brought to King Zedekiah, he told him that God had said they would be captured by the Babylonians. Jeremiah was taken from the dungeon and allowed to stay outside, where the guards could keep their eyes on him. For two more years he angered everyone by continuing to urge them to surrender.

Jeremiah wailed and Jeremiah pleaded.
Jeremiah cried his sad lament.
Jeremiah hoped he might prevent
God's wrath on those who would not repent.

Zedekiah finally agreed to execute this annoying prophet by lowering him into the mud at the bottom of a well. This kind of cruelty is called "torture." Many people whose ideas are different from others have had to suffer torture. This was especially terrible for Jeremiah, who had been trying so hard to also save the lives of the torturers!

Luckily, the king was persuaded to not to kill Jeremiah, and the poor, suffering prophet was carefully pulled out of the mud. Once again, the king asked for his advice. And once again Jeremiah told the king that if he surrendered Jerusalem, the city and its people would be saved. As usual, the king did not listen to Jeremiah. Many times, people ask for advice and then pay no attention to what they hear!

As the Babylonians continued their attack, Jerusalem began running out of food and water. Disease claimed many lives, and the people were desperate. The Babylonians were now preparing to hit the city walls with battering rams, huge wooden machines pushed by soldiers. By July, with the heat intense and the suffering great, Jerusalem could hold out no longer. The walls caved in and the Babylonians entered the city. The king was captured, tortured, and sent to Babylon. In August, Nebuchadnezzar sent orders to take everything of worth and then burn the temple and the city to the ground. Those people who were not killed were taken captive, and to this very day, their descendants mourn the great tragedy.

Although he had been allowed to remain in his homeland, Jeremiah eventually had to escape to Egypt. Though he never again saw his beloved country, he continued to bring words of hope to those in captivity:

"The Lord has said to me:

'Refrain from weeping, no more tears.
Your work shall be rewarded,
Put away your fears.
One day your people shall return
To Me,
From their captivity.'"

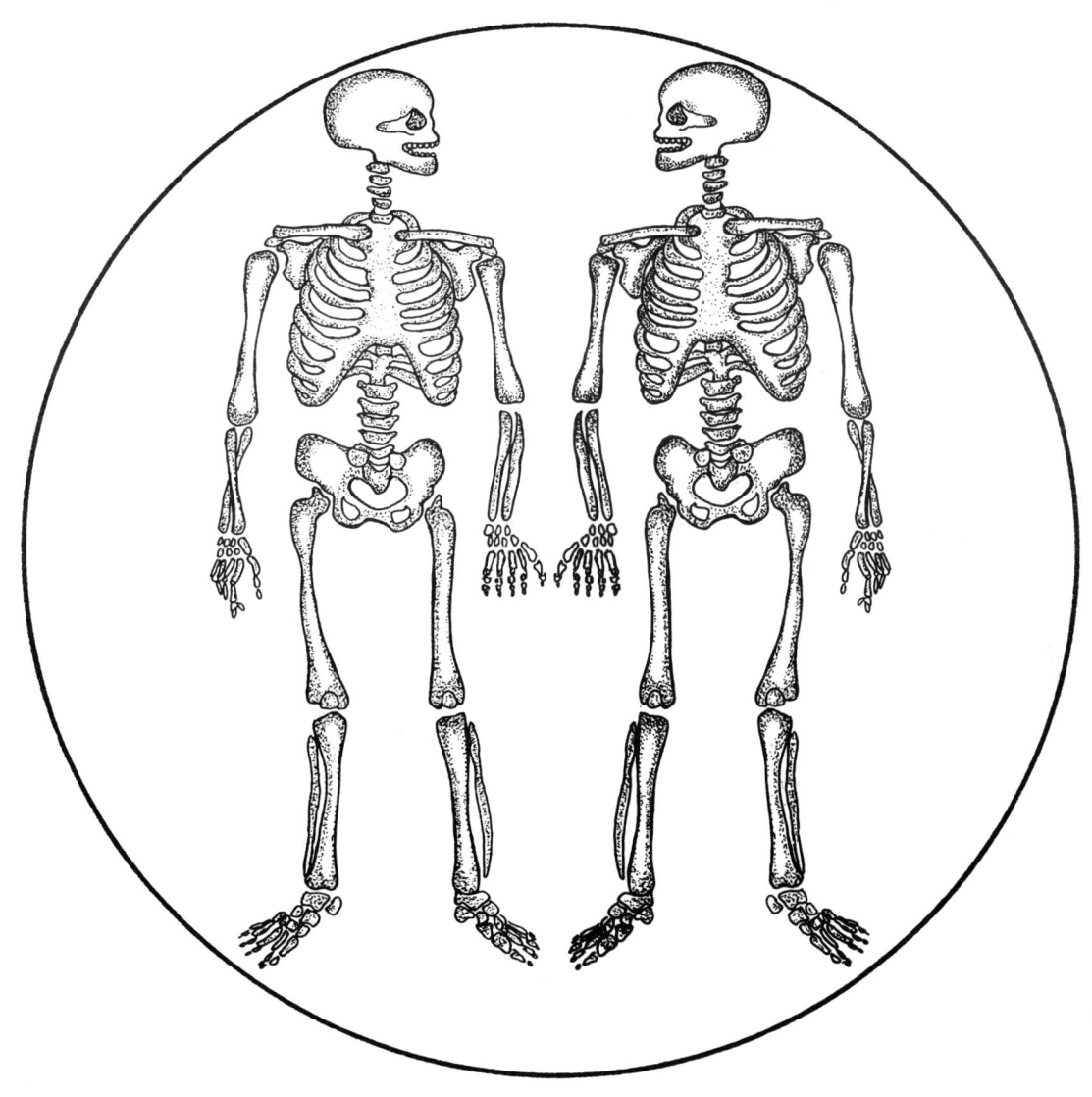

Ezekiel

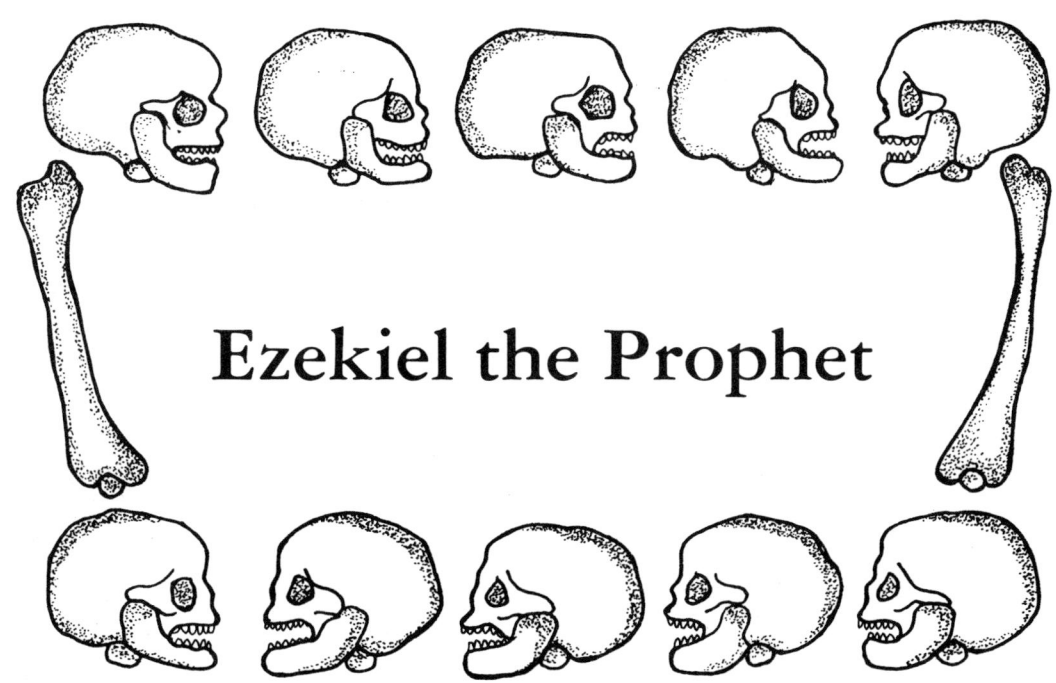

Ezekiel the Prophet

King Jehoiachin was eighteen years old when he and thousands of other important Judeans were taken into Babylonian captivity. Among the captives was the priest Ezekiel. It was a long, hot trip from Jerusalem to Babylon, and only the very strongest people survived. Weary and depressed, the captives bathed their sore feet in the cool waters of the river Chebar. The homesick travelers mourned:

> *"By the rivers of Babylon,*
> *There we sat down and wept*
> *When we remembered Zion."*

Eventually, after receiving the call to be God's prophet, it would be Ezekiel's job to renew the captives' hopes and help them keep God's covenant, as given to Moses so many years before. The remnant that remained would someday light the spark that once again would help them see God's light.

THE CALL OF EZEKIEL

On the fifth day of the fourth month
In the fifth year of captivity,
The word of the Lord came to Ezekiel the priest.
The hand of God was there upon him
When he saw the heavens open
As he sat among the captives by the river of Chebar.

A strong wind came from the north,
A great cloud with fire flashing,
And a brightness all around it.
Out of the fire something gleamed,
It seemed like metal in the flames,
And from its midst came four strange creatures.
From their features, their appearance
Looked very much like man.

Each one had four faces,
Each one had four wings.
Their legs were straight, their feet were sparkling
As if made of bronze.
Under their wings on all four sides
They had the hands of man.
Their faces were alike,
The front one being that of man.
On each right side there was a lion's face,
Each left side was an ox,
And behind each one, an eagle facing backward.
Two wings of each stretched upward,
While the other two wings covered
The body of each creature.

Every one of them went forward,
Since each faced the right direction

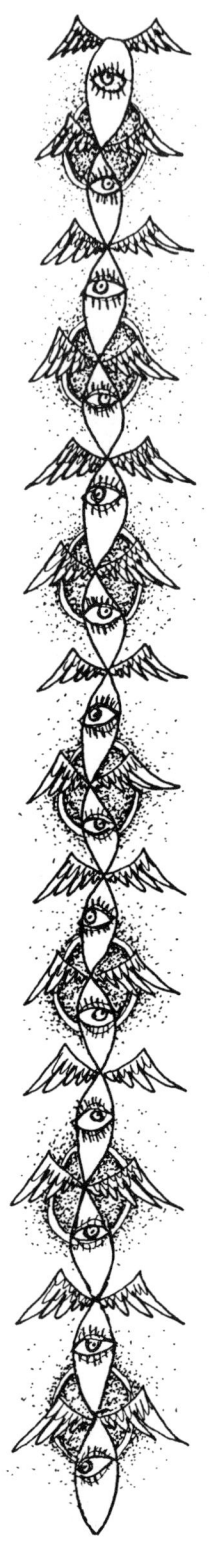

Toward the place they wished to go.
They galloped to and fro,
Looking just like coals of fire
Bright with lightning all around.

As I saw the living creatures,
There was one wheel at the bottom
Of each creature with four faces.
These wheels were of a topaz color,
Looking just like golden honey,
And each wheel was like a wheel within a wheel.
Whichever way the creature turned,
The wheel would easily obey.

The rings around the wheels were high,
Awesome in their height,
And the rings had eyes that told which way to go.
Where the living creatures went,
The whirring wheels went with them.
When the living creatures lifted up,
The wheels came along with them.
The spirit of each living creature
Lived inside the wheels.
The spirit knew the will of God
And the wheels knew what the spirit knew;
They moved about together;
When those went, these went,
And when those stood, these also stood,
When those were lifted up,
The wheels were lifted up beside them.
The spirit of each living creature
Lived inside the wheels.

Over the heads of each strange creature
Was a kind of sky
The color of the brightest, whitest ice.

And when the creatures moved,
I heard the noise
Of their great wings,
Like the noise of rushing waters,
Like the noise of a great army.
And when God's voice was heard
High above this blue-white sky,
The creatures let their wings down
And were still.

Over the sky above their heads
Was something like a throne,
Made of blue sapphire stone.
Upon this likeness of a throne,
Was what looked like a man.
From his middle upward
Was a look of fiery metal,
From his loins and downward
Was a look of fire round him.
Like the rainbow on a rainy day,
This brightness was the likeness
Of the Glory of the Lord.
When I saw it I fell on my face
And heard a voice that spoke.

And He said, "Son of man, stand on your feet
And I will speak with you."
Strength entered me and set me on my feet.
"Son of man," He said, "I send you
To the Children of Israel.
They're rebellious, they are sinful.
Brazen and stiff-necked.
I send you to them to tell them,
'Here is what the Lord God says.'
They may hear you or refuse you

But they'll know you came among them,
A prophet of the Lord.

"Son of man, don't be afraid of them,
Or what they say or do.
They are like briars, thorns, and scorpions.
Hear what I say to you:
Don't be rebellious like those people.
Open up your mouth and eat that which I give to you."
And when I looked,
There was a hand stretched out to me,
Holding a scroll.
He rolled it out and it was written on both sides
With lamentations, moaning, and with woe.

He said to me, "Now eat this scroll!"
I opened up my mouth and He said,
"You are to fill your belly with this scroll."
I did as God commanded.
I ate each and every sheet.
It tasted just like honey;
In my mouth it tasted sweet.

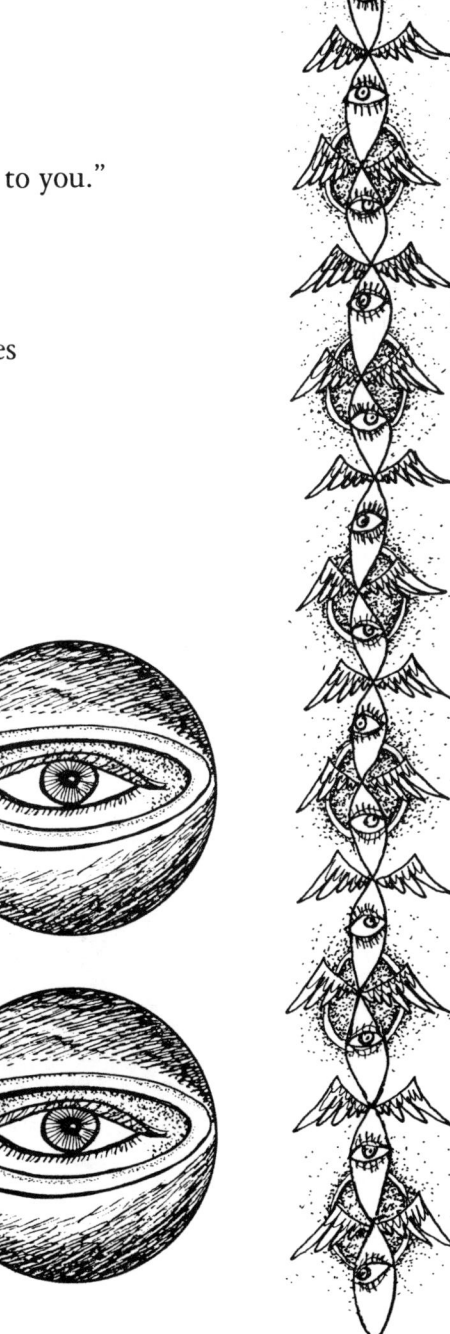

And then He said to me,
"Son of man, now you must go
To the Children of Israel
And tell them what I say.
I have given you the strength
To withstand their opposition.
Don't be dismayed by what they say,
They are a sinful people.

"Son of man, remember all My words
And take them to the captives.
Tell them, 'Hear the word of God,'
Though they may listen or refuse you."

313

Then a spirit raised me up
And I heard these words of praise:
"Blessed be the Glory of the Lord from His place."
I heard the noise of all the creatures
Touching wings,
And heard the noise of wheels beside them,
And the noise of a great rushing.
The spirit took me straight away;
I lay exhausted seven days.

And then the word of God came to me:
"Son of man, you are a watchman,
To all the house of Israel.
When you hear words from My Mouth,
You shall give to them the warning.
Ever after they must all return to God,
Or face disaster!"

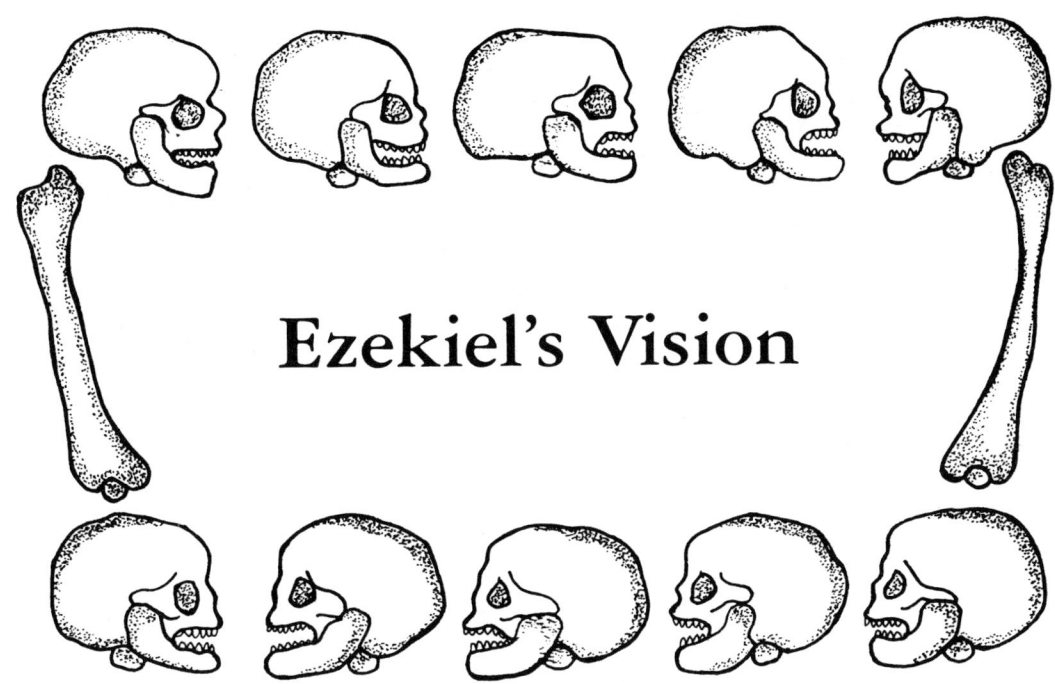

Ezekiel's Vision

The people of Israel and the people of Judah were once again united, this time as exiles in Babylonia. Babylon was the most beautiful city in the ancient world. Snarling lions made of colored bricks ornamented the walls lining each side of the paved road leading to the city. Bulls and dragons decorated the shiny blue-brick entrance gate. A double row of high walls and towers surrounded the city; the king's grand palace and a seven-story tower, built like a pyramid, were among its more impressive buildings.

King Nebuchadnezzar collected antiques and had built a museum to display them. He also loved to read and kept his books in a big library. His greatest pleasure was gardening. As a special gift for a homesick princess, he ordered the famous hanging gardens of Babylon to be built. Watered by wells and fountains, beautiful flowers, exotic plants, and lush vines tumbled over one another from a height of seventy-five feet. In the cool of early morning, the king was often seen kneeling on his special knee pads, weeding beds of orange poppies and yellow daisies.

The prophet Jeremiah had advised the people to build houses, settle down, plant gardens, marry, and have children. For once they followed his advice and, since they were not being mistreated, began to make new lives for themselves.

Some people worked on large farms that grew barley;
Some people learned how to make palm trees grow.
Some people were shepherds,
Some people were bankers,
Some people sewed clothes in a rainbow of colors.
But there were some people who couldn't stop thinking
About their past lives, which seemed so long ago.

The Children of Israel often gathered together to celebrate important occasions like the Sabbath, circumcisions, and weddings. Because he had been called by God, Ezekiel made use of these opportunities to speak to them. He knew that it was his job to keep the hope alive that someday his people would be allowed to return to their beloved homeland. And with this return would come a great reunion of the two kingdoms. No more would brothers and sisters fight with each other. All would live together, in one country ruled by one faithful king. After the final, terrible destruction of Jerusalem, Ezekiel had a vision describing the wonderful event yet to come:

THE VISION OF THE DRY BONES

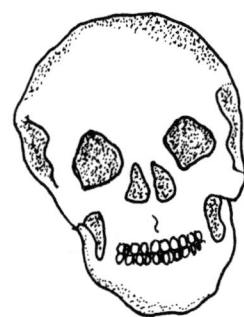

The Hand of the Lord was upon me,
And He set me down
In the midst of a valley,
A big, open valley
Full of dry bones.
There were
Head bones, neck bones,
Collar, back, and arm bones,
Wrist bones, finger bones,
Rib, hip, and thigh bones,
Knee bones, foot bones,
Ankle, toe, and jaw bones,
All kinds of dry bones
Lying on the ground.

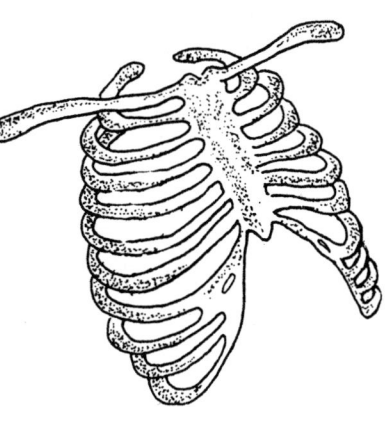

God said, "Son of man, tell Me,
Can these bones live?"
I answered, "Lord, only You know."
He said to me, "Prophesy over these bones and say,
'O you dry bones, hear the word of the Lord:
I'll give you muscles,
And new flesh and skin,
I'll put breath into you,
And you shall live
And know I am the Lord.'"

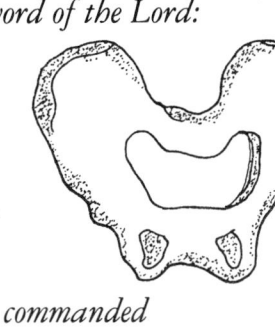

As I was doing what I was commanded
There was a noise, then a racket, a clatter,
A clanging commotion;
The bones were in motion!
Bone to bone they connected!
The Lord had directed these bones in their uprising!
Sometimes, the ways of the Lord are surprising!

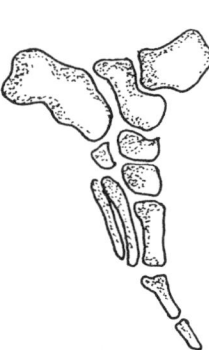

317

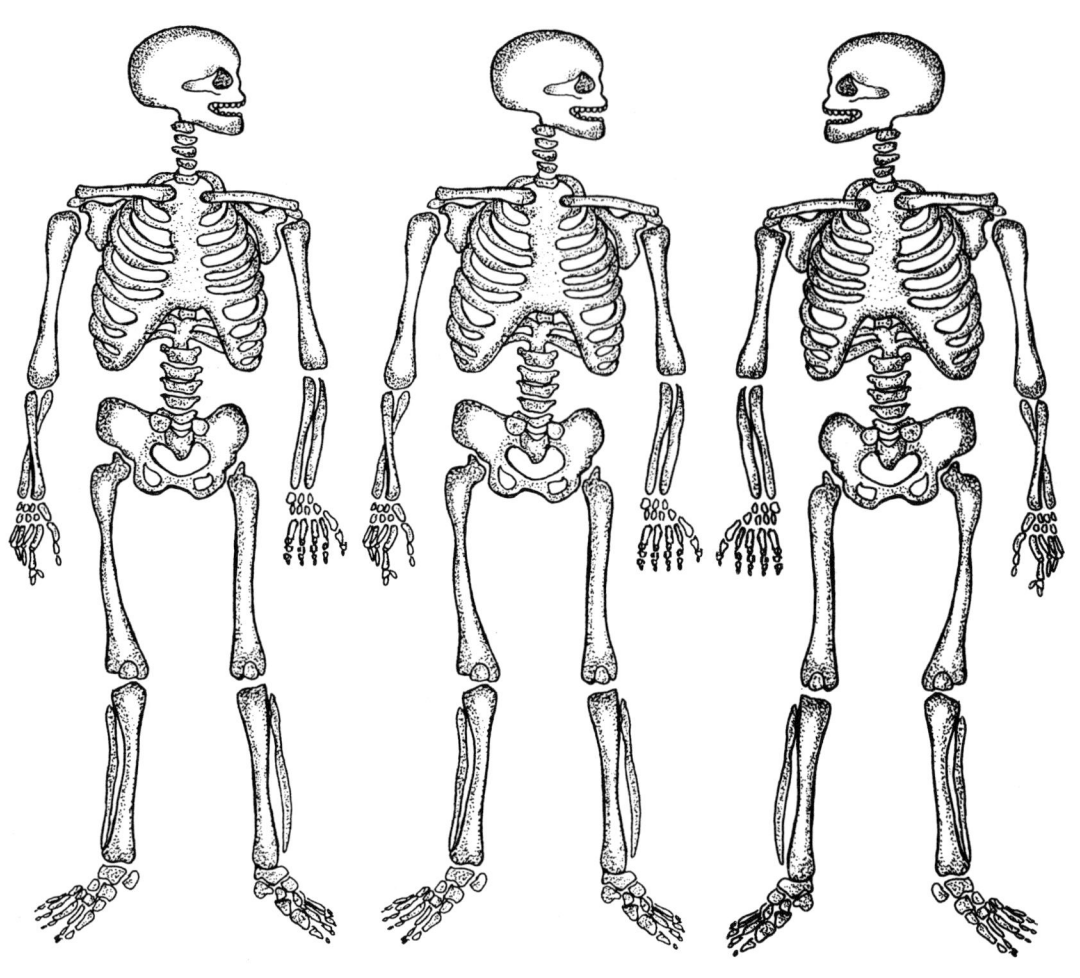

I looked and saw muscle, flesh, and skin on them,
But there wasn't the tiniest trace of breath in them.

God said, "Son of man,
Prophesy to the breath and say,
'Thus says the Lord God:
Come from the four ends of the earth
And breathe life
Into these bodies so that they might live.'"
I did as He told me,
And the breath came into them.
They lived and stood on their feet,
Both men and women!

318

Head bones nodding,
Neck bones swiveling,
Collar bones moving,
Back bones bending,
Arm bones flapping,
Wrist bones waving,
Hand bones clapping,
Finger bones pointing,
Rib bones rubbing,
Hip bones wiggling,
Thigh bones twisting,
Knee bones knocking,
Ankle bones creaking,
Toe bones tapping,
Jaw bones speaking!

God said to me, "Son of man,
These same bones
Are the Children of Israel.
They say,
'Our bones are dried up,
Our hope is lost;
We're like limbs without bodies.'
Now tell them My words:
'I will open your graves,
Bring you back to your land.
You will know I am God.
I'll put My Spirit in you,
The sweet breath of life,
And you shall live again
With the help of My Hand
In your own Promised Land.
And you'll know that I've spoken;
My word won't be broken.'"

319

After this amazing vision, the word of God again came to Ezekiel: "Son of man, take a piece of wood and write upon it: For the kingdom of Judah. Then take another piece of wood and write: For the kingdom of Israel. Then join them together to form a single plank in your hand. When your people ask, 'What does this mean?' tell them that the Lord God has said: 'I will gather them together from the nations to which they all have scattered and bring them into their own land. One king, like My servant David, the shepherd, shall be their king forever. No longer shall they be two kingdoms. I will make a covenant of peace with them, a promise that will never be broken. I will keep them, they will multiply, and My temple will be in their midst. My Presence shall always be over them and I shall bless them. They shall be My people and all the world shall know that I am the Lord.'"

The Twelve Prophets

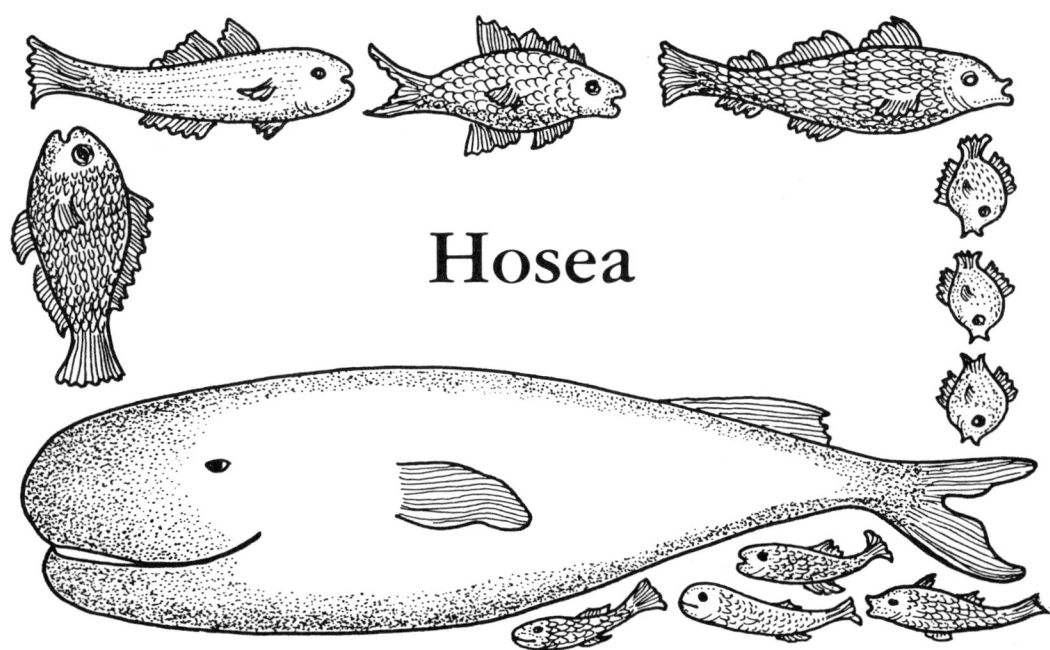

Hosea

Hosea the prophet lived in the kingdom of Israel. When God first spoke with him, he was told to marry a woman who would one day be unfaithful. At first he did not quite understand the meaning of God's command; after all, shouldn't a marriage be made with trust? However, Hosea knew that God has a reason for everything. He knew that someday, the meaning of this unusual command would be made known to him.

Hosea, a kind and tender man, soon asked a woman named Gomer to be his wife. Although he loved his wife dearly, she did not return his love. She betrayed him, hurt him, and did not tell the truth. He now understood God's command: the example of his own unhappy marriage showed him how God must feel when His special people disappoint Him.

Hosea had suffered a great deal. He did not want his people to suffer, and tried to teach them that God loved them like a father loves a child. God is willing to wait for His people to return His unlimited love. Although those who have turned away and walked down crooked paths will receive punishment from God, it will always be given with love. And although they may be sent far from home, they will remain forever in God's heart.

Hosea told his people that, as in a great and glorious marriage, the kingdoms of Israel and Judah would someday unite and live happily together in the light of the Lord. Here are God's words, as spoken to Hosea, the prophet:

"And in that day I will make a peaceful covenant for them
With the beasts of the field and with the fowls of heaven,
And with the creeping things of the ground;
I will break the bow and the sword;
There will be no more battles in their land.
I will keep them safe from harm.

"I will make the Children of Israel My bride;
As My gift I will give them
Righteousness,
Justice,
Loving-kindness,
And compassion.
Their gift to Me shall be their faithfulness;
And this marriage will be everlasting.
I will say to them:
You are my people.
And they shall say:
You are my God."

Joel

The name Joel means "The Lord is God." If you take the name Elijah, and place the second half first and the first half last, you will get the name Jaheli. This also means "The Lord is my God." Each time someone says the names of these two prophets, they are also praising the Lord!

The prophet Joel tells of a time when a terrible plague of locusts invaded the land of Judah. Millions and millions of flying insects, swift like horses, thundering like chariots, blackened the sky and ate up all the crops. And when the crops disappeared, no offerings to God could be made in the temple. Priests and ordinary people alike were filled with grief. But all was not lost. The Lord, Who is merciful, wanted His people to know how to make something good come of something so bad. In this way, they would understand the true meaning of the plague.

The prophet Joel spoke these words of the Lord:

"What the cutting locust left,
The swarming locust ate.
What the swarming locust left,
The hopping locust ate.
What the hopping locust left,

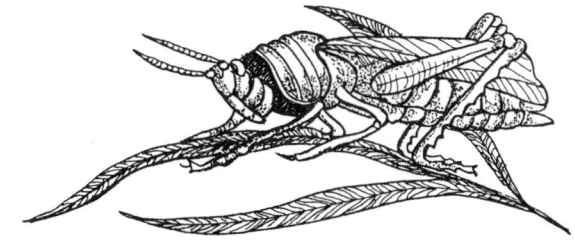

325

The destroying locust ate.
My land has been invaded by a people,
Without number;
With lion's teeth
They turned my vines to waste.
With great haste they stripped my fig trees,
Till their branches all gleamed white.
The fields are devastated,
The earth mourns at the sight.
The grain has been destroyed,
The vats that hold the wine are dry,
There's no more olive oil.

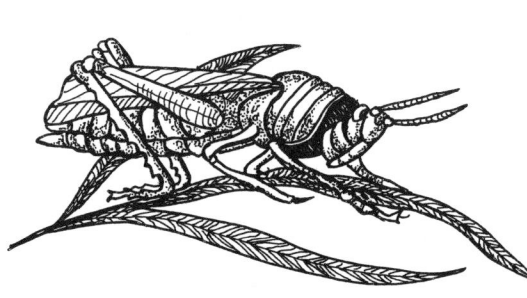

"Wail, farmers and vine-keepers,
The harvest has been spoiled.
Fig and palm and pomegranate trees,
Have also withered.
The people's joy is gone.
They mourn,
They too are withered."

To make matters worse, the prophet Joel gave his people
this warning from God:

"Proclaim a fast,
And cease from working.
Gather everyone together into the house of God.
The Almighty, with His Hand,
Shall cause a great destruction.
The day of God is coming to this land!"

"But have faith," said the prophet. "The Lord, in His mercy, will help His people if they ask forgiveness for their wrongdoings, give up their evil ways, and return to Him."

These are the words of the Lord that came to the prophet Joel:

"Turn to Me now with all your heart,
With fasting and lamentation.
Do not tear your clothes, but do tear your hearts out,
A true show of grief, and return to the Lord;
He will bring you relief.
He is gracious, and kind, slow to anger, and merciful.
Do not fear, O land, be glad and rejoice.
The Lord has done great things;
The locusts were His!
And with His mighty Hand he'll again do great things!
He'll make the ground fertile for growing and grazing.
Don't worry cows, goats, cattle, and sheep,
The pastures will bloom; you will have food to eat.
Trees will bear their sweet fruit,
The grapevines will blossom.

Rejoice in the Lord!
He'll bring enough rain; grain will fill all the barns.
The wine vats and oil vats will be overflowing
With wine and with oil.
The harvest won't spoil.
And there will be plenty to eat every day!
Before and after each meal you shall pray,
Praising the name of the Lord,
Your own God,
Who's been so good to you.
My people shall never more suffer and moan
Due to such devastation.
You'll know that My home is with you,
My own nation,
And that I, alone, am the Lord your God."

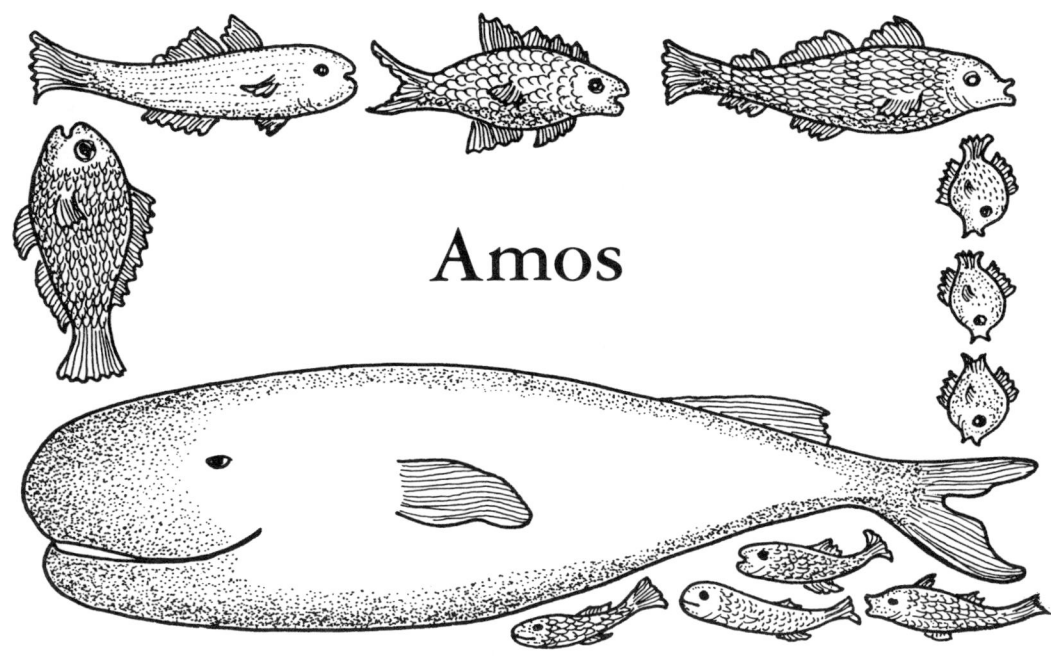

Amos

Amos the prophet called himself "a dresser of sycamore trees." These trees, also called mulberry figs, grow in Israel's warm lowlands. Popular with desert travelers, the sycamore's low, spreading branches can always be counted on for shade on the hottest days. Although their fruit is smaller and less sweet than that of regular fig trees, it is a very healthy snack. People who could not afford to buy grain would grind the figs into a flour for bread baking.

A "tree dresser" goes from tree to tree, putting a hole in each fig to help the bitterness escape. While tending to his trees and his sheep, Amos was called by God to become a prophet. His job was to warn the people that they were about to be punished for all their sins against God and against each other. He said:

"If God's people go astray,
Act unkindly and unfairly,
If they worship idols,
Disobeying God's commandments,
Then the Lord will punish them.
They'll have no one else to blame
But themselves."

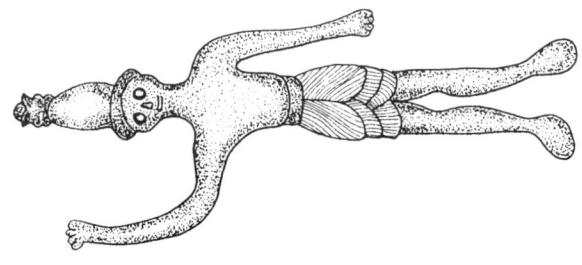

For Amos, honesty and fairness between all people and nations was very important. The Lord expects more of the Children of Israel than of any other people because He made His covenant with them so many years ago.

Amos the prophet relayed these words of God to the Children of Israel:

"You are My special people,
And you have betrayed Me.
Therefore, you'll be punished
For your sins against Me!
Will two people travel in the hot desert
If they don't agree on what's right and what's wrong?
Will a young lion roar if there is no prey?
Will a bird lay in a trap with no lure in it?
Shall a horn blow and the people not tremble?
Shall evil come without God having brought it?
The Lord will do nothing except tell His prophets
What is His intent.
The prophets, in turn, beg the people to listen,
And change their bad habits,
Return and repent!
The Lord has sent warnings
Like the roar of a lion,
The snap of a bird trap,
The sound of a horn.
His prophets speak for Him;
Won't His people hear?
The lion has roared!
Who will not fear?"

Amos lived a simple life; sun and rain, sweet fruit, and good pastures were all he needed to be happy in God's world. The rich life of the city-dwellers did not impress him. When God gave him these words to speak to the people, Amos understood them right away. God's people were like seedlings, and He was the One who would plant them wherever he wished.

Here are the words of the Lord, as spoken to Amos the prophet:

"Seek good and not evil so that you might live.
The Lord will be with you as you have implored.
Hate evil, love good,
Tell the truth, practice justice.
Perhaps then the Lord God will be good to you.
On that day I will raise up the temple of David,
Repair its ruins, rebuild it again.
The day will then come when the plowman replaces
The one who has pulled up the crops from the land.
And the sower of seeds will displace all of those
Who tread on the sweet grapes.
At that time the mountains shall drip with fine wine.
I will bring back My people from their captivity;
They shall plant vineyards, make gardens, drink wine.
With My Hand I will plant them on their land once more.
Never again will there come such a day
When they will be plucked up,
And taken away!"

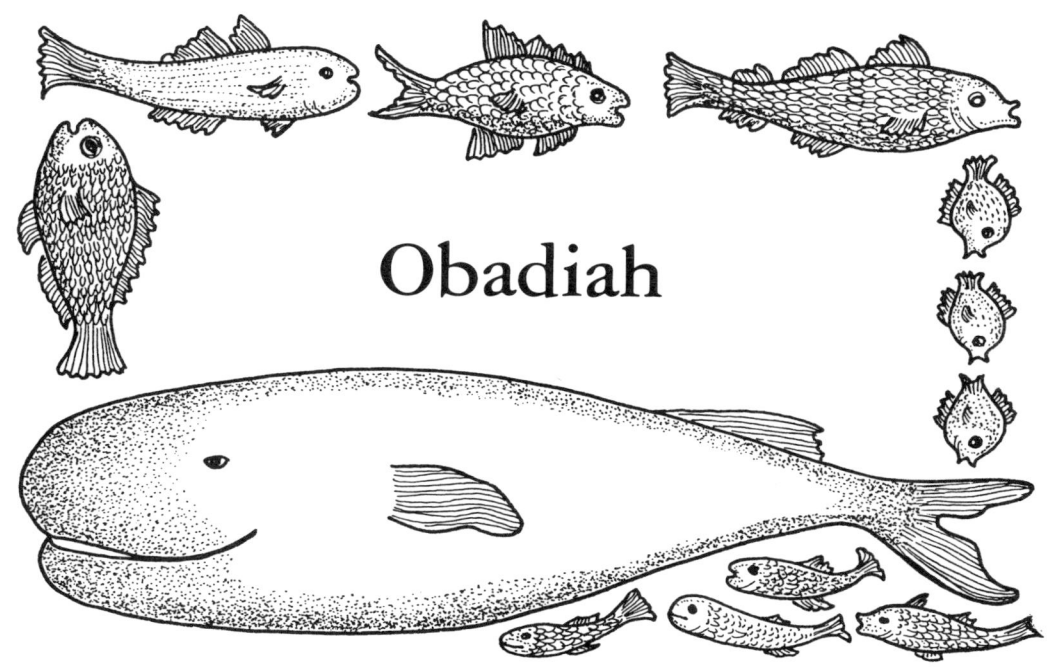

Obadiah

The people of Edom were said to be the descendants of Esau, the son of whom Isaac declared, "You shall live by the sword." Jacob, Esau's twin brother, eventually was given the name "Israel." Because these two countries had this common ancestor, it was especially terrible that Edom should want to fight against Israel. However, the Edomites had given the Children of Israel a hard time as far back as the days of the Exodus from Egypt. When Moses asked the king of Edom to allow the Israelites to pass through their land, he refused and threatened them with his army. King Saul fought against them, and King David conquered them. Back and forth during the times of different kings, Edom was always involved, either conquering or being conquered.

According to Obadiah the prophet, the Edomites had watched from a distance as Nebuchadnezzar destroyed Jerusalem. And when any of the Judeans escaped, the Edomites caught and killed them.

"Shame on you!" said the prophet, referring to this unbrotherly behavior. "God's prophets have heard a message concerning Edom. Listen to these words of the Lord:

'Rise up for war!
Edom, you are greatly despised!

332

You people who live high up in the rocks are mistaken
If you think that no one can bring you down.
Though your home is as high as an eagle's nest,
I will bring you down from there!
How you are cut off!
If thieves came to you at night,
They would steal everything.
If grape pickers came to you,
They would leave nothing behind for you.
The Edomites, Esau's descendants, have been discovered!
The men who once were your friends
Are now your enemies.
The men who once ate your bread
Have set a trap for you.
For the violence done to your brother, Jacob,
Shame on you!
And you shall be cut off forever.
You stood aloof on that terrible day
When Jerusalem was destroyed.
You should not have taken pleasure in Israel's disaster,
Nor been pleased with Judah's destruction.
You should not have entered My people's gate
In the day of their calamity,
Nor should you have stood at the crossroads
To capture those who escaped.
The day of the Lord is coming;
He will deal with the enemies of His people.
As you have done, it shall be done to you!'"

Obadiah believed that Edom's behavior through the years was a good example of anger without reason. He envisioned the great day when hostility and warfare would cease between nations. On that day, all the world would be nearer the time when "The Kingdom shall be the Lord's!"

Obadiah the prophet also believed with all his heart that the forces of evil would never destroy his people. Israel's faith, and the truth that goes with it, would last forever.

Jonah

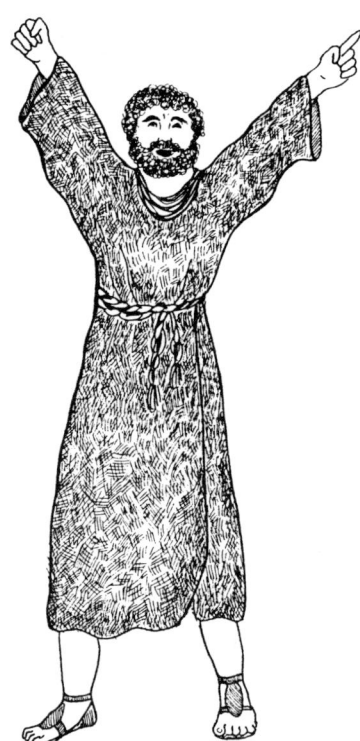

The word of the Lord came to Jonah the prophet:
     "Arise and go up to the city of Nineveh.
     Proclaim to the people, so wicked and selfish,
That God has been watching them,
And they are doomed."
But Jonah did not do as God had commanded;
He assumed that the Lord would forgive
All the sinners,
And he didn't think they deserved His forgiving.
Moreover, if after he told them God's words,
The people repented and God, in His mercy,
Kept them all living,
They'd say that God's words, through His prophet,
Were untrue.
A gloom fell on Jonah.
What was he to do?
Jonah fled from the Lord to the seacoast of Jaffa
In order to board a ship sailing to Tarshish,
A faraway place;

Jonah just couldn't face his problem with God.
He paid his fare and the crew took him on.
But the Lord hurled a furious wind toward the sea,
And a great storm began.
Angry waves, mighty breakers broke over the ship.
The crew thought they'd be wrecked,
And they prayed to their own gods to help them survive.
They tossed the ship's cargo over the sides
To lighten the boat so that it would still float.
While this was happening, Jonah, the prophet,
Had gone down below
And had fallen into a sleep,
Heavy and deep.
The captain approached him and said,
"We need help!
Why are you sleeping?
Get up and pray to your God; maybe He
Will do something for us so we do not die."
They said one to the other,
"Come let us cast lots and see who's to blame
For this stormy sea,
This calamity."
Casting lots was a way to determine the outcome
Of a situation,
An old game of chance that told who wins or loses.
And so they cast lots and the lot fell on Jonah.
The crew said to him, "What is your occupation?
Where do you come from and what is your nation?"
Jonah replied to them, "I am a Hebrew.
I worship the Lord, the God of the heavens
Who made both the raging sea
And the dry land."
The frightened sailors said, "What have you done?"
When Jonah first joined them he told everyone
That he was in flight from the sight of the Lord.
"What shall we do with you

335

So that this furious sea will be calm for us?"
Jonah said to them,
"Take me and cast me into the sea
So the sea may be calm for you.
Because of me, this storm is upon you."
The sailors, however, tried to be kind,
And they rowed just as hard as they could
Toward the shore.
But the sea raged and roared ever wilder around them.
They cried to Jonah's Lord
Who had sent this big storm,
"O Lord, we beg You,
Do not condemn us for what we must do."
Then, lifting Jonah, they threw him
Into the wild, churning sea!
And the sea ceased its fury,
Its raging, its roaring!
With respect for the Lord, the men made an offering.
They were astonished by what God accomplished!

Jonah bobbed up and down in the calm sea of blue
Treading water, and not knowing quite what to do.
Then the Lord caused a great whale to come up beside him.
Why did He do that?
Was Jonah to ride him?
The great whale opened up its gigantic jaws
And like milk through a straw
Sucked up Jonah inside him!

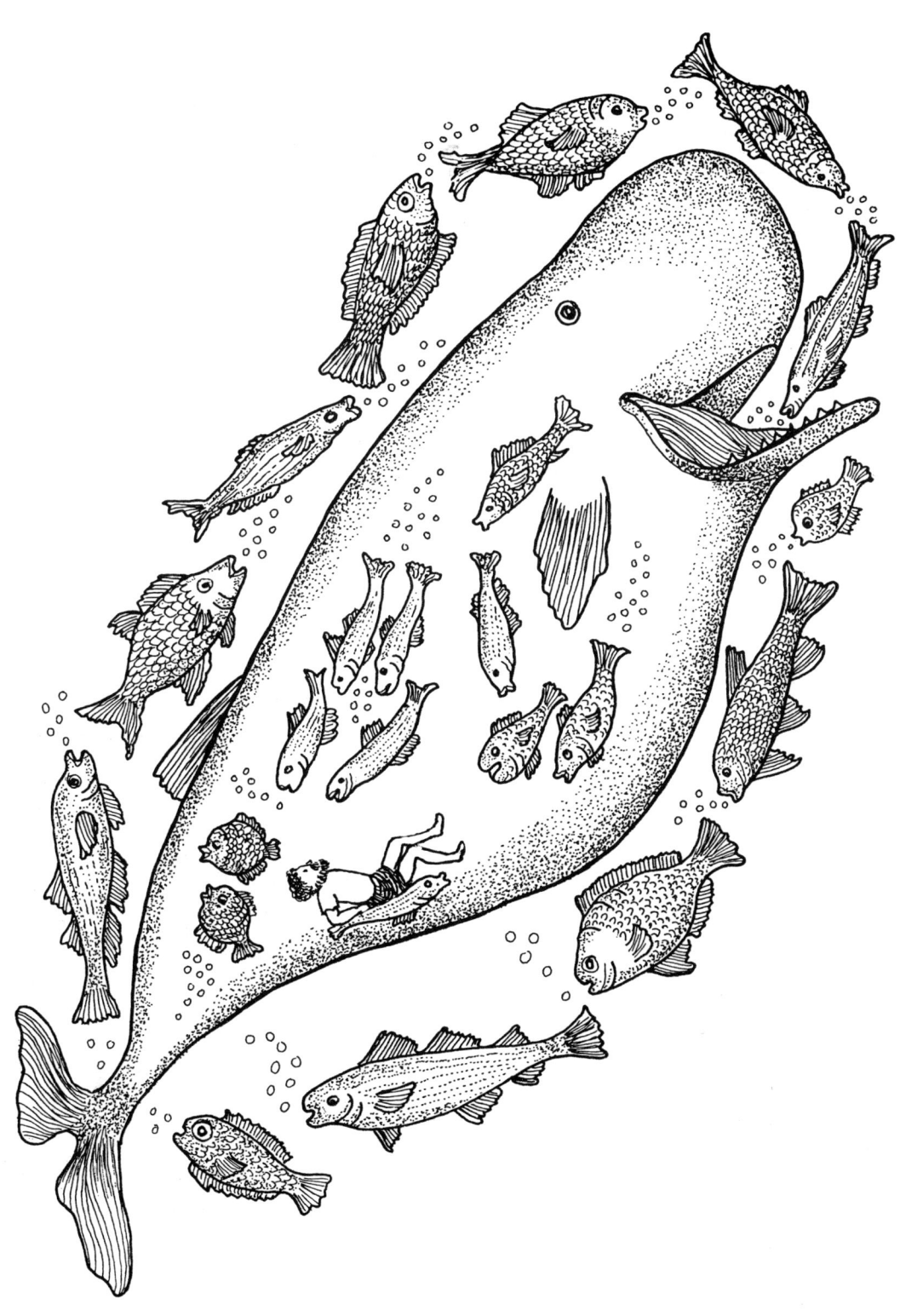

Jonah remained in the great whale's belly
Three days and three nights,
All the time seeing sights that he'd never imagined:
A whole school of sardines were swimming around him;
Tuna turned upside-down cartwheels behind him;
Flounders flapping their fins floated down the long throat
Of the great whale whose belly was now Jonah's home.
As a place to say prayers, this was certainly odd,
But the Lord always hears them wherever they come from:
On top of a mountain or down on a trail,
Or inside the belly of a great whale!
So Jonah recited this grand prayer to God:
"In my distress I called to the Lord
And He answered me.
From my watery grave I cried.
And You heard my voice.
You had me thrown
Into the sea;
Water flowed all around me;
Huge waves swept over me.
I thought, 'I am banished from the Lord's sight!
I wish I could once again
Look at Your temple!'
The waters surrounded me,
I'd soon be dead.
Sea weeds wound round my head
As I sank to the bottom.
It seemed like the earth's doors
Would open no more.
But You, Lord my God, raised me up
From my grave.
When I almost drowned,
I remembered the Lord.
And I prayed to You,
Toward Your own holy temple.
Those who believe in idols deceive themselves.

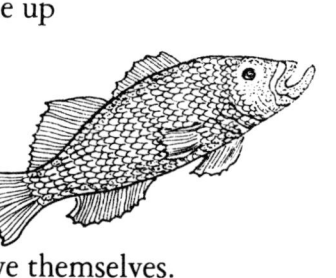

True loving-kindness comes from the Lord.
I shall bring You my offerings,
Full of thanksgiving
For the help that You gave me, on my accord.
That which I've promised to do, I will do.
Deliverance only comes from the Lord."
The Lord gave the great whale one last command.
The whale belly rumbled,
And out tumbled Jonah upon the dry land.

The word of the Lord came to Jonah a second time:
"Arise and go to the great city, Nineveh.
Tell them the message that I told to you."
Jonah did as God said and went to the city;
It would take three days just to walk through it.
Great limestone walls and high towers surrounded it.
When Jonah had journeyed one day's time into it,
He proclaimed to all:
"Forty days more and Nineveh shall fall!"
People were shaken!
Believing in God,
They trembled, they fasted!
And like poor souls grieving,
Put on coarse sackcloth,
The high and the lowly, the rich and the poor.
When the news reached the king,
He took off his royal robe,
Put on itchy sackcloth, and sat down in ashes.
Then he published a royal proclamation that read:
"In the name of the king
Neither people nor donkeys, cattle nor sheep,
Shall eat or drink anything,
All shall wear sackcloth as if they were mourning.
Everyone must pray sincerely to God,
Give up their evil ways and their bad deeds.
Who knows,

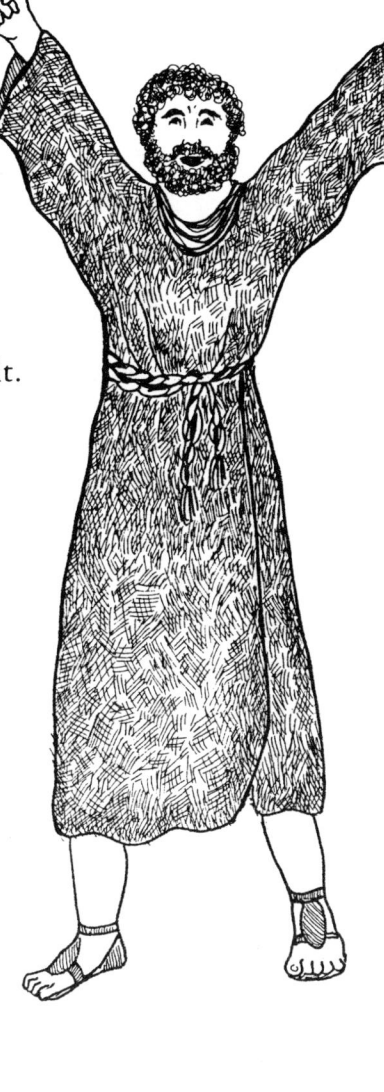

If they repent perhaps God will heed them,
Perhaps He'll relent and take back His decree."
Though people wore sackcloth, sat in ashes, and fasted,
Their outward appearance was only a small part
Of their true repentance.
The Lord saw their deeds,
He looked into their hearts,
He read all their thoughts.
Then God relented.
They would not be punished
With His final sentence.

This distressed Jonah greatly
Because, in the past,
The Assyrians, who were the people of Nineveh,
Behaved cruelly, were wicked, selfish, and mean.
Why then, through his efforts,
Should they be forgiven by God
And allowed to live in their own city?
Jonah the prophet had no pity for them.
He was very angry when he prayed to God:
"O my Lord,
I knew this was going to happen.
That's why I fled to the wild, churning sea.
My words, as a prophet, will now all seem false.
What will Nineveh and her king now think of me?
You are a gracious God,
And compassionate,
Slow to show anger,
Abounding in kindness.
I knew You'd relent if You saw them repent.
Now, Lord, I pray,
Take my life away.
I prefer death.
This is such a dark day."
God said gently to Jonah,

"Are you right to be angry?"
Jonah went from the city and stayed on the outside,
Where he made a hut of branches and sticks.
There he sat in its shadow to see what would happen.
Would God change His mind and hear Jonah's plea?
God caused a tree to grow up over Jonah.
It shaded his head and saved him discomfort.
Jonah was happy because of this tree;
Sitting beneath its cool leaves gave him joy.
The next morning, at daybreak,
God caused a worm to gnaw at the tree
Until it was destroyed.

With the sun now awake, God called for a wind,
A hot wind from the east, to blow.
And the sun's heat beat down on Jonah's head
Till he became faint, and wished he were dead.
Once more Jonah said,
"Take my life away.
I prefer death.
This is such a dark day!"
Then God spoke to Jonah,
"Are you very angry because of the tree?"
And Jonah replied, "Yes, to the point of death!"
The Lord said, "You had pity on the tree though
You did not make it grow.
It was only a plant that sprang up in the night,
And disappeared as the day became light.
But as for Me,
I was not to take pity
On Nineveh, the Assyrian city,
With thousands of babies
Who don't even know their right from their left hand.
And what of the cattle that live on this land?
These are the untaught,
The innocent,
The blameless.
They need compassion.
Am I to be merciless?"

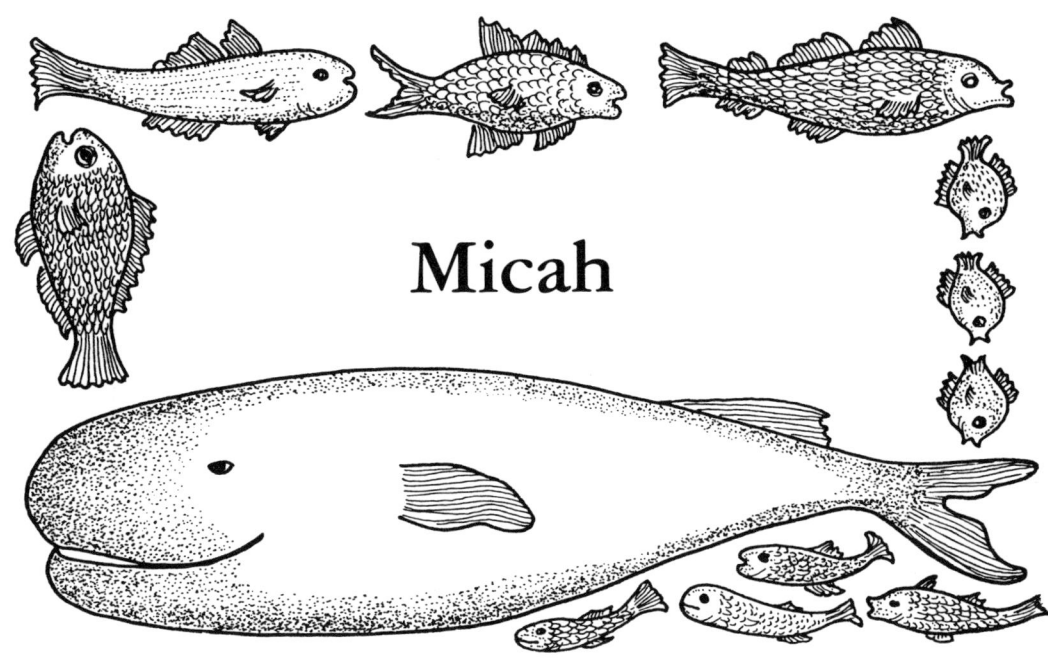

Micah

Micah the prophet was called the "prophet of the poor." He lived in a small village twenty-five miles from Jerusalem, where people had to work very hard all the time. They were called "peasants," and much of their farming and labor was done for the rich landowners who lived in Jerusalem. They were paid little, taxed heavily, and sometimes lost what little land they had. This was not fair, and many times Micah spoke out about this kind of mistreatment. He also warned them that God was going to punish His people by military defeat and exile:

"Woe to them who lay in their beds
Planning evil;
When the morning sun comes,
These bad deeds are done
By the rich to the poor:
They want somebody's field,
They go out and take it
By taxing and bribing,
By lying and cheating.
They want someone's house,

343

They devise ways to take it,
And with it, the owners,
Who now have no home.
They are taken by force
To work for the same ones
Who started this mess.
Therefore, the Lord says:
'Against these oppressors
I have also devised
Evil for evildoers,
For their sins and their lies,
Like animals bent
With their heads in a yoke
They will be sent away
And a tearful lament
Will be said for them all
On that dreadful, dark day.'"

Micah the prophet said that God does not only look for sacrificial offerings. It is more important to Him that His chosen people be examples of kindness, brotherhood, and good behavior. Among the prophet's gloomy predictions is this one sunny hope, in famous words passed down from generation to generation:

"Hear now what the Lord is saying:
'O My people, tell Me,
What have I done to you?
Why do I deserve such neglect?
I brought you up from the hard land of Egypt,
Redeemed you from bondage,
Sent Moses, and Aaron, and Miriam
To teach you,
I comforted you when you cried.
Remember, My people, what King Balak tried
To have Balaam do.
But with blessings, not curses,

344

He answered the king!
From Shittim to Gilgal I helped you come home
Across Jordan's river.
My power is known!'"
The people, remembering all of God's deeds,
Asked Micah the prophet to tell them, please,
"What does God want of us,
Burnt offerings, calves, thousands of rams?
Would olive oil suit Him, in vast amounts?
Shall we give Him our children,
The fruit of our bodies,
In atonement for the sins of our souls?"
And Micah the prophet said,
"It has already been told to you
By Abraham, Moses, Samuel, and Elijah,
That which is good,
And what the Lord God has said you must do:
'Only to do justly,
And to love mercy,
And to walk humbly with your God.'"

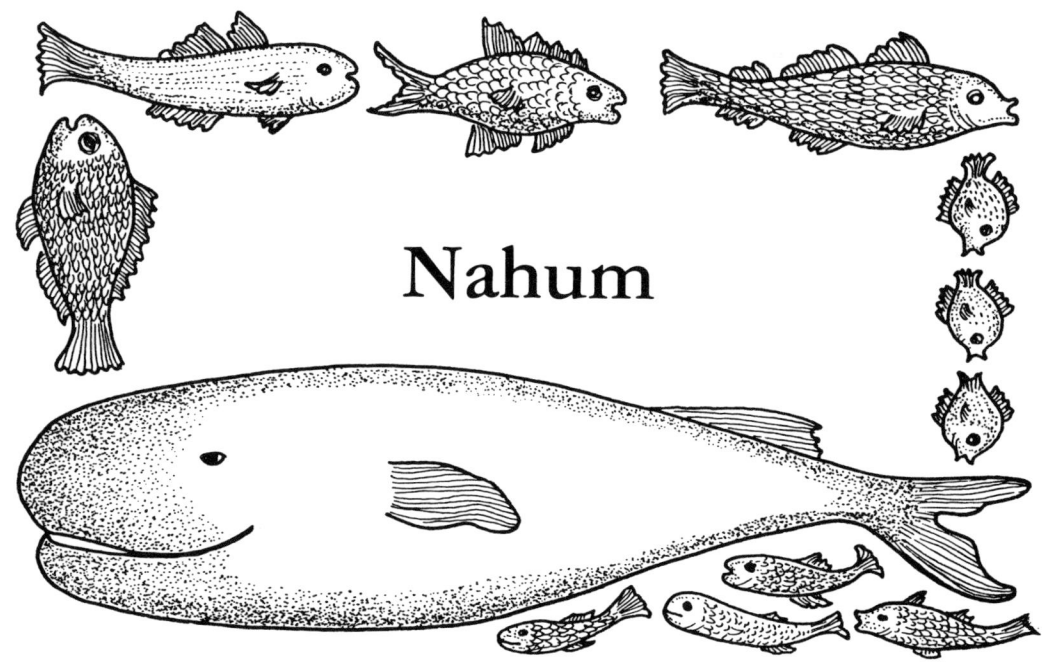

Nahum

The days were dark for the Children of Israel. One country or another continually attacked and terrorized them, especially Assyria, which, in its cruelty, always caused great suffering. Nahum, the prophet, had his own special way of reaching the people. Instead of denouncing his people's sins, he comforted them by predicting the fall of Nineveh, Assyria's main city, and the destruction of all who oppressed Israel. He spoke using vivid word pictures: the enemy were described as lions and their military men as grasshoppers. Though his manner was different from that of most other prophets, Nahum's main theme was familiar: what the Assyrians had done to others would finally be done to them.

DIFFERENT WAYS

There are many different ways
To get to the same place.
For instance, you can walk,
Or skip, or ride a wagon,
Run, or hop, or jump.

The road can bump you up and down,
Or be so smooth you slide,
Gliding to your destination
Like swans on a lake.
Some people take a different path
To teach us what they know.
Whichever way they choose
To say whatever they are saying
If we open up our brains a bit,
And let the words sink through,
If we listen carefully
And think,
We'll learn a thing or two.

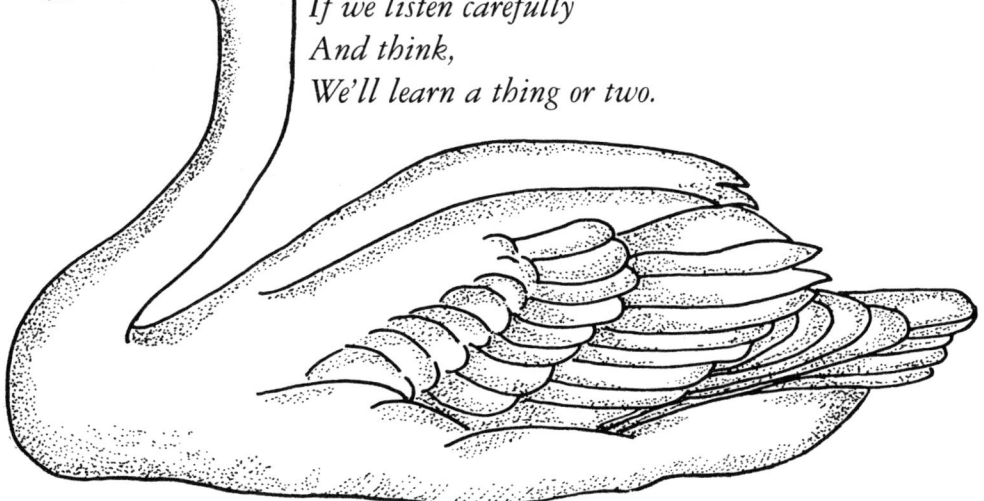

Here are the words of Nahum the prophet concerning the fate of Nineveh. When God is angry, all will suffer:

"The Lord is full of anger,
And will by no means clear the guilty.
The mountains quake at Him,
And the hills melt;
The earth is upheaved at His Presence.
Who can stand before His indignation?

"Where is this den of lions
Where the young lions fed
And where the lion and lioness walked?

347

The lion took what he wished for his family,
Killed to impress his lioness,
And filled his caves with that which he took.

"'I am against you,' says the Lord.
'I will burn her chariots,
The sword shall devour the young lions,
And the voice of your rulers shall be heard no more.

"'Your army generals are like swarms of grasshoppers,
Which take refuge in the cracks of walls on cold days,
And fly away when the sun shines.
Their whereabouts are unknown.

"'Your rulers and nobles are dead, Assyria.
Your people fled to the mountains
But there is no one to lead them home.

"'There is no healing for your pain;
Nineveh will never recover.
All who hear what has happened to you
Will clap their hands.
After all, who has not suffered from your wickedness?'"

Habakkuk

After the fall of Assyria, there was finally hope for peace in the land. But this was not to be. The Babylonians began where the Assyrians left off, and once again, the Children of Israel were the target of a terrible enemy.

During this time, Habakkuk the prophet compared Babylon to a fisherman who hauls in catch after catch with his net until he is delirious with pride at his own abilities. Babylon, filled with easy victories and conquests, bows down to worship its own power. Habakkuk asked God of the enemy: "Shall he keep emptying his net and never stop slaying nations? Why should the innocent suffer and the wicked grow rich?"

Turning his head toward heaven, Habakkuk waited in silence for the Lord's answer. When God's word came to him, Habakkuk was told to have patience; the enemy would be destroyed soon. And he was instructed to write His answer on clay tablets for the future, when the prophecy would be fulfilled.

Here are the woes that would befall Babylon, as relayed by the Lord to Habakkuk the prophet:

"Woe to them who take what is not their own. The victims will rebel against Babylon.

"Woe to him who has brought to his house things acquired by evil; they will bring nothing but bad luck.

"Woe to him who builds a town with blood; slave labor is wrong.

"Woe to him who terrorizes his victims, making them powerless as if they were drunk. They will be filled with shame instead of glory.

"Woe to him who says to a wooden idol 'awake,' and to a dumb stone 'arise.' See how they are covered with silver and gold, and there is no breath in them. But the Lord hears everything from His heavenly temple. Let all the earth wait silently for His will to be done."

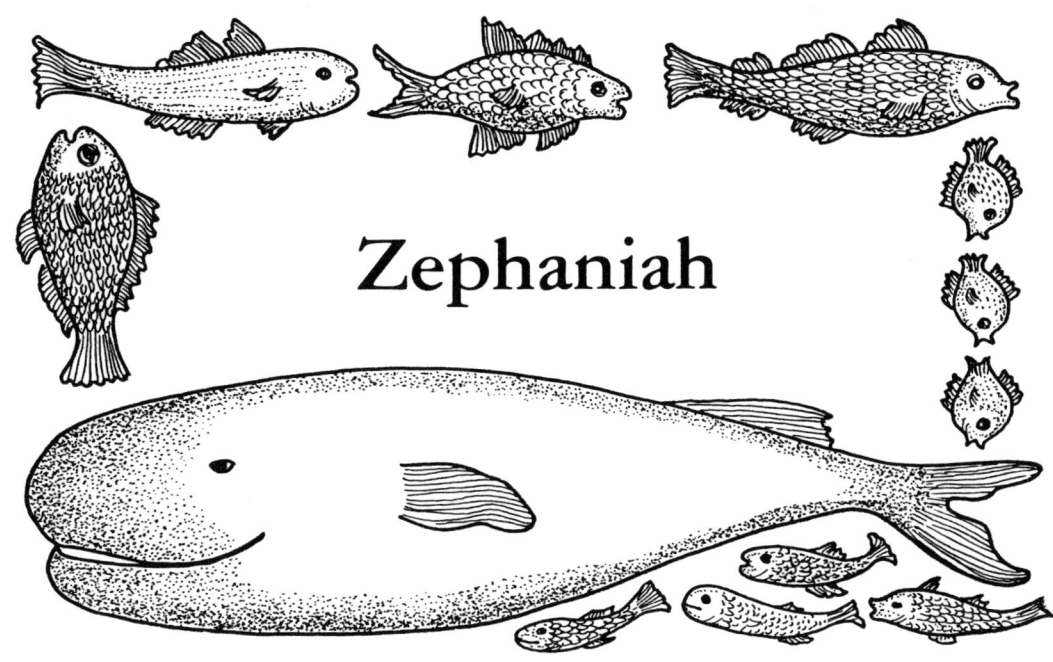

Zephaniah

When Jeremiah was proclaiming his message in the streets of Jerusalem and Huldah was teaching the Lord's word to women, Zephaniah the prophet was preaching his message about the wrath of God. This anger was not only directed at foreign people who were unbelievers, but at Israel and Judah. Many of Jerusalem's important people took advantage of those who were less fortunate.

"The day of the Lord will soon come," proclaimed the prophet, "when all sinners will be punished. God will keep only the humble and the poor safe."

Here are the words of the Lord that came to Zephaniah the prophet:

"With My Hand I will punish Judah,
The inhabitants of Jerusalem,
The idol worshipers,
Those who worship the moon and the stars,
And those who pretend to be loyal to God,
But do otherwise."

351

There will be no defense against God's own war. Those who come to destroy Jerusalem will bring torches to search dark hiding places. All will be punished! Here is how the Lord described this terrible day:

"The great day of the Lord is near,
Coming near with haste.
A day of wrath,
Of trouble, desolation,
Gloom and waste.
A day of cloud and darkness,
Of horn and battle cry.
I will bring distress to Judah.
Their walk shall be unsteady;
They have sinned against Me.
Neither silver nor their gold
Shall save them from My path
On My great day of wrath!"

Zephaniah the prophet urged the people of Judah to repent. Perhaps if they asked forgiveness, they might escape the Lord's anger:

"O shameless nation,
Gather together
Before the fierce anger
Of God comes upon you.
Here's what you can do:
Seek the Lord, all you people
Who've walked the right path,
And been humble and righteous;
You may be protected
On the day of God's wrath."

Haggai

When King Cyrus of Persia conquered Babylonia, he allowed the exiles to return to Jerusalem. Upon arriving at the rubble of what had been their glorious city, they found their great temple in ruins. The walls had been smashed and the beautiful ornaments destroyed or stolen; nothing remained except a heap of burned wood and stone. The people had no money and were barely able to feed themselves. The prophet Haggai believed that if they made the effort to rebuild His temple, God would reward them with good crops and prosperity.

On the twenty-first day of the seventh month, during the Festival of Tabernacles celebrating the autumn harvest, the word of the Lord came to Haggai the prophet, saying:

"Speak to all the remnant of the people and ask, 'Who remembers this house in its former glory?' If you had seen it, you would not be so slow in rebuilding it. Be strong, all you people, and get to work. I will be with you; My spirit lives in you. Do not fear.

"In a little while, after a few more problems are solved, I will shake up the nations and fill My house with their costly gifts. The wealth of these nations, all the silver and gold, shall be Mine. The glory of this temple shall be greater and last longer than that of the first. And with this temple's restoration, there will be peace in Jerusalem."

353

GOD'S HOUSES

God's houses are built in all kinds of shapes.
Some are red brick and square,
Some are plastered and round,
Some spread out on the ground,
Some reach toward the skies.
There are some made of dark wood,
And some made of stone.
Some have big windows,
And some have wide doors.
God's homes are all temples
No matter the size.

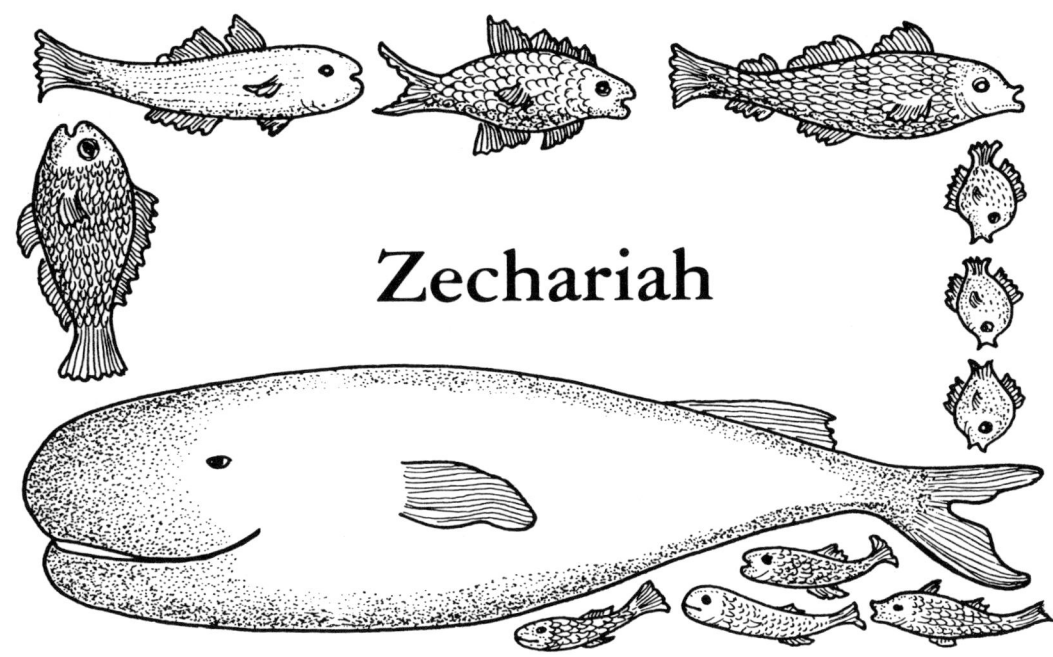

Zechariah

Like Haggai, the prophet Zechariah helped the people of Judah forget their sadness and encouraged them to rebuild God's temple. Unlike the other prophets, an angel brought the word of the Lord to Zechariah. Like an interpreter explaining foreign languages, the angel explained the prophet's visions to him.

One night I saw a man riding a red horse.
He stood by the myrtle trees down in the valley.
Behind him were horses, red, sorrel, and white.
I said to an angel, "My lord what are these?"
He said to me, "I will explain them to you."
The man on the red horse that stood by the trees
Answered, "These are whom the Lord sent
To walk to and fro
And report to Him how the conditions might be."
"We have walked to and fro through the earth,"
Said the men,
"And the earth is quite still,
And at rest."

355

The Lord had once promised to "shake up the nations,"
But nothing was happening,
All seemed too quiet.
Perhaps the Lord God
Was not ready yet.
The angel asked God, "O Lord, how long will You
Not have compassion on Jerusalem?
You've been angry with Judah sixty-seven years."
The Lord answered the angel that spoke with me
And He had good words to say,
That day,
Words of much comfort.
So the angel that spoke with me told me
What God said:

"I am full of love, deeply stirred by Jerusalem,
And I am displeased with the nations at ease.
They were told just to punish
But they have been cruel
And oppressed all My people,
And broken my rules about killing, and hurting.
They're arrogant, too.
Tell My people what I am about to tell you:
I'll return to Jerusalem, filled with compassion.
My house shall be built there.
A measuring line shall be stretched.
That's the first step in building a city.
One day all of Judah shall again have prosperity."

The people of Judah got to work rebuilding God's temple. Architects drew up plans, carpenters volunteered their time, and a cleanup squad began clearing the rubble. Keeping busy with an important job is one of the best ways to forget troubles. Soon the sound of singing could be heard coming from the building site; the lucky people who were working for God were happy.

Once more, Zechariah the prophet had a vision:

I looked up and saw a man with a measure.
"Where are you going?" said I to the man.
"To measure Jerusalem, its length and breadth."
Just then, the angel that spoke with me left
And met with another one who said to him,
"Run, speak to this young man and tell him:
Jerusalem shall be rebuilt without walls.
'For I,' said the Lord,
'Shall be a wall for her,
A wall made of fire,
For her population,
Men, women, and beasts.
I will protect her,
My people, My nation.'"

357

The prophet Zechariah taught that fasting and religious observances cannot take the place of good character and kind deeds. He reminded the people that God would return to His temple only after the people had returned to God. A pure and holy life was required if the future of the Lord's people was to be assured.

"Not by power, nor by might, but by My Spirit," said the Lord.

When he grew older, Zechariah the prophet no longer had angels visit him; now, his own message was understood by all who listened. The temple was being completed, and now the prophet concentrated on what was called the "Day of the Lord." On this wonderful day, a Messiah will come to lead Israel and the whole world into a time of justice and peace. Messiah means "anointed," and the great kings of Israel, Saul, David, and Solomon, were anointed with oil as God had commanded. This new Messiah, appointed by the Lord and perfect in all ways, will make a triumphant entry into Jerusalem, the earthly capital of the Kingdom of God. And on that great and glorious day, all the nations of the world will join together in peace with the God of Israel and His people.

May the words of Zechariah the prophet be fulfilled and live in the hearts of all:

"And the Lord shall be King over all the earth.
On that day, the Lord shall be one,
And His name one."

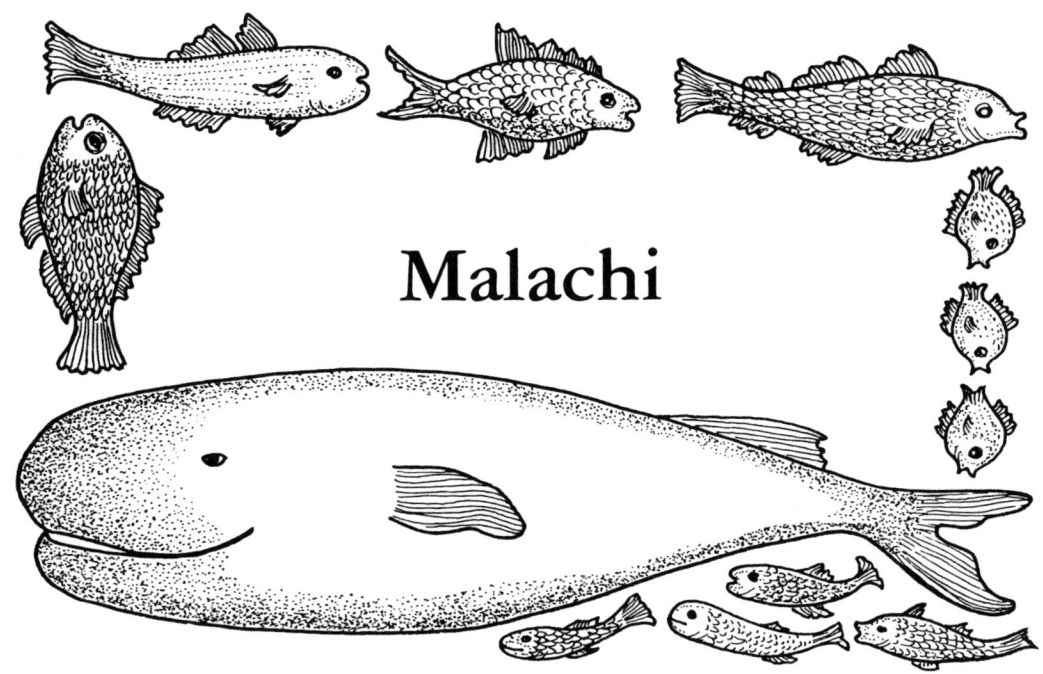

Malachi

The rebuilding of the temple had not brought about the changes in devotion, conduct, and prosperity predicted by Haggai the prophet. Malachi the prophet tried very hard to bring the people back to the Lord. But while those who distrusted religion and were impatient with God complained to each other, those who had remained devoted reassured themselves with words of faith and trust in God.

Malachi tried to reach those people who were turning aside from God and forsaking His rules and laws. He asked them:

"Have we not all one father?
Has not one God created us?
Why do we fight, every man against his brother,
Dishonoring the covenant of our forefathers?"

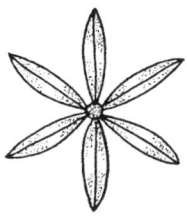

Malachi believed, with all his heart, that the "Day of the Lord" would be coming, a day of judgment for the Children of Israel. On this day, God will know who has been faithful to the law of Moses and who is wicked. However, before God decides His people's fate, the prophet Elijah will return to bring together quarreling parents and children and to turn the hearts of all once more to God. Here are the words of God as spoken by Malachi the prophet:

"Remember the law of My servant, Moses,
Which I gave to him on the mountain of God.
Remember, too, My commandments and rules.
Now I will send you
Elijah the prophet
Before the coming of the Lord's day.
And he shall turn
The hearts of the fathers
Back to the children,
And in the same way,
The hearts of the children
Back to the fathers.
If My people do not obey My instructions,
My Hand will smite this land with destruction.

Now I will send you
Elijah the prophet
Before the coming of the Lord's day.
He'll bring peace to the world,
There will be no more sorrow,
And he'll tell of God's Glory,
A brighter tomorrow."

About the Author

Esta Cassway is a painter, printmaker, and writer. The author and illustrator of *The Five Books of Moses for Young People*, she studied at the Philadelphia College of Art and received a Bachelor of Fine Arts degree from the Tyler School of Fine Art at Temple University. Esta Cassway's work has appeared in *The Jewish Exponent*, *Inside Magazine*, and *The Temple Review* at Temple University. She is also known for her performances of her own narratives, nostalgic essays, and poems, as well as numerous one-person exhibits of her art. The mother of three grown sons, Esta Cassway lives in Wyncote, Pennsylvania, a suburb of Philadelphia, with her husband, Robert, an architect.